D

HANDBUILT CERAMICS

HANDBUILT CERAMICS

- PINCHING
- COILING
- EXTRUDING
- MOLDING
- SLIP CASTING
- SLAB WORK

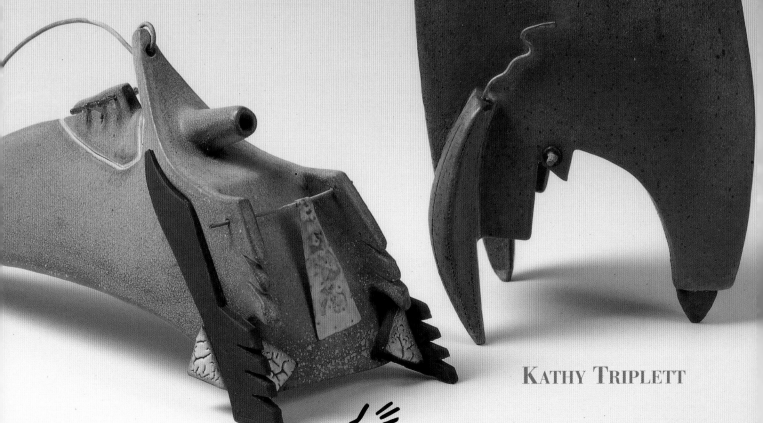

KATHY TRIPLETT

Lark Books
A Division of Sterling Publishing Co., Inc.
New York

Editor: Chris Rich
Assistant Editor: Laura Dover
Editorial Assistants: Rosemary Kast and Evans Carter
Art Director: Kathy Holmes
Production: Elaine Thompson
Production Assistant: Bobby Gold
Photographer (techniques): Evan Bracken

Library of Congress Cataloging-in-Publication Data
Triplett, Kathy.
        Handbuilt ceramics: pinching, coiling, extruding, molding, slip casting,
    slab work / by Kathy Triplett.
            p.   cm.
        Includes bibliographical references and index.
        ISBN 1-57990-184-0
        1. Pottery craft.   I. Title.
    TT920.T75   1997
    738.1--dc21   96-40099
                                             CIP

10 9

Published by Lark Books, a division of
Sterling Publishing Co., Inc.
387 Park Avenue South, New York, N.Y. 10016

First Paperback Edition 2000
© 1997 by Kathy Triplett

Distributed in Canada by Sterling Publishing,
c/o Canadian Manda Group, 165 Dufferin Street
Toronto, Ontario, Canada M6K 3H6

Distributed in the United Kingdom by GMC Distribution Services,
Castle Place, 166 High Street, Lewes, East Sussex, England BN7 1XU

Distributed in Australia by Capricorn Link (Australia) Pty Ltd.,
P.O. Box 704, Windsor, NSW 2756 Australia

If you have questions or comments about this book, please contact:
Lark Books
67 Broadway
Asheville, NC 28801
(828) 253-0467

Manufactured in China

ISBN 13: 978-1-57990-184-4
ISBN 10: 1-57990-184-0

For information about custom editions, special sales, premium and corporate
purchases, please contact Sterling Special Sales Department at 800-805-5489
or specialsales@sterlingpub.com.

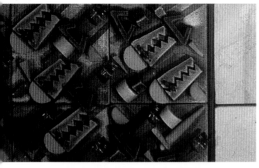

TABLE OF CONTENTS

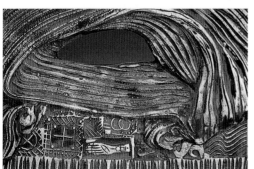

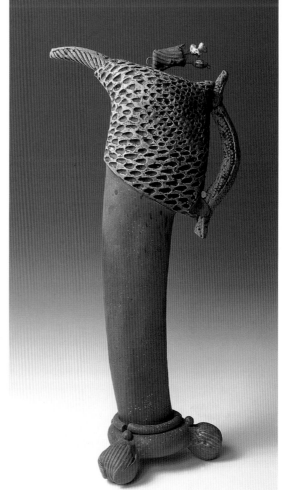

Left: Steve Smith, *Ritual Platter*. Diameter: 18" (45.5 cm), 1992. Slab over hump mold, carved; Δ10. Photo by Jerry Anthony

Center: Kathy Triplett, *Teapot*, 27" x 10" x 7" (68.5 x 25.5 x 18 cm), 1996. Slab, extruded, carved; layered underglazes, glaze; Δ3. Photo by Evan Bracken

Right: Joan F. Carcia, *Village Houses I, II, III*, 28" x 11" x 6" (71 x 28 x 15 cm), 1994. Slab; porcelain slip, oxides, stains; Δ9 reduction. Photo by artist

INTRODUCTION

Working with clay, as you're about to discover, is an art form like no other—a strange combination of seemingly disparate experiences that is, and has been for centuries, literally irresistible. Whether you're shaping moist clay into a simple cup or building a sculpture that will give voice to complex dreams and visions, the act itself can be as sensual as massage, as meditative as prayer, as challenging as tying shoelaces with one hand, as relaxing as a warm bath, or as rote—if we let it be—as sweeping the floor.

Ask any potter why he or she chose handbuilding. You're unlikely to get two identical answers, but you're

sure to hear one common thread—an astonishing depth of commitment. Ironically, this may be because handbuilding is no longer "necessary." In centuries past, potters inherited their craft and performed an essential role in fulfilling their communities' needs for functional

ware. Today, when a potter with a wheel can turn out fifty cups in an hour and when industry can reproduce endless, inexpensive, fiberglass architectural details, handsculpting clay seems especially slow and laborious. Yet people continue to shape clay by hand because doing so provides something beyond utility or expedience. Working with clay offers, as do very few activities in our mechanistic world, the opportunity to participate fully in an act of creation—to simultaneously express and fulfill a wide range of human needs.

Precisely because it invites creativity, handbuilding—working without a potter's wheel—is the most rewarding place for many beginners to start. Novice wheel-throwers have to practice (and practice and practice) before they can escape what a friend of mine used to call the "dog-bowl phenomenon"— the production of predictably heavy and lifeless work. Novice handbuilders, on the other hand, can achieve elegant results fairly quickly, with very few tools and very little practice.

This book was written with three basic goals in mind: to explain the ways in which clay can be shaped, decorated, and fired; to show you how to work with clay by walking you through a series of step-by-

step projects; and to share with you a wealth of work by different clay artists. You'll find most of the explanations and technical details in the first five chapters. Read these at a leisurely pace, but don't get bogged down in them. You don't need to be an expert before you start; knowledge will come with experience. Move on, instead, to chapter 6, where you'll find several projects, each designed to teach a different handbuilding technique, from working with coils to making and using molds. Try one out as soon as you can.

You won't be able to miss the photos of works by other artists, of course. When we put out a call for these, we received an astounding array of images, one which bore witness to the incredibly broad range of forms that contemporary claywork includes. As we selected slides and transparencies—an almost overwhelming process—we found ourselves asking very few questions about what the photographed objects "did." We didn't care whether a given piece was "functional." Our concern was its "voice." From simple tableware to sacred objects, the pieces we chose (and many we didn't) all pay exquisitely clear tribute to the hundreds of ways in which clay can speak—of those who shape it, of worlds within, and of the world without.

As you build your first projects, let these photos inspire and advise you. Let them encourage you—if you're the least bit reluctant to get dirty, to play, to treat clay not as taskmaster but as friend—to take the risk and reap the rewards that clay can bring.

CHAPTER ONE

GETTING STARTED

A s you contemplate setting up a work space and purchasing tools and supplies, remember the fact that for centuries, thousands of potters have worked with nothing more than clay, their hands, and hand-constructed kilns. Lack of access to a large studio space filled with high-tech equipment may be one of those limitations that actually works on your behalf— by bringing forth your ingenuity. There's no reason why you can't develop a well-equipped studio on a small scale, as long as you keep a few basic safety rules in mind.

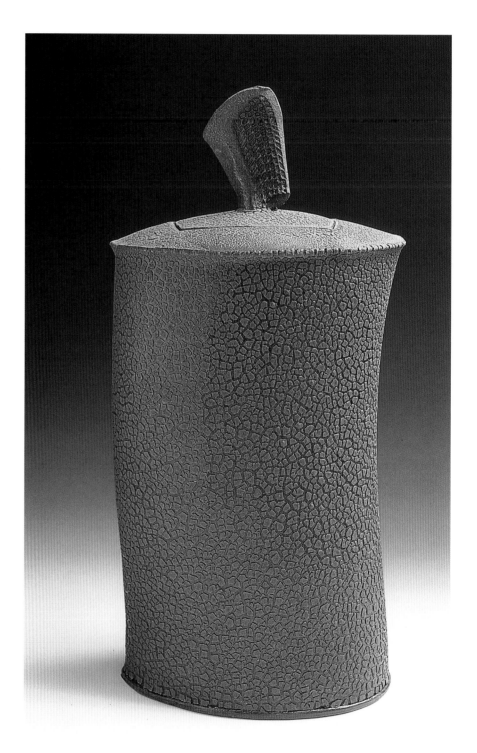

D. Hayne Bayless, *Oval Jar*, 18" x 7" x 4" (45.5 x 18 x 10 cm), 1995. Extruded; Δ10. Photo by artist

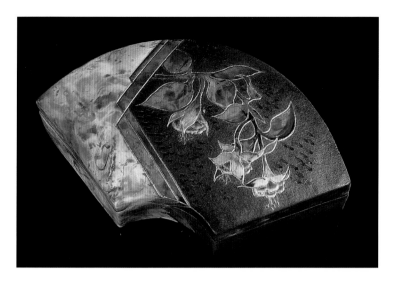

Above: Marcia Jestaedt, *Fuchsia Box*, 3-1/2" x 12" x 7" (9 x 30.5 x 18 cm), 1996. Slab; raku fired. Photo by Breger & Associates

Right: Phillip Sellers, *Untitled*, 13-1/2" x 8" (34.5 x 20.5 cm), 1996. Extruded, woven over mold; Δ5. Photo by Jerry Anthony

TOOLS AND SUPPLIES

Your initial collection of equipment, tools, and supplies certainly doesn't have to be expensive. In fact, you can make a pinch pot with nothing more than a bag of commercial clay and your hands. You'll have to fire your work in a kiln, of course, but you probably won't want to purchase this piece of equipment right away. Many beginning potters find it more practical to take a ceramics class, where there's usually an on-site kiln, or to locate a potter who will fire their work for a fee. Just be sure you have access to a kiln before you invest in other tools.

Rather than purchasing everything you could possibly want right away, equip your studio in stages, adding items as you expand your skills. **Photos 1** and **2** show some of the items that a professional potter will have on hand.

A BASIC SET-UP

Start out with the items described in the following list:

■ A work surface. While a sturdy workbench with access from all four sides is best, a single piece of plywood placed on a sturdy surface will do. Sturdy is the key here. Even a simple table made with 2 x 4s and plywood will do, as long as it doesn't jiggle around.

■ A few pieces of plywood or other boards. You'll use these to move slabs of clay and projects.

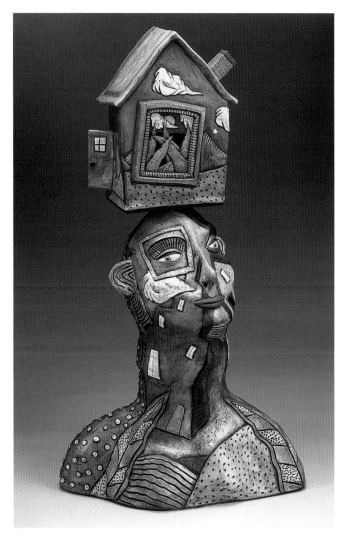

Left: David A. Stabley, *Large Head and House*, 48" x 12" x 11" (122 x 30.5 x 28 cm), 1994. Slab, coiled, pinched, carved; Δ05. Photo by Robert Brown

Above: J. Paul Sires, *Platter*, 24" x 20" x 3" (61 x 51 x 7.5 cm), 1990. Slab; Δ6. Photo by artist

■ A few sheets of canvas or newspaper. You'll cover your work surface with these to keep clay from sticking to it.

■ A respirator that's been rated effective for dust. You must wear this whenever you work with clay that is no longer moist, powdered glaze components, or dry plaster.

■ Rubber gloves. Wear these whenever you work with glazes or plaster.

■ A ruler. Besides being handy for taking measurements, your ruler will serve as a cutting guide. A metal ruler is best, as your knife won't slice into it, and it won't warp when it's exposed to moisture.

■ A spray water bottle. Misting your clay will help keep it moist.

■ Several sheets of lightweight plastic. Covering clay with these sheets will prevent it from drying out too quickly. Recycled dry-cleaning bags work well.

■ A small sharp knife. You'll use this to cut clay.

■ A length of wire. This is the perfect tool for slicing slabs from a block of soft clay. Cutting wires with small dowel handles are available from ceramic suppliers.

■ A wooden rolling pin or fat wooden dowel. You'll roll out slabs of clay just as if you were rolling out pie dough.

■ A kitchen fork. To join stiff clay pieces, you'll *score* (scratch) their edges, apply clay *slurry* (a soupy mixture of clay and water) with a stiff-bristled brush, and then press

the pieces together. A fork works well for scoring.

■ A small sponge. You'll use this to smooth out rough clay surfaces.

■ A mop and sponges. Wet-cleaning is critical in any clay studio. Never use a broom or duster; inhaling clay dust is hazardous.

■ Buckets. These are necessary for mixing the plaster from which you'll make molds and for pouring and dipping glazes. Keep a few stirring sticks on hand, too. For descriptions of other glazing tools and supplies, see chapter 4.

■ A selection of paintbrushes. You'll need these to apply stains and glazes. Include one small brush with stiff bristles, a 1/2" (1.3 cm) brush, and a pointed touch-up brush.

Above: Elyse Saperstein, *Shielded Voyage*, 14" x 12" x 4" (35.5 x 30.5 x 10 cm), 1995. Slab; Δ05. Photo by John Carlano

Right: Antonio Fink, *The Veiled One*, 23" x 16" x 16" (58.5 x 40.5 x 40.5 cm), 1995. Slab; Δ06. Photo by Guillermo Kahlo

ADDITIONS

When you're ready to expand your collection, add the items in this next list. Many are available from ceramic suppliers. Others you'll collect from a variety of sources.

■ A *pin tool* (one is shown in **Photo 1**) looks like an enlarged pin set into a handle and is the instrument you'll use for cutting clay.

■ A *scoring tool* (shown in **Photo 2**) takes the place of a kitchen fork. It consists of a handle with several stiff, crinkled wires extending from one end.

■ A wooden or rubber *rib* is the tool potters use to smooth moist clay.

■ A flat metal rib with a serrated edge works well for texturing clay surfaces and for scoring.

■ A *loop trimming tool* (two are shown against the green template in **Photo 2**) is used to carve designs into stiff clay. Dental tools also work well.

■ Several 1/2"-thick (1.3 cm) sticks will come in handy when you want to cut consistently thick slabs.

■ An electric drill with a paint-mixing attachment will make mixing plaster and glazes much easier.

■ A scale is necessary for measuring plaster, water, and glazes.

■ A rasp or file will help you sand down clay that isn't moist.

■ A pair of scissors and some cardboard will let you make templates, which will help you reproduce projects quickly.

■ Large craft knives have a myriad uses.

■ Metal hole cutters, which are available from ceramic suppliers, are also easy to make. I use a hacksaw to cut lengths of copper tubing at an angle and then sharpen the angled edges with a file. A small knife will also cut holes.

■ A turntable is especially helpful when you're making coiled projects, but has other uses as well.

■ A wooden spatula that is curved on one side and flat on the other is indispensable for paddling clay to shape it or to strengthen joints.

■ A mini-extruder (see "Major Equipment" in this chapter) will allow you to press out narrow, shaped tubes of moist clay.

■ A 90° angle or square and paper and pencils will prove useful for measuring, marking, and design work.

FOUND TOOLS

I also collect tools made for other purposes. As you grow more familiar with the various ways in which you can texture and shape clay, you'll find that kitchen-supply and hardware stores are great places to look for unusual finds. My own collection includes the items shown in **Photo 3** and described in the following list:

■ A ridged wooden roller that I found at a kitchen-supply store. This is just one of dozens of objects and implements I use for texturing clay, ranging from fabrics to wires from spiral-bound notebooks. See chapter 3 for details.

■ A pizza cutter will cut soft clay without distorting it too much.

Metal cookie cutters are also fun to use.

■ Wooden sticks and dowels in various sizes and shapes are useful for incising and shaping slabs.

■ Spoons or polished stones are the tools used to burnish clay.

■ Dental tools and knives are used to incise and carve clay.

MAJOR EQUIPMENT

When you're sure that working with clay will be more than a hobby, you may want to purchase some of the major equipment that makes the studio potter's life easier, including a slab roller, extruder, and clay cutter. Most professional studios invest in these time- and labor-saving devices, but beginners may not use them enough to justify their expense.

■ A *slab roller* (both manual and electric models are available) rolls out many slabs of clay quickly and produces wonderfully consistent results (**Photo 4**). This piece of equipment can also double as a work table.

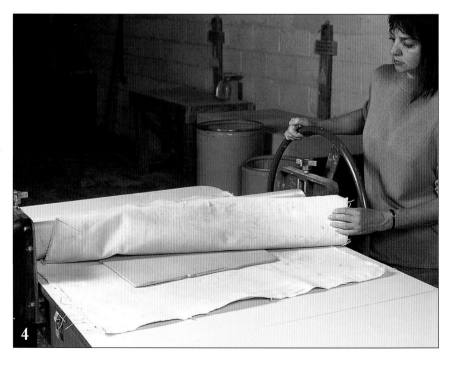

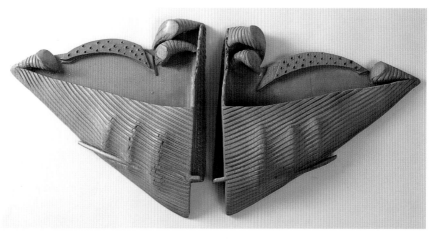

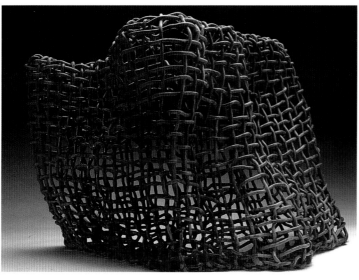

Top left: Tom Latka, *Vase,* 10" x 4" x 3" (25.5 x 10 x 7.5 cm), 1996. Extruded; Δ01. Photo by artist

Top right: Kathy Triplett, *Wall Planter,* 15" x 36" x 7" (38 x 91.5 x 18 cm), 1996. Slab; Δ3. Photo by Evan Bracken

Center left: Phyllis Kudder-Sullivan, *POD 31,* 16-1/2" x 22-1/2" x 10" (42 x 57 x 25.5 cm), 1993. Extruded and woven coils; Δ6. Photo by Joseph D. Sullivan

Center right: Michael Kifer, *Dome Basket,* 24" x 13" x 7" (61 x 33 x 18 cm), 1995. Slabs over hump mold, extruded base, slab handle; Δ05. Photo by artist

Bottom: Mark W. Forman, *Earthslam #1,* 17" x 13" x 14" (43 x 33 x 35.5 cm), 1995. Pulled and slammed slab. Photo by Joseph D. Chielli

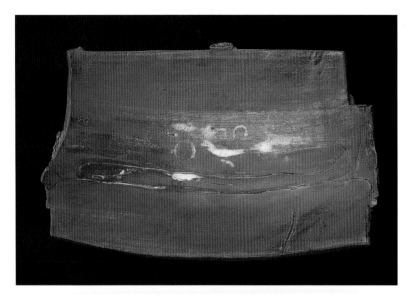

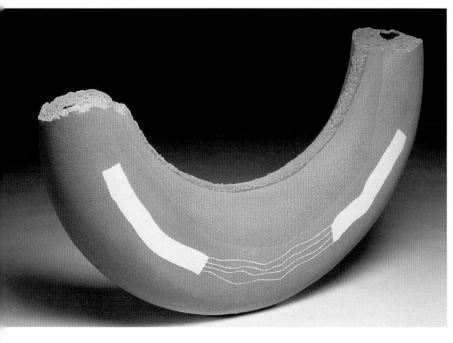

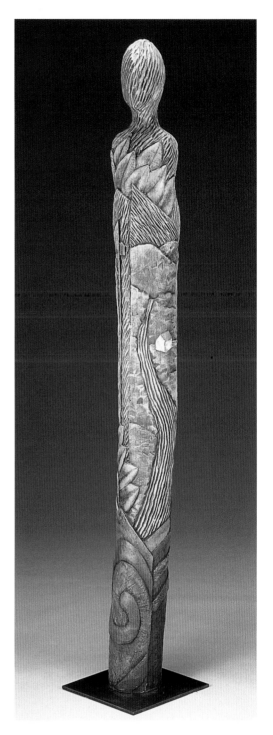

Top left: Anita McIntyre, *Inland Sea. Series II. Cooper Creek Ancient Carvings*, 3-1/2" x 20-1/2" x 12-1/4" (9 x 52 x 31 cm), 1995. Slab; terra sigillata, porcelain slip; Δ4. Photo by Johannes Kuhnen

Center left: Gordon R. Andrus, *Teapot*, 7" x 7-1/2" x 4" (18 x 19 x 10 cm), 1995. Soft slab, cast spout, pulled handle; terra sigillata; Δ04. Photo by artist

Bottom left: Nick Latka, *Rocking*, 20" x 40" x 12" (51 x 101.5 x 30.5 cm), 1990. Slip cast; Δ03. Photo by artist

Above: Christine Federighi, *Long Leaf House*, 70" x 9" x 8" (178 x 23 x 20.5 cm), 1994. Coiled, carved; Δ05; oil patina. Photo by Bridget Parlato

Marjolaine Renfro, *La Cage aux Clay*, 13" x 15" x 3" (33 x 38 x 7.5 cm), 1996. Slab; terra sigillata; Δ04. Photo by Michael Olenick

Ken Eastman, *Here*, 12-1/2" x 16-1/2" x 14-1/4" (32 x 42 x 36 cm), 1995. Slab; Δ4. Photo by artist

■ A manual or electric *extruder* produces seamless tubes of clay, either hollow or solid, and in many shapes and sizes (**Photo 5**). A wide variety of metal or wooden extruder dies (a few are shown in **Photo 6**) make it possible to extrude different shapes, from molding-like strips of clay to tubes with shaped surfaces. Some models come with expansion boxes that produce pieces as wide as 14" (35.6 cm).

■ A commercial clay cutter resembles a large cheese cutter and is ideal for slicing off uniform sections from blocks of clay or extrusions and for making small slabs quickly.

STAYING FIT

Your hands may be the most important tools you'll ever need, so keep them well oiled. The ceramics profession can be brutal on them, especially during cold weather. I apply pure lanolin to mine every night.

Keep your whole body fit as well. Bending over to load heavy pots into a kiln and lugging tons of clay into your work space can strain a weak back. There's another good reason for maintaining body strength. Like playing tennis, forming clay is akin to dance; it requires a fluidity of motion that doesn't stop at the wrist. A quick slash of a glaze-filled brush across a

5

6

Left: Karen Estelle Koblitz, *Denver Della Robbia with Nuptial Vase*, 20-1/2" x 15" x 9" (52 x 38 x 23 cm), 1989. Slab, slip cast; bisque, Δ04; glaze, Δ06. Photo by Michael Bush

Above: Jon Burke, *Terra-Cotta Clock*, 10" x 9" x 2" (25.5 x 23 x 5 cm), 1996. Slab; Δ06. Photo by Lamping Photography

clay piece several feet away or one solid whack from a stick can push a stodgy clay form into life. To ensure robust, spontaneous, direct, and sure marks on clay, your entire body must sometimes participate. As you work, alternate periods of standing and sitting, stretch frequently, observe all safety precautions, and try to relax.

WORK SPACE

■

Important safety factors (these are detailed in Appendix A on page 146) will influence where you choose to work. Inhaling or ingesting clay dust and glaze chemicals is very hazardous, so keep your work space as far from the kitchen and other living areas as possible. A well-ventilated basement, garage, or outbuilding are all possibilities.

A water source is important. If your selected site doesn't include

one, plan on transporting buckets of water to the site and changing this water regularly. Water containing clay, glazes, and plaster should never be poured into your drainage system, whether it's a public system or a septic tank. Use the clay water left over from rinsing tools and hands when you mix recycled dry clay or allow the water to evaporate and dispose of the sediment in the garbage. Water left over from rinsing glazing tools and containers should also be allowed to evaporate; the sediment can then be placed in the trash.

Few professional potters ever seem to have enough studio shelving. Rolling racks of shelves with removable ware boards are available commercially, but almost any open shelving will do. For shallow clay pieces such as plates and tiles, make your own stacking shelves by nailing 1" x 1" (2.5 x 2.5 cm) strips to each end of several

boards. These spacers will keep the boards separated when you stack them, leaving spaces for your ware.

No studio is complete—or potter safe—unless the work space is properly ventilated. A full treatment of ventilation is provided in Appendix A. Take the time to read it!

If you can't find space to call your own, enroll in a local ceramics class. These courses offer more than equipment and space. The skilled potters who teach them are there to help you when you need expert advice and will offer you the kind of hands-on learning experience that no book—even this one—can provide. If you're interested in taking a ceramics course or attending a short workshop (and I strongly recommend doing both), look for one at a nearby college or university, ceramic hobby shop, or clay supplier. Individual potters sometimes conduct classes, too.

CHAPTER TWO

EXPLORING THE NATURE OF CLAY

Michael Sherrill, *Rising Cross*, 24" x 19" x 8" (61 x 48.5 x 20.5 cm), 1995. Extruded and pulled forms, carved; low fire. Photo by Tim Barnwell

Beginning potters are sometimes dismayed by what strikes them as the vast amount of information they need to absorb. Although it's true that the technical details related to clay, glazing, and firing can sometimes seem overwhelming, it's equally true that successful potters lived centuries before many of these details were known or shared.

Treat this chapter on clay as reference material. Read it, of course, but don't get bogged down in trying to memorize every nuance of clay composition before you've experienced the thrill of touching moist clay itself. When you have questions, come back to the information offered here. It won't go away!

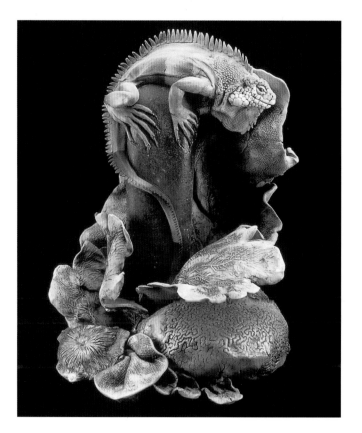

PURCHASING AND STORING CLAY

■

One-fourth of the earth is composed of this amazing substance, and because nature composes it continuously, we don't need to worry about limited supplies. Clay is often found in creek beds and along river banks and may very well be outside your back door. Whole villages have grown up around particularly fine sources.

Clay is plastic and holds together as well as it does because when its small, flat particles are moist, they stick and slide around like a wet deck of cards. It's fun to dig up some of this slippery stuff and see how it feels to mold it. I've often thought that the desire to plunge hands into clay's wet, unblemished surfaces must be a human instinct. Judging from the number of paw prints in my living room tiles, it must be an animal instinct as well. If you have clay soil in your yard, try digging some up. If you can

roll a small coil and wrap it around your finger without the clay cracking, it may be plastic enough to use.

Commercially prepared clay, sold in plastic bags, comes cleaned and prepared. No sticks or rocks to remove, and no air bubbles to make your work blow up in the kiln. The only difficult part about purchasing clay is choosing the type best suited to your needs. You'll find helpful information on this topic on pages 20-27.

Buy in quantity, but if the clay will sit unused for months, take care to keep it moist by double-bagging it. Even plastic-wrapped clay will dry out a little, and partly dried clay is very hard to re-wet, so keep the clay damp by opening the bags and misting it with a little water from time to time. Let the misted clay sit in the sealed bags for a day or two before using it so that the water will disperse evenly throughout it.

If your stored clay has dried out slightly, slice it into pieces 1/2"

(1.3 cm) thick. Dip each slice into water and return the slices to the bag. Seal the bag and let the clay sit for a few days. Wedge it well (see the next section) before using it.

Clay that is stored in an unheated area may freeze. Although it won't be ruined if it does, when it thaws, much of the water in it will probably have pooled in one area. To redistribute the moisture, slice the clay thinly (some areas will be mushy; others will be too dry), arrange the slices in the bag, and let them sit for a few weeks. You'll need to wedge this clay before you use it.

As you work with clay, you'll often find yourself setting aside a lump for later use in the same project. To prevent this lump from drying out, cover it tightly with a sheet of lightweight plastic. When you're ready to use it, re-wedge it, as its outer surface may have dried out somewhat.

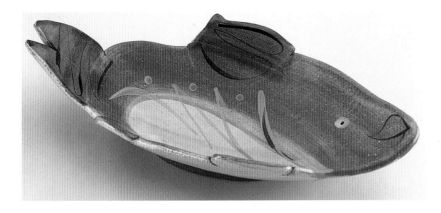

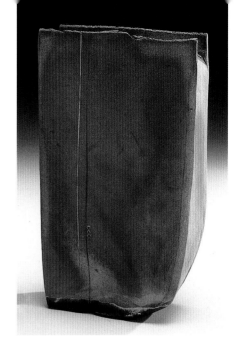

Above: Suzanne Storer, *Fish Whatnot Bowl*, 3-1/2" x 7" x 10" (9 x 18 x 25.5 cm), 1996. Slab on drape mold; Δ6. Photo by Robert Casey

Right: Penny Truitt, *Untitled*, 12-3/4" x 7-1/2" x 3" (32.5 x 19 x 7.5 cm), 1995. Slab; copper matt glaze with iron-manganese wash; raku fired. Photo by Tim Barnwell

WEDGING CLAY

■

Clay, like wine, improves with age. As more of its smaller particles get wet, the clay becomes more plastic. In Japan, one generation used to prepare clay for the next, and this in spite of the fact that plastic storage bags hadn't been invented yet!

A new bag of commercially prepared clay rarely needs any preparation. You won't always be working with clay fresh from the bag, however. More often, you'll have opened the bag, removed some clay to work with, and wrapped the rest in plastic sheets to keep it readily accessible. By the time you need it, this clay may have dried out a little. You may even be working with clay that you've recycled or mixed yourself. These clays will be uneven in consistency and may contain air bubbles or lumps. Although inconsistencies aren't as critical to the handbuilder as they are to the wheel thrower, an air bubble can ruin a handbuilt piece by showing up on a smooth surface after the piece is fired.

To redistribute moisture and eliminate lumps and bubbles, you must *wedge* (or knead) the clay (**Photo 1**). Wedging makes moist clay easier to manipulate and also helps

prepare your body by loosening it up. Because the level of moisture in your clay may dictate which forms you can shape with it that day and which will need to wait until the clay has dried out a bit, some potters also use wedging time to decide what to make.

Do your wedging on a thick, canvas-covered plaster slab, canvas-covered board, piece of smooth wood, or slab of concrete set on a very sturdy surface. (Professional wedging tables are usually heavy.) A plaster surface will quickly dry clay that is too wet, but be sure that no pieces of plaster break off, as plaster bits in the clay can explode during firing. You won't have this problem with concrete. No matter which surface you use, it should rest at a level lower than that of your work table. Your palms

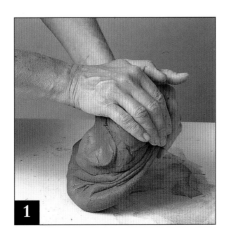

1

should sit comfortably on the wedging surface when your arms are at rest.

Use your whole body for this task, not just your arms. Start by pressing down on the lump of clay with the heel of one hand. Then use the other hand to rotate the mass of clay slightly. Push and rotate the lump of clay about 20 to 40 times, removing any foreign objects as you spot them. If the clay is especially sticky, a longer wedging will help dry it out. Don't treat wedging as if you were kneading bread. Bread dough is folded over onto itself, trapping air in the process—the exact opposite of your goal with clay.

When you perform the rocking motion of wedging correctly, a spiral pattern resembling flower petals develops in the clay. In fact, the Japanese call this process "kikumomi," which means "chrysanthemum wedging."

An alternative to wedging is to cut the clay lump in half with a wire and check the two pieces for unwanted material and air bubbles. Inspect the cut surfaces, remove any foreign objects, slice through air bubbles with a knife, and then slam the pieces together again. Repeat this process until the clay

Left: Jan Richardson, *Stone House* (lidded), 12" x 8" x 7" (30.5 x 20.5 x 18 cm), 1995. Slab, extruded, colored clay; Δ9. Photo by T. R. Wailes

Above: Geri Camarda, *The Table*, 17" x 21" x 9" (43 x 53.5 x 23 cm), 1996. Hand sculpted; Δ8; oil paints. Photo by artist

is consistently malleable. For recycled clay, I find that this process of amalgamation is sufficient. I use a slab roller to roll the clay out, cut into air bubbles when I spot them, fold the clay over, and roll it out again, repeating until the clay is lump- and air-free.

RECYCLING CLAY

■

Preparing clay that is partly dried out is difficult, which is why many clay suppliers package their clay slightly on the wet side. Because recycling dry clay is a job I detest (working with it creates hazardous clay dust), I make a practice of throwing leftover scraps of moist clay right into a plastic bag while I work. I spray the bagged scraps thoroughly with water, seal the bag, let the clay sit for a month so that it will absorb the moisture evenly, and then wedge the clay before I use it.

If you choose to recycle clay that has hardened, first let it dry out completely. Then put on your respirator (this is essential), go outdoors, and break the clay up into small pieces. Soak the pieces in water to make a slurry and allow the slurry to sit until it is thick and muddy. Then pour the slurry in a thick layer onto a large board, cover it lightly with plastic, and allow it to dry to a malleable, moist state. You'll need to check to make sure that the edges aren't drying too quickly. If they are, work them back into the center. Don't forget to wedge the clay well before you use it.

No matter how you choose to recycle your clay, be careful never to mix different types of clay together. You'll learn more about these different types (or bodies) in the next section.

SELECTING CLAY

■

As you can see in **Photo 2**, not all clays are alike. Although you'll use the same basic handbuilding methods no matter which type of clay you use, the qualities of the clay you select will affect the outcomes of the ideas you explore with it. Your clay must be suited to the purposes it will serve as well as to your own aesthetic taste.

In the pages that follow, you'll find

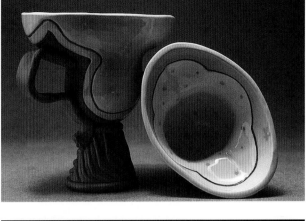

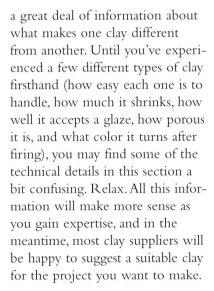

Above: Dina Wilde-Ramsing, *Talking to the Beast*, 14" x 12" x 4" (35.5 x 30.5 x 10 cm), 1994. Slab, modeled; terra sigillata; Δ03. Photo by Melva Calder

Top right: Joanna Borlase, *Two Cups*, 4" x 4" x 3" (10 x 10 x 7.5 cm), 1995. Press molded in cardboard cut-out mold, coiled, incised; slips, terra sigillata, clear glaze; Δ04. Photo by artist

Bottom right: Dennis Meiners, *Rescue Teapot*, 18" x 20" x 5" (45.5 x 51 x 12.5 cm), 1994. Stretched slab; reduction fired. Photo by Bill Bachhuber

a great deal of information about what makes one clay different from another. Until you've experienced a few different types of clay firsthand (how easy each one is to handle, how much it shrinks, how well it accepts a glaze, how porous it is, and what color it turns after firing), you may find some of the technical details in this section a bit confusing. Relax. All this information will make more sense as you gain expertise, and in the meantime, most clay suppliers will be happy to suggest a suitable clay for the project you want to make.

Primary clays are found in the earth, close to their source of origin; nature hasn't transported them to other locations. Because they're the clays closest to the chemical definition of clay (a clay, incidentally, that doesn't actually exist), they're considered to be the "purest" clays. *China clay*, from which porcelain is made, is a primary clay.

Secondary clays are those that over the aeons have been carried by water and ice to new locations. These clays are usually filled with minerals and organic matter that they've picked up along the way, impurities that tend to make them fire to many different colors. The iron oxide in *terra-cotta*, for example, makes this secondary clay fire to a warm red.

The clays available from suppliers have been formulated and vary both in their ingredients and the proportions in which those ingredients are mixed. Because each *body* (or type) has its own characteristics, it will be better suited to some projects and processes than to others.

I learned a good lesson on clay suitability and on life dictating art years ago, when I worked in Mexico with a clay from a local pottery. Whenever I used this clay to make shapes that varied a great deal from the forms typical of that locale, my pieces collapsed, warped, or cracked. Potters in that area knew their clay and what could be done with it; the forms they designed were the only ones that survived.

Experimentation is the best way to get to know different clay bodies, but knowing a bit about their various characteristics will help guide your experiments. A clay's firing temperature, texture, porosity and absorption rate, color, plasticity, tendency to warp, and degree of shrinkage will all affect your final product.

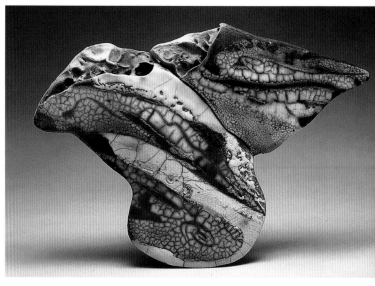

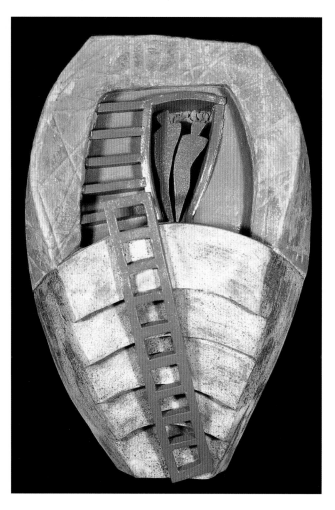

Left: Glenda E. Guion, *Anasazi Ladder*, 23" x 18" x 5" (58.5 x 45.5 x 12.5 cm), 1995. Slab; lithium glaze; Δ04; acrylic paint. Photo by artist

Above: Steven Forbes-deSoule, *Time Shard #5*, 18" x 3" x 25" (45.5 x 7.5 x 63.5 cm), 1995. Slab; raku fired. Photo by artist

FIRING TEMPERATURES

The wet clay with which potters work bears little resemblance to the fired clay of their final products. When clay is *fired* (or baked) in the intense heat of a kiln, it becomes hard and brittle. Each clay body, depending upon its composition, has its own *maturation point* during firing—a point at which the clay vitrifies, becoming dense, waterproof, glasslike, and impervious to acids.

Earthenware clays, for example, are low-firing secondary clays that mature at temperatures below 2000°F (1093°C). *Stoneware* and *porcelain*, on the other hand, are high-firing clays that vitrify only at temperatures over 2000°F. *Raku clays* are low-firing clays that are mixed to withstand the stress of being fired quickly and then cooled quickly.

If a clay is fired beyond its maturation point, it may warp and will eventually melt. The upper range of temperatures to which a given clay can be fired—its *cone-firing range*—is designated by the symbol Δ, followed by one or more numbers—Δ02, for example. A complete list of these ranges is provided in Appendix B on page 147. (The cone-numbering system may confuse you at first. Δ022 is extremely low, Δ02 is higher, Δ2 is higher still, and Δ10 is very high.) When you purchase commercial clay, the cone-firing range is provided by the manufacturer. Pay attention to these ranges. If you fire a low-firing earthenware at a stoneware range, it will melt in the kiln!

Clay is not always fired to its vitrification point. It should be, however, when the finished product will be displayed or used outdoors or in wet areas indoors. Clay that has not vitrified may absorb water, which in turn may cause the glaze to flake off and allow repeated freezing and thawing to crack the piece. Professional potters often tap a piece of fired ware to check its "ring." A higher-fired clay will give a clearer and higher-pitched tone than low-fired ware.

How might the firing range of a clay affect your work? Suppose you wanted to make an unglazed indoor planter that would hold water. You'd probably choose a high-firing clay that would become so dense when fired to maturity that it wouldn't absorb water. Even when low-firing clays are fired to their maturity point, they can still be somewhat porous.

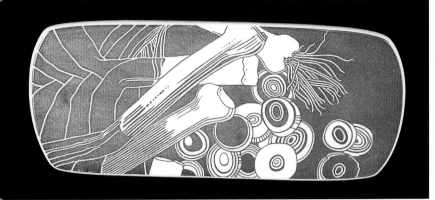

Top left: Laura Jane Nuchols, *Leeks*, 1-1/2"
x 5-1/2" x 13" (4 x 14 x 33 cm), 1994.
Slab; sgraffito on porcelain; Δ10. Photo by
David Andersen

Top right: Ginny Marsh, *Garden Vessel*,
27" x 16" x 14" (68.5 x 40.5 x 35.5 cm),
1994. Coiled, scraped with surform;
stained exterior; Δ9 reduction. Photo by
Bob Payne

Center left: Bernadette Stillo, *Fins—Spiral
Fish Ceremonial Rattle*, 5" x 3" x 2" (12.5 x
7.5 x 5 cm), 1996. Two pinch pots joined
with clay balls inside, slab additions,
stamped with hand-carved bisqued stamps;
iron oxide; Δ02. Photo by John Carlano

Center right: Carrie Anne Parks, *Bird House
with Squash*, 14" x 9-1/2" x 11-1/2"
(35.5 x 24 x 29 cm), 1993. Slab,
pinched; slip, underglaze; Δ05. Photo
by artist

Bottom: Karen Orsillo, *Cream and Sugar*,
3" x 4" x 3" (7.5 x 10 x 7.5 cm), 1994.
Slab, colored porcelain; Δ8. Photo by
Charley Freiberg

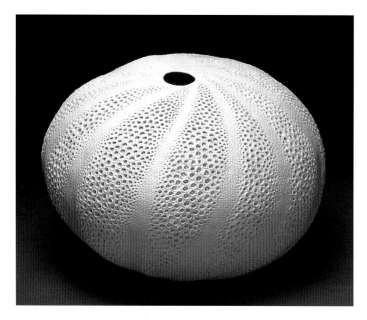

Top left: Bernadette Stillo, *Spiked Squash with a Twist—Ceremonial Rattle*, 7" x 4" x 4" (18 x 10 x 10 cm), 1995. Two pinch pots joined with hand-rolled clay balls inside, coiled additions; iron oxide; Δ02. Photo by John Bender

Top right: Sandi Pierantozzi, *Pumpkin Creamer/Sugar Set*. Creamer: 5" x 5" x 4" (12.5 x 12.5 x 10 cm), 1994. Slab; glaze, terra sigillata; Δ04. Photo by artist

Center right: Georgina Holt, *Porcelain Dinnerware: Two Plates with Translucent Cups*. Plate diameter: 11-1/4" (28.5 cm), 1996. Slab, incised decorations; clear glaze; Δ10. Photo by Paul Figura

Bottom: Carol Sevick, *Tunicate*, 10" x 12" x 12" (25.5 x 30.5 x 30.5 cm), 1990. Pinched; Δ10. Photo by Michael Cohen

Left: Ginny Marsh, *Garden Sentinel*, 21-1/2" x 18" x 7" (54.5 x 45.5 x 18 cm), 1994. Stretched slab; white slip; Δ9 reduction. Photo by artist

Above: Curtis and Suzan Benzle, *Diminuendo*, 4" x 5" x 5" (10 x 12.5 x 12.5 cm), 1994. Inlaid colored porcelain; unglazed; Δ7. Photo by Curtis Benzle

COLOR

The color of a fired clay depends upon its mineral content and the temperature to which you fire it. The lack of certain minerals in porcelain make it a pure white color, for example; those in Georgia Lizella make the fired clay dark brown; and the iron in a fired earthenware terra-cotta turns it the color of warm, sun-baked earth.

If you don't plan to glaze your project, the fired color of the clay body you choose will be especially important because it will show in the finished piece. If you do plan to use glazes, you might want to choose a white clay body such as porcelain because glaze colors tend to be brighter on white clay.

HARDNESS AND POROSITY

Fired stoneware and porcelain clays are harder than fired earthenware. Stoneware, as its name suggests, is much like stone in its texture and density, and porcelain—a very high-firing clay—has the same smooth, dense translucency and sheen as a seashell.

Again, these clay characteristics will influence your decisions regarding what to make with them. Because they are harder and denser, stoneware and porcelain make dinnerware that is more chip-resistant than that made with earthenware.

Different clays also vary in their degree of porosity at maturity. Earthenwares are still porous; high-firing stoneware and porcelain clays aren't. If you make an earthenware vessel and want it to hold liquid, you'll have to glaze it because only a glaze will make it impervious to water.

Because less porous clays absorb less water, they also withstand the effects of freezing and thawing better than porous clays. For these reasons, nonporous clays work very well for outdoor projects such as the coiled planter presented on pages 99–103.

A potter working with a new clay might want to perform an easy test to measure the clay's *porosity* (or absorption rate). He or she would first fire an unglazed clay sample to maturity and then weigh it on a gram scale. After soaking the sample overnight in water and wiping it clean, the potter would weigh it again. The percentage gain in weight is the figure used to indicate the porosity of the clay body. Stoneware will average 1% to 6%. An earthenware might be 12% at Δ06 and 6% at Δ2. Porcelain might be only .5% at Δ10.

The *saturation coefficient* of a clay is also important, as it affects the clay's ability to withstand harsh weather conditions. To find out what the saturation coefficient of a clay is, the potter would take the porosity test one step further by boiling the unglazed piece and weighing it once again. The potter would then divide the piece's soaked weight by its boiled weight. The result is the saturation coefficient of that clay. This figure should be at least .8 (preferably .85) or higher if the clay will be used outdoors.

Above: Linda Bourne, *Untitled*, 10" x 8" x 3" (25.5 x 20.5 x 7.5 cm), 1994. Colored clay; Δ7. Photo by Bill Bachhuber

Right: Jeffery Kaller, *Lamp*, 24" x 12" x 12" (61 x 30.5 x 30.5 cm), 1995. Metallic sulfates. Photo by John Carlano

TEXTURE, STRENGTH, AND PLASTICITY

Texture, too, makes a difference. Porcelain, so translucent in appearance, is especially appropriate for delicate shell-like forms. Not surprisingly, the word "porcelain" is derived from the Italian word for cowrie shell—"porcella."

Some clays have more naturally occurring aggregates such as sand in them. Long ago, people discovered that pots made from these coarse-textured clays had more *tooth*. They were usually stronger and were less likely to shrink, crack, or explode when used as cooking vessels. Early potters deliberately added sand, straw, or ground seashells to their clay to open up its pores, which in turn "tempered" the clay, allowing it to dry evenly and expand and contract without stress.

Today, *grog* (ground fired clay) or other tempering materials are added to clay to serve the same purposes. Fine-particled clays such as porcelain, which don't contain much grog (or have much tooth), tend to shrink more when they dry. To make a very large coiled planter, you probably wouldn't use a porcelain clay unless grog had been added to it.

Some clays are more plastic than others. Aging improves plasticity as well. Handbuilders can usually sacrifice some of the plasticity that a wheel-thrower needs, but if you're working with tightly curved forms rather than angular ones, you'll need a more plastic clay that will bend easily without cracking. Plastic clays do have one disadvantage: they will shrink more when they dry and when they're fired (all clays shrink to some extent), and shrinkage can cause cracking. The more plastic the clay, the more attention you must pay to matching moisture levels when you join two pieces together.

SHRINKAGE

All clay shrinks when it dries and again when it is fired. If you want to make a piece of a specific size (a planter that will fit perfectly into your kitchen windowsill, for example), you must know the shrinkage rate of the clay you're using and then calculate how large the piece should be before drying and firing. Shrinkage rates are often provided by the clay supplier, but whenever you start working with a new clay, it's wise to test and record this rate yourself, as it will vary both with the clay body and the temperature to which you fire it. The higher the temperature, the greater the shrinkage; some porcelains may shrink as much as 15%.

To calculate the shrinkage rate of any clay, start by making a *clay ruler* (**Photo 3**). Roll out a strip of the clay from which you intend to make your project, making it about 1/4" to 3/8" (6 to 9 mm)

Cristina Acosta, *Bold Floral Variation* and *Assorted Geometric Variation*. Each: 12" x 7" x 12" (30.5 x 18 x 30.5 cm), 1996. Slip cast; underglazes, clear glaze; Δ06. Photo by Gary Alvis

thick. Cut a 6"-long (15.2 cm) strip from it. Then, either press a ruler with raised numbers into the clay strip in order to create impressions of the dimensions, or just place the ruler next to the clay strip and transfer the dimension markings to the clay. Also mark the clay strip with the temperature to which you'll be firing it and with the type of clay from which you made it.

Allow the clay strip to dry. Then hold it against the ruler to compare the dimension markings. You'll note that the clay ruler has shrunk and that the 5" (12.7 cm) mark on the actual ruler now corresponds with a different dimension on the clay ruler—perhaps 5-1/4" (13.3 cm).

Now fire the clay strip and compare it with the ruler again. The clay will have shrunk even more. The 5" mark on the ruler may now correspond with the 5-1/2" (14 cm) mark on the strip. Note that approximately half the clay

shrinkage occurs in drying and half in firing.

How would you use this clay ruler when making a project? Let's consider an example. Suppose you wanted to end up with a 5"-long fired piece of clay. Hold the two rulers side by side and look for the 5" mark on the real ruler. The corresponding mark on the clay ruler, perhaps 5-1/2", will let you know how long your moist clay piece should be before drying and firing.

Coming up with a percentage figure for shrinkage of a given clay is fairly easy. Following is an example in which the length of the original wet clay strip was 6" and its dried, fired length is 5-1/2".

■ Subtract the length of the dried, fired clay ruler from the length of the wet clay ruler.

6 minus 5-1/2 = 1/2

■ Divide the result by the length of the wet clay ruler.

1/2 divided by 6 = .09

■ Multiply the result by 100.

.09 x 100 = 9

The shrinkage rate of this clay is 9%. To use this percentage figure when making a project, first decide how long or wide you want the finished piece to be. We'll use 5-1/2" in the following example:

■ Subtract the percentage shrinkage rate from 100 and divide the desired dimension by the result.

100 minus 9 = 91

5-1/2 divided by 91 = .06

■ Multiply the result by 100.

.06 x 100 = 6

■ Your moist clay piece should be 6" long.

A clay ruler is especially handy when you're trying to fit a clay shape to a particular space. Let's say that you want to make a two-hole switch plate cover for an electrical outlet. Rather than measure the distance between the two holes with a real ruler, measure it with your dried, fired clay ruler and make a moist clay switch plate with a center section as wide as the clay-ruler measurement you recorded. After the switch plate is fired, the distance between its holes should be perfect.

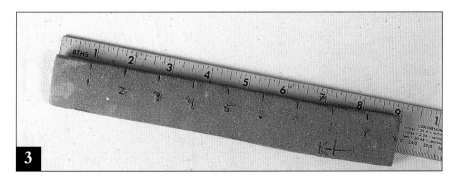

3

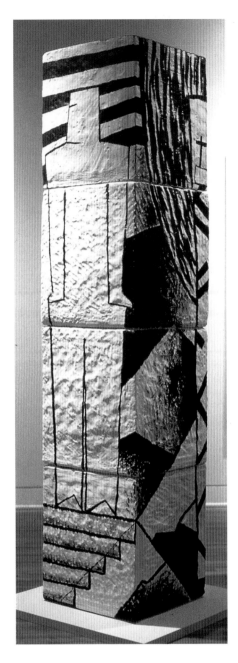

Left: J. Paul Sires, *Column of Vision*, 2' x 2' x 8' (.6 x .6 x 2.4 m), 1988. Slab; white and black slip; Δ6. Photo by artist

Above: Andra Ellis, *Myself a Scream*, 22" x 25" x 2" (56 x 63.5 x 5 cm), 1990. Slab; matt and gloss glazes; Δ04. Photo by Bill Moritz

WARPING

Warping is a potential problem to consider when you're making a large sculpture consisting of several pieces that must fit together. To test a clay for warping, fire a 4-3/4"-long (12 cm) strip of it, supporting it with two kiln posts (see page 73) spaced about 3-1/2" (9 cm) apart. If the strip sags, consider underfiring your project—firing it to a temperature below the maturation point of the clay. This will decrease warping and is a good method to use for clay pieces that will end up indoors and stay dry.

Another way to prevent warping is to build and include in your sculpture an internal structure of supporting clay ribs and buttresses. (Think of bridge and road designs when designing these.) Also keep in mind that curved forms have more structural integrity than long, flat, unsupported forms. Temporary supports used only during firing can also help. The braces described on page 91 are a good example.

MATCHING CLAY BODIES

■

Because different clay bodies shrink at different rates, you can't make a project by joining one type of clay to another unless they have the same shrinkage rates. If you try, you'll find that the parts of the project are likely to crack or separate at the joints. Be sure never to combine scraps of different clays either. If you have more than one type of clay in your studio, label their bags clearly.

CHAPTER THREE

HANDBUILDING TECHNIQUES

Trying out each of the classic handbuilding techniques, which you'll do when you make the projects in chapter 6, is the best way to acquaint yourself with the ways in which professional potters manipulate clay. In the meantime, a preview of these techniques and a brief introduction to some of the terms that potters use will help make the project instructions easier to follow once you get to them.

Richard Zane Smith, *Fluted Vessel,* 26" x 19" (66 x 48.5 cm), 1988. Coiled native clays and slips with stains; wood fired. Photo by Robert Sherwood

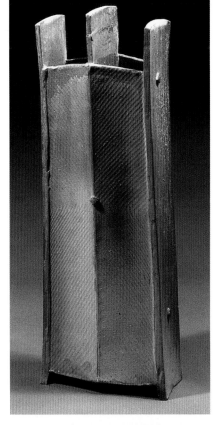

Top left: Mark Lueders, *Form I*, 24" x 16" x 12"
(61 x 40.5 x 30.5 cm), 1996. Precolored slabs;
printed with silkscreens, low-fire slips; Δ1. Photo
by artist

Top right: Larry Halvorsen, *Spires*. Height: 18" to
21" (45.5 x 53.5 cm), 1995. Coiled, carved; slip,
sgraffito; Δ10 reduction. Photo by Lynn Thompson-
Hamrick

Center: Tim Crane, *Box*, 20" x 5" x 2-1/2" (51 x
12.5 x 6.5 cm), 1987. Slab-built stoneware; salt
fired in wood and oil kiln. Photo by artist

Far right: Kathryn Allen, *Prairie School Vase Series*,
28" x 5-1/2" x 5-1/2" (71 x 14 x 14 cm), 1996.
Slab, carved, inlaid copper; glazes; raku fired.
Photo by Tom Holt

Bottom: Lana Wilson, *Cedar Creek Teapot*, 8" x
17" x 5" (20.5 x 43 x 12.5 cm), 1996. Soft slab;
stamped; Δ6, Δ06. Photo by artist

The Potter's Language

■

Ceramists, like people in any professional group, have developed a work-specific vocabulary that makes their lives easier. In this section, you'll find definitions of some terms you'll need to know and explanations of a few basic processes.

At each stage of dryness, clay exhibits certain characteristics. These are important because in each handbuilding technique, you'll use clay at a particular level of dryness.

■ *Moist* (or *plastic*) clay is soft and pliable. Take a look at **Photo 1**, which shows clay at three different moisture levels. At the left of this photo is a moist clay slab, sliced right from a new bag. For some handbuilding techniques, you'll work with clay in this plastic state.

■ *Stiff* clay is clay that has dried just enough to stand on its own without sagging. At the center of **Photo 1** is a slab that has dried and stiffened somewhat. To construct tall, straight pieces, you'll work with clay in this state so that the walls of your project won't collapse as you build them.

■ *Leather-hard* clay has dried even more. At the right of **Photo 1** is a leather-hard slab; it's too dry to bend without cracking. In its early leather-hard stages, clay is still somewhat flexible. In later stages, although the clay can't be bent, it is still moist enough to retain impressions, so you can easily incise its surface to create a texture. Wear a respirator whenever you're working with leather-hard clay that is dry enough to create clay dust.

■ *Bone-dry* clay is completely dry and warm to the touch. It is rigid, water-absorbent, uniform in color, and very fragile. You may work on clay at this stage, incising designs in it and using a kitchen scouring pad or sandpaper to smooth rough edges, but many potters avoid doing so, both because the clay is so fragile and because the clay dust created is hazardous. (Never forget to wear a respirator when you work on bone-dry clay.) Any clay piece you make must be bone-dry before you can fire it.

■ *Greenware* is bone-dry clay that has not yet been fired.

■ *Casting slip* is a liquid mixture of clay, water, and electrolytic substances, which can be purchased or mixed by hand. Slip-cast pieces are made by pouring casting slip into plaster molds and allowing it to harden.

Moisture levels are also important because clay pieces generally adhere better to one another if they have the same moisture content. Although there are situations in which you'll seal joints between stiff slabs with coils of moist clay, pressing a stiff clay slab against a moist one

Marsha McCarthy, *Paradise*, 18" x 11" x 4" (45.5 x 28 x 10 cm), 1995. Incised; underglaze; Δ06; dyed and waxed. Photo by Dean Powell

won't usually yield a very strong joint. For this reason, as you work on a project, you may need to cover some pieces with sheets of plastic to keep them from drying out as you work on other pieces. You may also need to even out the moisture level of a number of pieces before you can continue working. One way to do this is to place the pieces closely together, cover them loosely with plastic, and leave them overnight to distribute the moisture evenly among them.

Making a seam between two pieces of soft, moist clay is easy; you'll simply press the pieces together. To join pieces of leather-hard clay, you must first score their surfaces in a criss-cross fashion, using a kitchen fork or scoring tool. (For more precise fits when joining narrow edges, you'll cut the edges at matching angles.) Then you'll brush the scored areas with water or with a clay slurry made from the same clay

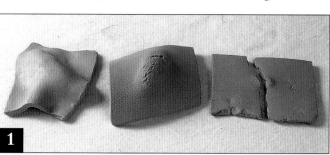

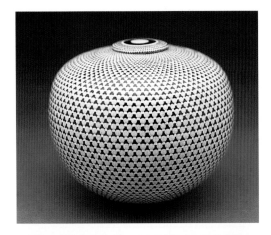

Top left: Roddy Brownlee Reed, *10,482 Spot Series*, 4-1/4" x 5-3/16" (11 x 13.5 cm), 1994. Pinched from single ball of clay; brush-applied glaze; Δ04. Photo by Robert Polzer

Bottom left: Roddy Brownlee Reed, *Scallop Series*, 4-9/16" x 5" (11.5 x 12.5 cm), 1995. Pinched from one lump of clay; brush-applied glaze, Δ04. overfired gold overglaze. Photo by Robert Polzer

Above: Wesley Anderegg, *Salt and Pepper Shakers*. Each shaker: 6" x 3" x 3" (15 x 7.5 x 7.5 cm), 1995. Pinched, coiled; slips, matt glaze; Δ06. Photo by artist

you're using, and press the pieces firmly together.

One other set of terms, both related to firing clay, will make it easier for you to understand the information that's coming up.

■ *Bisque firing* is the process of heating a bone-dry clay or slip-cast piece in the kiln in order to harden it so that it will be less fragile. It is usually the first of two firings a piece undergoes and takes place at relatively low kiln temperatures.

■ *Glaze firing* is usually the second firing that a clay or slip-cast piece undergoes. Its purpose is to melt the glaze you've applied to bisqued ware and fuse it with the clay or casting slip. Glaze-firing temperatures are generally high.

Now you're ready to begin exploring handbuilding techniques. We'll cover these one at a time.

PINCHING

■

Pinching is simply the manipulation of a single lump of clay with one's hands. Although it's an easy process to describe and, at one level, easy to learn, true expertise in this technique is rare. Roddy Reed, whose work is shown on this page, can create magnificent pieces without using a single tool to shape the clay.

Basic pinch pots are started by using the thumbs to indent the center of a fist-sized lump of clay. The walls of the lump are then thinned and shaped by holding the lump in the palm of one hand while pinching the clay with the other hand. By rotating the lump and working gradually from its bottom upward, the artist creates a natural organic shape—symmetric for some people, asymmetric for others (**Photo 2**). Many variations

are possible; you'll find several described on page 106.

Extended pinch is a technique in which a piece is built by pinching moist lumps of clay to make objects as small or as large as you like. The shaped and interlocking sections of handsculpted clay make extended pinch work very strong.

Above: Carol Stirton-Broad, *Raku Teapot*, 6" x 8" x 4-1/2" (15 x 20.5 x 11.5 cm), 1995. Press molded, coiled additions; raku fired. Photo by artist

Top right: Mark Cavatorta, *Untitled*, 9" x 15" (23 x 38 cm), 1991. Coiled; unglazed; wood fired, Δ10 reduction. Photo by Dennis Maxwell

Right: Janet Braley, *Lattice Bowl*, 13" x 5" (33 x 12.5 cm), 1996. Cut slab; Shino glaze; Δ10. Photo by Jack Pettee

COILING

■

Coiled work is formed by wrapping a rope of clay around itself, stacking the coils to build height and adding new coils as necessary. Many coiled pieces are round, but a coiled work certainly doesn't have to be.

To make the coils by hand, you'll roll the clay out on a flat surface while exerting gentle pressure with your fingers (**Photo 3**). Some potters roll the clay vertically between their palms, allowing the suspended coil to develop downward. It's also possible to make coils with an extruder.

The diameter of the coils will depend on the size, use, and desired appearance of your project. Thick coils make the work progress rapidly, of course, and can be smoothed and flattened to add height quickly. Some very successful large but delicate pots, however, are made with narrow coils.

To start a simple coiled pot, the potter rolls out a small round slab, as thick as the coils to be used. This slab, which will serve as the base of the pot, is placed on a turntable that has been covered with a sheet of paper to prevent the clay from sticking to it. After scoring the edges of the slab, the potter wraps a coil around it, pinching it in place well. Then, to build the walls of the pot, the coil is wrapped around and on top of itself, and the coils are pushed together to join them (**Photo 4**). Several coils are usually necessary.

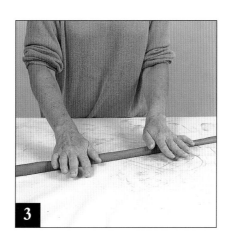

3

4

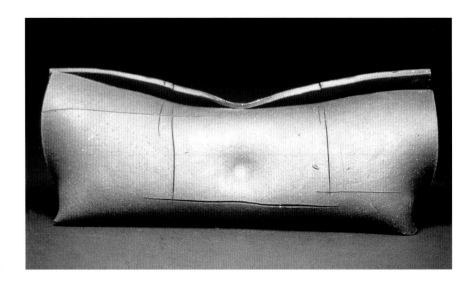

Left: Hazel Mae Rotimi, *Bremen Town—Musicians* (multiple planter), 25" x 15" x 6" (63.5 x 38 x 15 cm), 1996. Beaten joined pots, coiled animals, incised; unglazed. Photo by Sharon Howard (Double Exposure)

Above: Mary Kay Botkins, *Untitled*, 2" x 6" x 1-1/2" (5 x 15 x 4 cm), 1994. Folded slab; unglazed; Δ1 reduction. Photo by Neil Pickett

To join one coil to the next, the potter either butts their ends together and smooths the joint or tapers one end of each coil, overlaps the tapered ends, and smooths them together.

The coils only need to be pinched together on one surface of a pot (either interior or exterior), but they must be pinched together firmly so that the pot will be strong enough not to crack along its joints. Sometimes the potter leaves the pinched surfaces intact to add visual texture; at other times, the surfaces are smoothed out (many ancient pieces were made in this fashion), first with the fingers and then with a paddle or rib (**Photo 5**).

WORKING WITH SLABS

■

Slabs are flat pieces of clay that have been sliced directly from a block of clay or rolled out to the desired thickness on an absorbent surface. Some projects are made with moist slabs while others are constructed with slabs that have been allowed to dry and stiffen a bit. Unlike moist slabs, which won't stand up well when you're trying to build tall, straight pieces and which must be handled with a light touch in order not to lose crispness of definition, stiff slabs can be bent but are firm. Shaping soft slabs, allowing them to stiffen, and then joining them to other stiff slabs is also possible.

MAKING SLABS

If your moist clay is lumpy or its moisture level is inconsistent, start by wedging it well. Then use any of the methods described in this section to make slabs from it.

To roll slabs out by hand, first place a lump of wedged clay on a canvas-covered work surface. Hit it several times with the edge of your palm to thin it out a bit. Then roll out the clay with a wooden rolling pin or dowel, varying directions, just as if you were rolling out a pie crust (**Photo 6**). To ensure consistent thickness, turn the slab over several times as you do this.

One way to produce multiple slabs of equal thickness is to use a cut-off wire and two sticks with equidistant notches carved in them. As shown in **Photo 7**, by fitting the

5

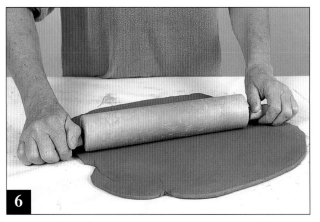

6

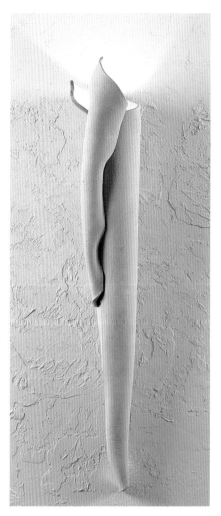

Above: Trudy Evard Chiddix, *Boogie-Woogie Brew*. Teapot: 10-1/2" x 11" x 7" (26.5 x 28 x 18 cm), 1991. Slab, coiled, impressed; black slip; clear glaze, Δ5; black luster, Δ018. Photo by Allen Bryan

Right: Gordon R. Andrus, *Box Series* (leather lined), 5" x 4-1/2" x 4-1/2" (12.5 x 11.5 x 11.5 cm), 1995. Soft slab, press-molded feet; terra sigillata; Δ04. *Photo by artist*

Far right: Janet Braley, *Wall Sconce Blue Twin*, 32" x 6" x 6" (81.5 x 15 x 15 cm), 1994. Slumped slab; Δ1. Photo by Jack Pettee

wire into a pair of notches and drawing the sticks back towards yourself, you can slice off an even slab. Each time you slice another slab, lower the wire to the next set of notches so that all your slabs will be of equal thickness.

Another way to guarantee slabs of equal thickness is to roll out each one between two sticks of equal thickness until the rolling pin comes

to rest on the sticks. You may also use two stacks of flat sticks, each stick the same thickness as the others. Place a lump of clay between the stacks and draw a tightly gripped cutting wire flat along the uppermost sticks to slice off one slab (**Photo 8**). Remove a stick from each stack and slice off another slab in the same fashion. Remove another pair of sticks, and slice again.

Each slab you slice off will be the same thickness—that of one stick.

With a little practice, you can produce thin, even slabs rapidly without using sticks or rolling pins. Slice a piece of clay from a lump, lift it up, and throw it flat on the work surface. Using both hands, lift the slab by its far edge, flip it over, and slam it hard on the table (**Photo 9**). Repeat this "throwing"

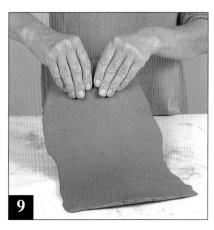

process several times until the slab is as thin as you want. Note that the edges of slabs made in this fashion may be a bit thinner than their centers.

A slab roller (shown on page 12) saves a lot of time and work by producing perfectly even slabs in a wide range of thicknesses. Some slab rollers force the clay between adjustable rollers; others have a movable roller that passes over the canvas-covered clay.

When you plan to make a project with leather-hard slabs, make more slabs than you think you'll actually need so that they can all dry to leather hard together. Nothing is more frustrating than nearing the end of a project only to discover that you have to speed-dry one more stiff piece of clay!

MOVING ROLLED SLABS

Once you've rolled out a slab, how do you move it around without tearing or distorting it? Cover it first with a piece of canvas or newspaper and then with a piece of wallboard or plywood. (I use a painted or sealed piece of plywood, which won't warp from the moisture in the clay.) Then flip the slab over, lifting it by grasping the canvas on which you rolled it rather than by touching the clay. If you need to dry the slab before working with it, remove the canvas that now rests on top of it and cover the slab loosely with plastic. To dry several slabs, roll each one out on a separate canvas-covered board, cover each slab with either a piece of newspaper or canvas, and then just stack up the boards. For relatively slow drying, cover the stack lightly with plastic; for faster drying, leave the stack uncovered.

If you didn't roll out your slab on a loose piece of canvas and have to handle the clay with your hands, give it a few licks with a rolling pin. Although the clay may look flat, it has a "memory," so you must reorient its particles to flatten it again.

SOFT SLAB WORK

Pieces made with soft slabs are characteristically fluid in appearance, as the moist, pliable clay is easy to fold, bend, press into open-face molds, drape over hump molds (convex objects such as carved styrofoam blocks), or drape into concave sling molds made by tacking loose fabric to frames. Making seams in soft clay is easy as well. You'll learn how to make a variety of soft-slab projects in chapter 6, but you'll want to experiment with texturing the surface of soft clay before you start these.

If you've never worked with moist slabs before, roll out several and start by using your fingers to make impressions in one. Then gather objects—from your kitchen to your yard—and experiment by pressing them into the other slabs. Try anything from ravioli cutters to acorns and fabric to metal lath. **Photos 10**, **11**, **12**, and **13** show a range of textures and the objects with which they were made. Some

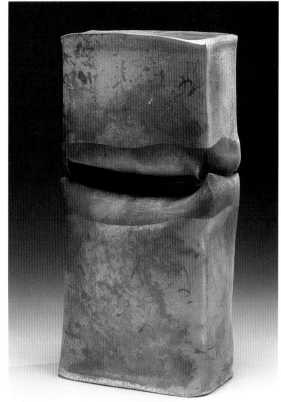

Above: Linda Workman-Morelli, *Night of the Falling Stars*, 17" x 16" x 5" (43 x 40.5 x 12.5 cm), 1990. Slab; copper oxide, salt; pit fired. Photo by Bill Bachhuber

Right: Penny Truitt, *Canyon Walls II*, 18" x 9" x 5" (45.5 x 23 x 12.5 cm), 1994. Slabs folded over a form; raku fired. Photo by Tim Barnwell

artists make and use bisque-fired clay stamps such as those shown in **Photo 13**.

You can also texture a soft or stiff slab by adding pieces of clay to it (**Photo 13**). If the slab and clay pieces are both stiff, score them and brush on some slurry before pressing them together. If the slabs are moist, just press them together.

For a soft texture, try placing a soft slab on a piece of foam rubber or a pillow filled with wadded plastic and pressing into the upper surface of the slab with any hard instrument (**Photo 14**).

For a fluid effect, place a soft slab on a small piece of plywood. Rest some objects such as clay shapes, beans, or seeds on the slab (**Photo 15**). Cover these with another slab (**Photo 16**). Then lift the plywood and drop it hard on the table or floor (**Photo 17**). The uppermost slab will take on the shape of the objects beneath it (**Photo 18**). If you've used natural objects such as beans or seeds, you can press the

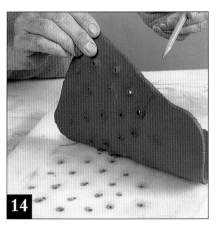

14

15

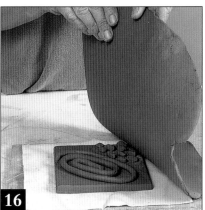

16

17

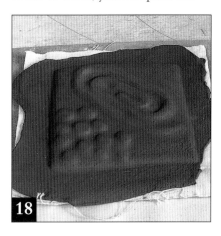

18

Left: Margaret F. Patterson, *Sprung-Spring String*, 9-1/2" x 8-1/2" x 3" (24 x 21.5 x 7.5 cm), 1996. Slab cut with sprung spring wire, coiled additions; ∆6. Photo by Rick Lubrant

Above: Mary Kay Botkins, *Untitled*, 5" x 5" x 1-1/2" (12.5 x 12.5 x 4 cm), 1994. Folded slab; unglazed porcelain; ∆10 reduction. Photo by Neil Pickett

slabs together at the edges, pierce holes in the bottom slab to allow moisture to escape during firing, and fire the entire sandwiched piece. The objects inside will burn out during the firing. Alternatively, you can texture a single slab by placing the objects directly onto the plywood; just lift the slab away from them after is has stiffened.

One of the most intriguing textures comes from slicing off a piece of soft clay with the spring wire from a spiral notebook or screen door (**Photo 19**). Resist the urge to touch, sponge, or otherwise alter this texture or others. Overmanipulating clay destroys the crispness and delicacy of its texture and soon gives the clay an overworked look. Also, keep your work surface clean. Bits and pieces of clay on it will mar clay surfaces.

As you work with moist clay, one of the most important lessons you'll learn is when to stop! Keeping a project simple is often the best rule and not just for beginners. When moist clay is handled too much, its structure breaks down. As a result, it loses elasticity and freshness and actually looks tired.

STIFF SLAB WORK

If you're building a slab project that requires clay flexible enough to be bent but stiff enough to stand on its own, you must allow your moist slabs to dry and harden somewhat. Timing is critical in the drying process; I can't emphasize this enough. Trying to work with a slab that is too dry and that cracks at the slightest attempt to bend it is endlessly frustrating. Equally frustrating is trying to work with a slab that sags and bends when it's supposed to stand up. Unfortunately, a number of unpredictable factors can influence drying times—humidity, for example. Be patient, keep an eye on the slabs as they dry, and have several different

projects going at the same time so that you can work on one while another is drying.

To dry moist slabs to stiffness, transfer them to pieces of plywood or plasterboard, cover them loosely with plastic, and allow them to rest for several hours or overnight. The slabs will still be somewhat flexible, but they should stand up without buckling. If they get too dry, spray them with water, cover them tightly with plastic, and let them sit, repeating the spraying from time to time.

Occasionally, you'll need to dry a moist slab quickly. One way to do this is to set the slab in direct sunlight, where it will dry very quickly indeed, so quickly, in fact, that you'd be wise to wrap its edges in plastic, as the edges dry out first. Some potters use hairdryers for quick drying jobs; others even use propane torches.

Stiff slabs may be "textured" by incising designs into their surface. A loop tool is made for this purpose, but many sharp instruments will work, including dental tools, which are especially useful for incising very fine textures and lines.

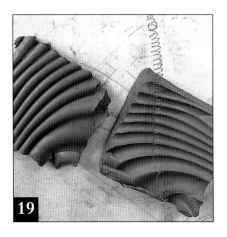

19

Top left: Tim Crane, *Vase*, 10" x 3" x 14" (25.5 x 7.5 x 35.5 cm), 1984. Slab, wire-cut with stretched spring; salt fired in wood and oil kiln. Photo by artist

Top right: Theresa M. Archuleta, *Golden Glitz*, 15" x 18" x 3" (38 x 45.5 x 7.5 cm), 1995. Slab, carved; raku fired. Photo by Lynn Huton

Center left: Steve Smith, *Ritual Platter*. Diameter: 18" (45.5 cm), 1992. Slab over hump mold, carved; Δ10. Photo by Jerry Anthony

Center right: Eric Nelsen, *Traveler #25*, 16" x 18" x 6" (40.5 x 45.5 x 15 cm), 1994. Press molded, carved; unglazed; Δ12, wood fired. Photo by Roger Schreiber

Bottom: Glenda E. Guion, *Within an Ancient Space*, 20" x 12" x 3-1/2" (51 x 30.5 x 9 cm), 1992. Slab; glazed; Δ04, acrylic paint. Photo by artist

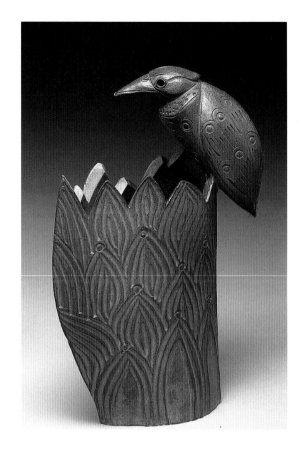

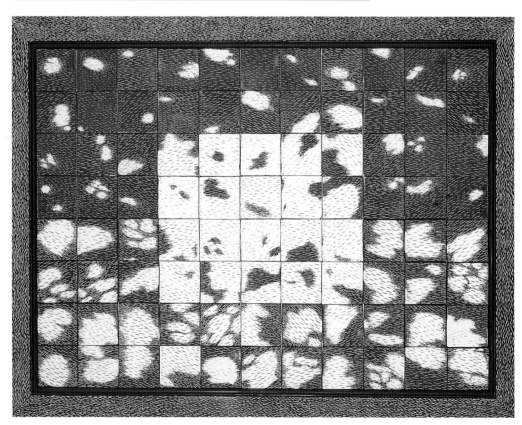

Top left: Craig A. Bird, *Runningman Teapot*, 16" x 16" x 1-1/2" (40.5 x 40.5 x 4 cm), 1995. Layered and inlaid engobes; Δ7. Photo by artist

Top right: Peter Rose, *Waiting*, 15" x 12" (38 x 30.5 cm), 1996. Extruded, molded; wood fired. Photo by John Cummings

Center left: Patrick L. Dougherty, *Spirits in the Night*, 4" x 17" x 22-1/2" (10 x 43 x 57 cm), 1996. Draped slab; underglaze, clear glaze; Δ03. Photo by Tom Mills

Bottom: Amanda Jaffe, *Black Spots*, 32" x 24" x 1" (81.5 x 61 x 2.5 cm), 1990. Cast and carved tile; terra sigillata, black stain; Δ4. Photo by artist

Right: Bernadette Stillo, *Flying Turtles*, 5" x 3" x 1" (12.5 x 7.5 x 2.5 cm), 1996. Slump-molded slab, stamped with hand-carved bisqued stamps; underglazes, clear glaze; Δ03. Photo by John Carlano

Far right: Joanna Borlase, *Two Pouring Bottles*, 7" x 3" x 2" (18 x 7.5 x 5 cm), 1995. Press molded in cardboard cut-out mold; slips, stains, underglazes, terra sigillata; Δ04. Photo by artist

MAKING AND USING MOLDS

■

People have used molds to shape clay since 2000 B.C. Some of the earliest clay containers were made by smearing a layer of clay onto the inside of a basket and then burning the basket away to leave a hardened clay shell. Ancient one-piece terra-cotta molds have been found in China, Greece, Rome, the Middle East, and the Americas.

Today, most mass-produced ceramics, from tableware to toilets and teeth, are molded, but only recently have potters started to make their own molds regularly. Doing so helps them achieve special effects and speeds up the uni-

form replication of complicated clay pieces. The four most common varieties of molds are hump molds; slump molds; one-piece, open-face molds; and two- or more-piece molds.

Hump molds are convex molds over which moist clay is draped in order to shape it. Any number of objects can serve as hump molds, including rounded mounds of plaster, stones, beach balls, carved pieces of rigid polystyrene foam, bags of sand, gourds, or bisqued clay forms (**Photo 20**). The clay is removed from a hump mold as soon as it has stiffened enough to be separated from the mold without distortion. If you wait too long, it will crack.

Slump molds are similar to hump molds, but their shapes are concave rather than convex. Clay in slump molds will shrink away from the mold rather than tightening around it, so you won't have to cope with the clay cracking as it shrinks. One simple form of slump mold is the canvas *sling mold*; instructions for making one are on page 97.

An *open-face press mold* is a one-piece mold with one open "face" and is usually made from plaster (**Photo 21**). This type of mold produces a relief, so it's perfect for molding sculptural tiles or plates. *Two-* or *more-piece molds* are molds that are made to create objects with undercuts in them—pieces the shapes of which would make it impossible to remove them from a one-piece mold once they'd stiffened or dried. Molds of two or more pieces may be used in two ways. You may press moist clay into the separate mold pieces, allow the clay pieces to stiffen, remove them from the mold sections, and then join them together. Alternatively,

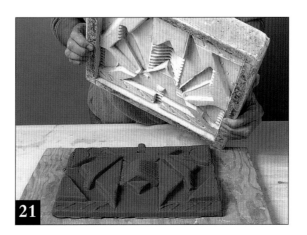

20

21

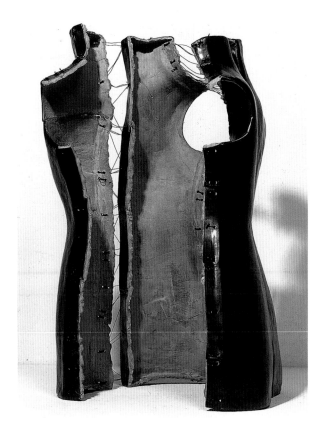

Left: Linda Marbach, *Interior*, 29" x 30" (73.5 x 76 cm), 1996. Slab; Δ6. Photo by Gary Mamay

Above: Barbara E. Doll, *Growth & Potential*, 28" x 32" x 11" (71 x 81.5 x 28 cm), 1995. Coiled; oil paints. Photo by Bart Kasten

you may bind the mold pieces together securely and pour casting slip into them. When the slip hardens, the mold pieces are removed from the cast object.

UNDERCUTS

The concept of *undercuts* is one you must grasp before you tackle mold-making. A simple cup without a handle, similar to the cone-shaped paper cups dispensed at water fountains, could be slip-cast in a one-piece mold. You'd simply pour casting slip into the hollow in the mold, swirl it around, and pour the excess out. After the slip in the mold hardened, you'd turn the mold upside down, and the slip-cast cup would drop out. But what about a cup that flared out at the base, that had protrusions such as handles or knobs, or that had surface ridges or even scratches? This cup would be impossible to remove from a one-piece mold, as any of these design elements in the mold would constitute the dreaded undercut.

Let's consider an example. Take a look at the small pitcher shown in **Photo 22**. Imagine a single block of plaster, hollowed out in the shape of this pitcher. Now imagine pouring clay slip into the hollow of this plaster mold. So far, so good, but what would happen when you tried to remove the hardened slip-cast piece from the mold? You'd probably go crazy because the flaring base of the pitcher rests in a mold undercut and would be trapped by the portion of the mold above it. To create three-dimensional shapes such as cups with handles, potters avoid

22

undercuts by designing molds that consist of more than one piece, each of which can be removed from the clay easily.

MAKING ONE-PIECE MOLDS

A one-piece mold is usually made by creating a moist clay model of the desired piece, building a mold form around it, pouring plaster into the mold form, allowing the plaster to harden, and removing and discarding the clay model. To use the hardened plaster mold, the potter presses clay into its hollowed-out portion, allows the clay to stiffen, and then removes the stiff clay. One-piece molds of this type may also be used with casting slip rather than with moist clay. As long as the mold has no undercuts in it, the clay or slip in a press mold dries, shrinks, and releases easily.

MAKING THE MODEL

Models are often made with fine clay that includes no grog or sand, as this type of clay can be shaped

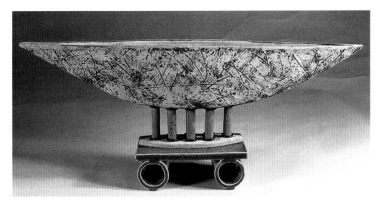

Above: Kathy Triplett, *Bowl*, 11" x 5" x 16" (28 x 12.5 x 40.5 cm), 1993. Slab, extruded; layered underglazes; Δ3. Photo by artist

Right: Leroy Johnson, *Blues in the Night*, 13-1/2" x 8-1/2" x 15" (34.5 x 21.5 x 38 cm), 1994-95. Mixed media; Δ04. Photo by John Carlano

to create fine details in the completed mold. You won't need to fire the clay model for an open-face press mold or coat it with any sort of releasing agent because after the poured plaster has hardened around it, you'll peel the model out of the mold and discard it.

You can certainly use materials other than clay to make your models, but if you use a material that is nonabsorbent, you'll need to seal the model before pouring plaster over it to keep it from sticking to the plaster. I've made interesting models by sealing polystyrene packing material with shellac. Wooden tools and egg cartons sealed with polyurethane or shellac—even parts of your own body, coated with petroleum jelly—will work.

Plaster is sometimes used to make models as well, but both plaster and bisque-fired clay models must be coated well with a release known as *mold soap* (available from clay suppliers) and buffed with a natural-bristle brush when the soap dries. Several coats of buffed soap will ensure a good release. Especially when working with a plaster model, be sure to fill every crevice with soap, as plaster adheres all too readily to itself.

Yes, you can oil these surfaces instead, but mold soap will preserve details better and won't add unwanted texture.

CONSTRUCTING A MOLD FORM

Once you've made a model for an open-face press mold, the next step is to construct a *mold form* (traditionally known as a *cottle*) around it (**Photo 23**). The walls of this form, which will contain the liquid plaster that you pour over the model, should be long enough to allow an even margin of 1" to 2" (2.5 to 5.1 cm) around the outer edges of the model and wide enough to extend a couple of inches above its top.

Sealed wooden boards or acrylic sheets, fastened together with

23

screws or C-clamps, make good mold forms, as do bent strips of linoleum or sheet metal held together with bands or web clamps. Even slabs of leather-hard clay may be used as mold-form walls.

MIXING AND POURING PLASTER

Complete instructions for mixing plaster are provided in the project on pages 112-115. This task isn't as difficult as you might think, but you'll need to study the information in this section before you begin.

Most potters use plaster (commonly known as plaster of paris) to make their molds because this porous material draws moisture evenly from both clay and casting slip. Plaster also picks up extremely fine details, and a plaster press mold that is handled with care can last for hundreds of impressions. This material's only disadvantage is that it is somewhat fragile and chips easily.

Top left: Bernadette Stillo, *The Energy Between Two—Ceremonial Candlestick*, 7" x 4" x 2-3/4" (18 x 10 x 7 cm), 1992. Slab, coiled, pinched, press molded; glaze watercolors/pastels; Δ04, gold paint. Photo by David Coulter

Top right: Judy Brater-Rose, *Double Vase*, 6" x 8" (15 x 20.5 cm), 1995. Slab; hand-painted glazes. Photo by John Cummings

Center left: Meg Largey, *Pinch Pot*, 5-1/2" x 4" (14 x 10 cm), 1993. Pinched stoneware. Photo by Ken Burris

Center right: Patz Fowle, *Rush Hour ... Rodeo*, 6-1/2" x 9" x 4-1/2" (16.5 x 23 x 11.5 cm), 1985-1987. Slab, sculpted; underglaze, engobes, oxides, stains; high fired; overglaze. Photo by Joe Sullivan

Bottom left: Carolyn Genders, *Ochre Vessel*, 20" x 11" x 11" (51 x 28 x 28 cm), 1995. Coiled; engobes and resists; Δ01. Photo by artist

Above: Michael Cohen, *Two Baskets*, 3" x 10" x 7" (7.6 x 25.4 x 17.8 cm), 1995. Extruded coils handbuilt over form; Δ10 reduction. Photo by artist

Right: Kathy Triplett, *Teapot*, 26" x 11" x 5" (66 x 28 x 12.5 cm), 1996. Slab, extruded; layered underglazes, glaze; Δ3. Photo by Evan Bracken

Special-purpose molds, with which other molds are created, as well as some press molds, are occasionally made with nonporous materials such as rubber. The latter must be covered with wet paper, plastic, or fabric to prevent the clay from sticking to them.

Dry plaster (calcium sulfate) is a white powdered substance that becomes hard when mixed with water. There are many different types of plaster, some of which are very hard and are used only to make molds for ram presses or to create master molds from which duplicate molds will be made. These plasters are less absorbent than the plaster most potters use— No. 1 Pottery Plaster—which usually comes from clay suppliers in 50- to 100-pound (22.7 to 45.4 kg) bags. If you want to purchase smaller amounts, try your local hardware or paint-supply store.

Store dry plaster in a dry place, as its shelf life is limited by its ten-

dency to absorb moisture. If you plan to keep the plaster for any great length of time, double-bag it and seal the bags tightly.

To mix up liquid plaster, you'll start by weighing out the required amount of plaster and water. The strength and absorbency of your completed mold will depend in part on the ratio of these two ingredients. That ratio is usually 140 parts plaster to 100 parts water (or roughly three parts plaster to two parts water). A higher proportion of plaster makes a denser, less absorbent mold. Too much water may result in a soft, crumbly mold, but you do have some leeway here, so don't worry about precision too much.

As you add the plaster to the water (water is never added to plaster) and stir, the mixture will begin to thicken. When it does, you'll pour it over your model and allow it to harden. Then you'll dismantle the mold form, remove and discard the

model, and allow the plaster mold to dry before using it.

Always pour any excess plaster into a waste bucket, allow it to harden, break it up, and discard it. Never pour liquid plaster down the drain, as it will harden in the pipes. Clean your gloves and tools immediately in a bucket of water. If you wait, the hardened plaster will be more difficult to remove. Allow the plaster that you've rinsed off in the waste water to set up in the bottom, decant the water, and throw away the solid plaster.

After you've made a number of molds, you'll have a much better sense of how much plaster to mix in order to fill a mold form of a given size. In the meantime, the molded projects in chapter 6 come with recommendations as to the quantities of plaster and water you'll need, and the chart of plaster and water ratios provided in Appendix C on page 147 will help

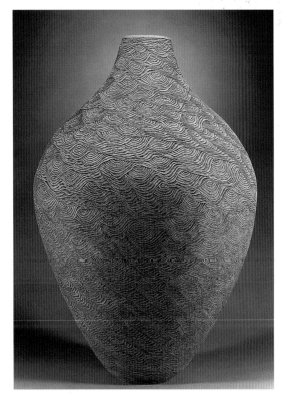

Left: Richard Zane Smith, *Untitled*, 24" x 19" (61 x 48.5 cm), 1991. Coiled native clays and slips with stains; wood fired. Photo by Robert Sherwood

Above: Phillip Sellers, *Untitled*, 9" x 10" x 14" (23 x 25.5 x 35.5 cm), 1996. Extruded coils woven over a mold; Δ5. Photo by Jerry Anthony

MAKING TWO- OR MORE-PIECE MOLDS

To make a two-piece mold (which you'll do when you make the project on pages 116-121), you'll first handbuild and bisque fire a clay model, one designed to require only two mold pieces. Next, you'll bury a portion of the model in moist clay. Then you'll construct a mold form around the model and clay (**Photo 24**) and pour plaster into it to cover the exposed portion of the model. What you'll end up with is a plaster mold with a hollowed-out portion that matches the exposed portion of the model. You'll repeat this process to make a separate mold of the other portion of the model.

DRYING WORK BEFORE FIRING IT

■

No matter which technique you use to construct it, your finished clay or slip-cast piece must be slowly dried to the bone-dry stage before it can be glazed and/or fired. To prevent the piece from drying too quickly, cover it lightly with plastic. Because small appendages of clay dry more quickly than interior portions, you may need to wrap these areas of a project more tightly in order to increase their drying time. If the piece is drying too slowly (you've kept it under plastic for a week now, and it's still leather hard), try draping the piece with fabric instead of plastic or drying it under a piece of plastic that you've folded and then perforated with a hole punch.

What happens if your drying pot freezes, develops a shinglelike texture on its surface, and then returns to normal after thawing? (By this time, you probably think I live in the Arctic Circle. I don't, but I do heat my studio with an unpredictable wood stove.) Unless you find the frozen look appealing, jettison the pot, as the texture almost always pops back out again later.

Many potters say that a clay piece will never look as good again as it does in the leather-hard state. I agree. Glaze won't often rescue an unconvincing piece, so if you're not happy with what you're setting aside to dry, recycle the clay and start over. Your next piece will almost always be better.

24

CHAPTER FOUR

SURFACE DECORATION

Elaine Carhartt, *Rocket Man*, 60" x 16" x 28" (152.5 x 40.5 x 71 cm), 1995. Slab; underglaze, glaze; ∆06.
Photo by Artworks

The word "decoration" in a discussion of surface treatments for clay is somewhat deceptive. It suggests, among other things, that surface treatments are afterthoughts—colorful veneers applied after the fact. They shouldn't be. A glaze applied with no forethought can overwhelm rather than complement the form of a piece. Contemplating a finish while you design and make a piece is critical.

This chapter begins with descriptions of some of the substances that are applied to clay as surface decoration—from clay slip and engobes to underglazes and glazes. Once you understand what these various materials are, you'll be introduced to a few of the ways in which they're used. Then you'll learn how to test and apply glazes, and finally. how to mix glazes from powdered ingredients.

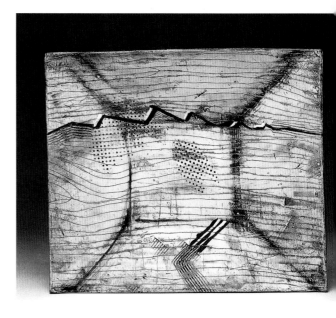

SURFACE DECORATION MATERIALS

■

When beginners think about surface decoration, they generally assume that glazes are their only choice. This couldn't be further from the truth. Glazes are only one of several substances that a potter has at his or her disposal, and a piece may only need to be glazed if it will be used to hold food or beverages.

COLORANTS

Oxides and *carbonates*, both of which are available from ceramic suppliers and come in powdered form, are chemical compounds that act as coloring agents in clay, glazes, and slips. Cobalt oxide, for example, turns clay blue, and copper oxide yields green. Both oxides and carbonates may also be diluted with water and applied directly to clay. When the piece is fired, most oxide or carbonate colorings will be permanent.

Stains, which come in a wider variety of colors than oxides, are commercially prepared combinations of ingredients that may be incorporated into clay or clay slip to color it and that are also added in small amounts to glazes. Stains may also be applied directly onto clay, but unlike oxides and carbonates, they won't fuse with clay unless they're first mixed with *frits* (pulverized, glasslike materials that help clays, glazes, slips, and stains to melt when fired), *gum suspenders* (to help keep the stains suspended in the mixture), and water. By mixing these ingredients together, you're making what's known as an underglaze. In Appendix D on page 148, you'll find a formula for one.

COLORED CLAYS

One way to add color to a piece is to incorporate colored clays (light-colored clays mixed with stains or oxides). Premixed clays in a wide range of colors are available through clay suppliers. The important thing to remember is that the shrinkage rate and firing range of a colored clay must match the body of any base clay to which it is added. If the clays don't match, they're likely to crack and separate during drying or after firing.

Making your own colored clay is relatively easy. Start off with the simplest method—making marbled or pink clay by wedging together a red clay and white clay that have the same maturing temperature and shrinkage rate. Adding oxides to clay is another method. Combining 1% (by weight) cobalt oxide with a white clay base, for example, will give you blue clay. Adding ceramic stains is another method. (The advantage to using stains over oxides is that you'll have more color choices.) Powdered stains may be wedged into the clay but you'll get a more consistent color if you add 3%–5% to a batch of dry clay, mix this into a slurry, and then dry the slurry to a plastic state.

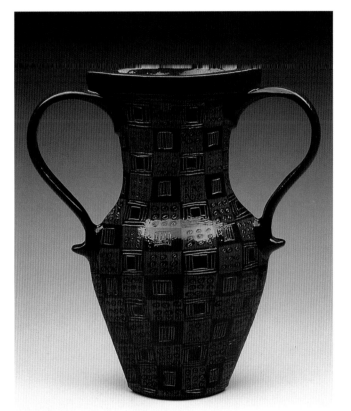

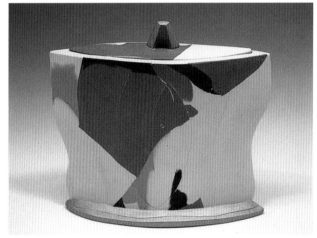

Top left: Hanna Lore Hombordy, *Three Pods.* Pod length: 9-3/4" to 10" (25 to 25.5 cm), 1995. Slab; underglaze, clear glaze (pod); unglazed seeds; entire piece bisqued to Δ5, then fired at Δ05. Photo by artist

Top right: Patz Fowle, *Gone Fishing ... In His Head*, 11" x 8" x 5" (28 x 20.5 x 12.5 cm), 1989. Sculpted; airbrushed underglazes, engobes, stains; high fired; gold luster. *Photo by Joe Sullivan*

Center left: Lynn Peters. *"Baden Baden" Amphora*, 20" x 15" x 7" (51 x 38 x 18 cm), 1995. Press molded, coiled; clear glaze over slip; Δ04. Photo by Jeff Martin Studio

Center right: Hiroshi Sueyoshi, *Covered Jar*, 10" x 14" x 5" (25.5 x 35.5 x 12.5 cm), 1996. Colored porcelain; unglazed exterior, glazed interior; Δ7, gold luster. Photo by artist

Bottom: Kaete Brittin Shaw, *Dancing Teapots*, 12-1/2" x 24" x 4" (32 x 61 x 10 cm), 1996. Slab; inlaid colored clay, matt glaze; Δ9. Photo by artist

Top left: Richard Zane Smith, *Illusions*, 19" x 20" (48.5 x 51 cm), 1994. Coiled native clays and slips with stains; wood fired. Photo by Robert Sherwood

Top right: Chrissie Callejas, *Creamer/Sugar Set with Tray and Spoon*. Tray length: 10" (25.5 cm), 1996. Slab; slips; Δ5. Photo by Michael Siede

Center right: Sarah Frederick, *Penland Teapot*, 11" x 16" x 5" (28 x 40.5 x 12.5 cm), 1994. Slab; glaze stains and glazes; Δ2. Photo by Ron Forth

Bottom left: Richard Garriott-Stejskal, *Box Man II*, 33-1/2" x 9-1/2" x 12" (85 x 24 x 30.5 cm), 1995. Coiled, slab addition; stains, underglazes; Δ6. Photo by Alan Labb

Bottom right: Terry Gess, *Vase Set*. Each: 10" x 3" x 2" (25.5 x 7.5 x 5 cm), 1996. Press molded stoneware; slips on exterior, glaze on interior; salt fired. Photo by Tom Mills

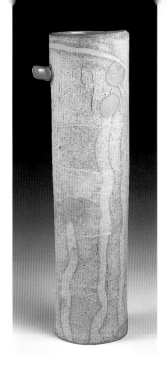

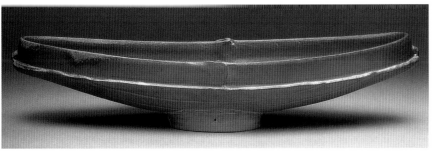

Top left: Amedeo Salamoni, *Stoneware Vase*, 14" x 3" x 3" (35.5 x 7.5 x 7.5 cm), 1995. Slab, colored inlays, slip designs; unglazed exterior; Δ10 reduction. Photo by artist

Top right: Joan F. Carcia, *Village Houses I, II, III*, 28" x 11" x 6" (71 x 28 x 15 cm), 1994. Slab; porcelain slip, oxides, stains; Δ9 reduction. Photo by artist

Bottom left: Randy J. Johnston, *Long Bowl Form*, 27" x 7" x 8" (68.5 x 18 x 20.5 cm), 1995. Slab, extruded; slips; Δ10, wood fired. Photo by Peter Lee

Bottom right: Trudy Evard Chiddix, *Tango*, 23-1/2" x 19" x 4-3/4" (60 x 48.5 x 12 cm), 1992. Slab, carved, stamped; colored slips; Δ06. Photo by Allen Bryan

COLORED SLIPS

Colored slips are mixtures of either clay slurry or casting slip and oxides or ceramic stains. Available premixed through clay suppliers, most colored slips are formulated for application to clay in the early leather-hard stages but some slips are formulated for bisqued clay or greenware. Because slips made with slurry will shrink much more than those made with casting slip, they won't adhere as well unless special ingredients are included to minimize shrinkage.

Beginners often enjoy working with colored slips. Unlike glazes,

they don't run when they're fired, so it's easier to keep the fired colors separate. You'll find many formulas for effective slips in books on ceramics, and most will specify whether the slip is best suited for use on leather-hard clay, bisqued clay, or greenware. To try your hand at mixing slip yourself, add 3% to 5% ceramic stain to any of the casting slip formulas provided in Appendix G on page 149.

Like colored clays, slips must match the firing range and shrinkage rate of the clay to which you apply them, or they may crack and separate. Testing any slip on a small

tile before using it on a project is always a good idea. See page 56 for testing instructions.

ENGOBES

Engobes, which are applied to greenware or bisqued ware, are similar to clay slips, but include flint, feldspar, and fluxes to make them melt and shrink to fit the clay body to which they're applied. Because they're often used as a smooth, single-color surface over which a different colored glaze is applied, they're sometimes called underglazes. Engobe formulas are widely available; one is provided in Appendix E on page 148.

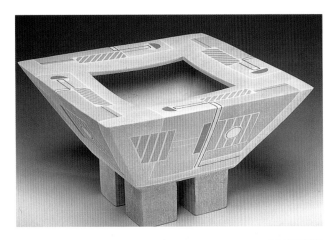

Top left: Andrew Van Assche, *Untitled*, 6" x 9-1/2" x 9-1/2" (15 x 24 x 24 cm), 1993. Slab; slips, underglaze pencil; Δ6. Photo by Bob Barrett

Top right: Mary Lou Zeek, *Birdhouse Clocks*. Larger clock: 15" x 6" x 6" (38 x 15 x 15 cm), 1996. Slab; underglazes, clear glaze; Δ6. Photo by Michele Mogle

Left: MaryLou Higgins, *Guardians*, 9-1/2" x 12" x 10-1/2" (24 x 30.5 x 26.5 cm), 1996. Slab, press molded; underglazes, underglaze pencils, clear glaze; Δ7, luster. Photo by Edward K. Higgins

UNDERGLAZES

For two reasons, this category of surface treatment substances may be the most confusing. First, commercial underglazes are liquid mixtures of ceramic stains, flux, refractory materials, and binders, but you'll sometimes hear the word "underglaze" used to describe engobes or even oxides applied under glazes. Second, although underglazes are usually applied under glazes to add color, they're occasionally applied on top of glazes instead. They may also be used without glazes to create a flat dry effect.

Underglazes are available for both greenware and bisqued ware and are sold in a wide variety of forms, including liquids, chalks and pencils, and tubes or small pans. The liquids are generally sold in 2-ounce (29.6-ml) and larger bottles. **Photo 1** shows a bisqued tile with a design that was sketched with an underglaze pencil. The completed, fired design, with a clear glaze on top of it, is shown to the right.

Firing temperatures will affect underglaze colors noticeably. A layer of glaze on top of them will affect them as well. The two tiles shown in **Photo 2** are both coated with the same series of underglaze colors, and half of each tile is covered with a transparent glaze. The right-hand tile was fired at Δ6 and the left-hand one at Δ05. Notice how some of the colors have burned out at the higher-temperature, Δ6 firing. In spite of the fact that an underglaze color can vary somewhat, beginners will appreciate the fact that, unlike glaze colors, they look almost the same before and after firing.

Above: Eric Nelsen, *Traveler #27*, 27" x 17" x 11" (68.5 x 43 x 28 cm), 1995. Slab, coiled, extruded, press molded, carved; unglazed; wood fired. Photo by Robert Schreiber

Top right: Jane Perryman, *Smoke Fired Vase*, 11" x 14" x 14" (28 x 35.5 x 35.5 cm), 1995. Coiled, burnished; sawdust fired. Photo by James Austin

Right: Sang Roberson, *Rico!*, 7" x 8" x 8" (18 x 20.5 x 20.5 cm), 1993. Cast, burnished with terra sigillata; pit fired; bound with waxed linen. Photo by Tim Tew

GLAZES

All glazes, whether they're matt or shiny, textured or glossy, colored or clear, include three essential components:

■ *Silica* (glass), also called flint, which melts at around 3100°F (1705°C)

■ *Fluxes*, which are compounds that combine with silica to make it melt at a lower temperature

■ *Alumina*, a refractory element that makes the glaze stronger and harder and prevents excessive running

Additional ingredients, including coloring oxides and stains, opacifiers, and fluxes suited to different firing temperatures, yield different glazing effects.

Clay certainly doesn't have to be glazed to be attractive. The texture of a warm, brown stoneware clay is very beautiful when left bare. A smoothly burnished terra-sigillata surface (see pages 62-63) can be as soft and inviting to the touch as a bird's egg. Color is very seductive, however, and glazes do make a piece waterproof and therefore hygienic.

Unfortunately, there's no way around the fact that using glazes can be frustrating for the beginner. Hundreds of different glazes exist; their application can be tricky, especially on large pieces; they can obliterate a delicate texture; and a blister or drip of glaze can ruin a carefully made piece. What's more, the chalky look of an unfired glaze never reflects the actual color or gloss that will result after firing, so you can never tell exactly what the color and appearance of a fired glaze will be. In spite of all these drawbacks, however, learning about glazes and how to use them

can be a great deal of fun!

Ceramic suppliers offer many prepared glazes for all firing temperatures, both ready-mixed and in dry powdered form. These are almost all water-based except for some of the low-fire metallics and lusters. The cost of glazing very large pieces with these commercial preparations is significant, but their convenience and reliability are certainly benefits.

Glazes are usually applied to bisque-fired work, and the glazed piece is then fired again to melt the glaze. Some glazes, however, are formulated for use on greenware so that the work need only be fired once. These glazes usually contain a higher percentage of clay.

Glazes are usually grouped into three categories: low-fire (Δ020 to Δ04), medium-fire (Δ03 to Δ4), and high-fire (Δ5 to Δ10). Some will cross over these boundaries.

Said to have "good range," these cross-over glazes are very useful in kilns with uneven temperatures. Into these three categories fall a vast array of types, a few of which I'll describe in this section. You'll need to know what kind of kiln you'll be using before you can choose one.

ASH GLAZES

These were probably discovered when a potter first noticed that ash on the shoulders of pots removed from a wood-fired kiln had melted to form a glassy surface. Potters still create natural glazes by wood-firing unglazed ware, but ash glazes are also formulated by "washing" ashes and adding them to high-fire glazes in percentages around 40%. Ash glazes can be used in any kiln, but will not melt at low temperatures.

SALT GLAZES

High-fired salt glazes form a glassy coating, with a texture similar to that of a lemon peel. They're created by throwing salt (sodium chloride) into the kiln chamber when the maturing temperature of the clay body has been reached. The vapors from which the glaze is formed don't usually enter the interior of a pot, so the potter must glaze the interior first.

We now know that salt-glaze fumes are highly toxic, so many potters substitute less hazardous substances for sodium chloride.

SLIP GLAZES

Slip glazes, commonly used by early American stoneware potteries, are glazes made from clays that contain natural fluxes. They're usually high-fire glazes but do come in many temperature ranges. Because they're made from clay, slip glazes must match the clay body to which they're applied so that the clay in the glaze will shrink at the same rate as the base clay.

MAJOLICA GLAZES

These tin glazes are historically associated with Spain. The term "majolica" actually refers not to the glazes but to a particular glazing style in which earthenware clay is glazed with a white, tin-opacified viscous glaze, then decorated with colored brush-work, and fired at Δ04 to Δ03.

MATT GLAZES

Matt glazes, unlike other glazes, produce a nonshiny fired surface. High alumina levels in these glazes, combined with slow kiln cooling of the fired piece, produce very small crystals in the glaze, and these crystals create the matt appearance.

Top left: Penny Truitt, *Untitled*, 9" x 15" x 3" (23 x 38 x 7.5 cm), 1995. Folded slab; raku fired. Photo by Tim Barnwell

Top right: Mark Lueders, *Form II*, 14" x 12" x 8" (35.5 x 30.5 x 20.5 cm), 1996. Precolored slabs; silkscreened slip; Δ1. Photo by artist

Right: Jane Peiser, *Untitled*, 2" x 9" x 7" (5 x 23 x 18 cm), 1994. Colored porcelain; salt glazed. Photo by Tim Barnwell

Far right: Keiko Fukazawa, *Tea Set*, 5" x 8" x 5" (12.5 x 20.5 x 12.5 cm), 1991. Underglazes, glazes; low fire, lusters. Photo by Gary Schwartz

CRYSTALLINE GLAZES

The crystalline pattern that these glazes develop is caused by certain ingredients (zinc, borax, or potassium, for example) and by the manner in which the kiln is cooled during firing. Because crystalline glazes are very runny, the glazed ware is placed on special alumina-coated supports in the kiln so that the melting glaze won't cause the ware to stick to the kiln shelf.

RAKU GLAZES

These low-fire glazes are formulated especially for use with raku firing, a firing technique unlike any other. The glazed ware is first warmed and then placed in a kiln that is already hot. When the glaze melts, the piece is quickly removed from the kiln in its red–hot state and plunged into a combustible material such as sawdust. When this material ignites, it reduces the amount of oxygen available to the glaze surface, creating striking glaze lusters and crackles as a result.

OVERGLAZES

Overglazes provide a way of applying a colored glaze design over another glaze. They include enamels, china paints, lusters, and metallic lusters, each of which is applied either after the piece is glazed but before it is fired, or more often, on top of a fired glaze. In the latter case, the piece is returned to the kiln for a low-temperature firing. Overglazes are also used to silkscreen images onto glazed surfaces.

Left: Christine Federighi, *Head West*, 18" x 8" x 10" (45.5 x 20.5 x 25.5 cm), 1992. Coiled, carved; Δ05, oil patina. Photo by Dave Holloway

Above: Randy J. Johnston, *Coffee Pot*, 10-1/2" x 10-1/2" x 5-1/2" (26.5 x 26.5 x 14 cm), 1994. Slab; slip; Δ10, wood fired. Photo by Peter Lee

TESTING GLAZES AND UNDERGLAZES

■

Glazes, unfortunately, aren't like paints; what they look like in the bottle isn't what they look like after they're applied and fired. In fact, a dried, unfired glaze just looks chalky. After the clay and glaze interact in the kiln, the glaze color and texture will be entirely different. The only way to tell what a glaze will look like on the clay you're using, whether the glaze is one you've purchased or one you've prepared yourself, is to test it by firing it on that clay. It's always wise to test-fire a glaze before you apply it to a whole kiln-load of ware. Testing underglazes is a good idea, too.

You'll need to have access to a kiln, of course. A small test kiln will do, but your results will be more accurate if you fire your test pieces in a regular firing, as small kilns tend to heat and cool more quickly than large ones. You'll also need to make some small, bisque-fired tiles. I make a small hole in one corner of each (**Photo 3**) so that I can hang them up on a wall for easy reference. A notebook and good record-keeping habits will work to your advantage, too.

When I test glazes, I write down the name of the glaze and its formula in my notebook. If I'm experimenting with a formula, I also record the variation I'm testing. Then, on the back of a small, bisqued tile, I use a glaze stain to record the notebook page number, the variation,

and the cone to which the glazed tile will be fired. I apply the glaze, fire the tile, and hang the tile up on my wall. After I've tested a glaze on a tile, I also test it on a bisqued vertical piece with a base. (I make these shapes by attaching small extruded tubes to small tiles.) If the glaze melts too energetically, the base prevents the runny glaze from cementing the piece to the kiln shelf.

Not every test you perform will yield interesting results; only one in every ten is even mildly interesting to me. Even a glaze formula with an intriguing title (what about "Large Crystalline Breaking to Aqua Rust with Rabbit's Fur Texture"?) may turn out to be a boring opaque olive. Nevertheless, taking those little test chips out of the kiln is sometimes the most exciting part of my day. I make them frequently and include some with every firing.

Occasionally, mixing two glazes together can yield the perfect glaze. My ceramics professor had a great glaze that he'd made up from the glaze coating scraped out of his glaze-spraying booth!

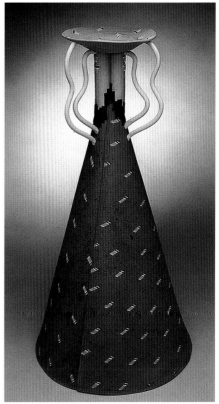

Above: Karen Estelle Koblitz, *Still Life: Plate with Leaf on Blue Water*, 13" x 22" x 22" (33 x 56 x 56 cm), 1987. Slab, slip cast; underglazes; bisque, Δ04; glaze, Δ06. Photo by Susan Einstein

Right: Diana Crain, *Cone Vase*, 22" x 8" (56 x 20.5 cm), 1989. Slab, inlaid and painted colored porcelain slip; Δ10. Photo by George Post

PREPARING GLAZES FROM POWDERED INGREDIENTS

■

You don't have to be a chemist to mix glazes from powdered ingredients. Books on ceramics offer hundreds of glaze formulas (you'll find some in Appendix H on page 151), and potters trade formulas all the time. If you do decide to use formulas to mix glazes, you'll need the items shown in **Photo 4**: a triple-beam balance gram scale and some small sheets of paper for weighing the ingredients, an excellent respirator (many glaze chemicals are toxic), gloves, a stirring stick or electric drill with a mixing attachment, a 50- to 80-mesh glaze sieve, a measuring cup, and glaze application tools. Some empty plastic buckets with lids will also come in handy.

Ingredients in glaze formulas are listed as a percentage of the total weight of the glaze; the total weight of the ingredients is 100%. This percentage system makes it easy to increase the quantity of a formula proportionately. When you're mixing up a test glaze, always use at least 100 to 200 grams of the dry ingredients. Two hundred grams will yield about one cup of glaze.

The correct cone-firing temperature for a glaze is provided with the formula, and many formulas will also specify the finished color, the matt or shiny quality of the glaze, and whether the glaze should be oxidation or reduction fired. (You'll learn more about firing in the next chapter.)

Start by weighing out the dry ingredients and placing them in an empty bucket. Because many glaze ingredients are white, check each one off on your formula so that you won't lose your place. Then mix the dry ingredients together. Doing this is especially important if your glaze formula calls for *bentonite* (a glaze suspender), as unless

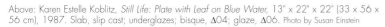

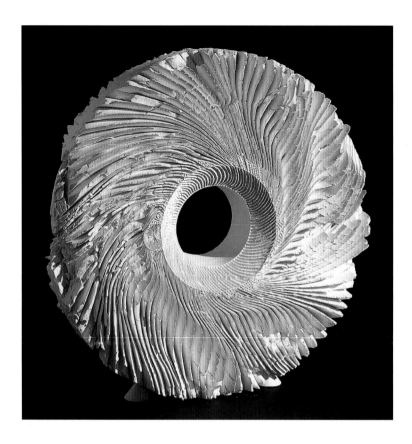

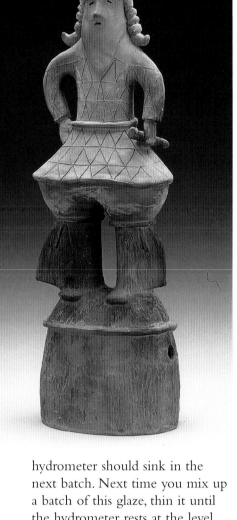

Above: Marc Leuthold, *White Wheel*, 11" x 11" x, 1-1/2" (28 x 28 x 4 cm), 1996. Carved; unglazed; Δ04. Photo by Robert McDonald

Right: Matthew Lyon, *Haniwa: Old Man in Ceremonial Garb*, 17" x 5" x 4" (43 x 12.5 x 10 cm), 1994. Slip cast, incised; unglazed; smoked after Δ1 firing. Photo by Bill Bachhuber

you disperse this material throughout the other dry ingredients, it will gum up into blobs when you add water.

Deciding how much water to add to the dry ingredients can be tricky. The consistency of a glaze should be similar to that of thick cream. First, add some water to the dry ingredients and allow them to soak down. Then add some more water and stir the mixture well. Sometimes just stirring the glaze can give you a feel for getting the right amount of water.

The thickness of any glaze makes quite a difference in its application and firing and is especially important with matt glazes, so you may want to purchase or make a *hydrometer*—a tool that will help you gauge the thickness of a mixed glaze. This tool is usually tubular in

shape and has calibrations and numbers marked along its length. When it's placed into the liquid glaze, part of it will sink and part will remain above the surface. The more of the hydrometer that remains above the surface, the thicker your glaze is. Homemade hydrometers run the gamut from wooden dowels with weighted bottoms and weighted candy thermometers to straws with 1"-long (2.5 cm) steel rods in one end.

Although this piece of equipment won't tell you what the correct thickness of a glaze should be, once you figure out what that thickness is, it will help you to make future batches. By placing the hydrometer in a glaze of the correct thickness and recording the number at the calibration that rests just at the surface of the glaze, you'll know how deep the

hydrometer should sink in the next batch. Next time you mix up a batch of this glaze, thin it until the hydrometer rests at the level you recorded.

When the glaze is the correct thickness, sieve it through a 50- to 80-mesh glaze sieve. (These sieves are available in large and small sizes.) If you plan to spray the glaze on, you may need to use a finer-mesh screen. Pantyhose will work if you have nothing else. Mechanisms to push the glaze through the sieve—a tedious job when it's done by hand—are available commercially.

Most glazes that are stored in lidded plastic buckets or jars will keep indefinitely and won't be harmed if they freeze, although their containers may crack.

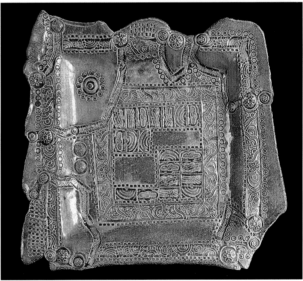

Top left: Chrissie Callejas, *Goblets*. Height: 10" to 12" (25.5 to 30.5 cm), 1996. Slab; colored slips; Δ5. Photo by Michael Siede

Top right: Sandi Pierantozzi, *Water Pitcher*, 10" x 6" x 5-1/2" (25.5 x 15 x 14 cm), 1993. Slab; terra sigillatas, glaze; Δ04. Photo by Neil Patterson

Bottom left: Richard Montgomery, *Wood-Fired Cup*, 5-1/2" x 6-1/2" x 3" (14 x 16.5 x 7.5 cm), 1993. Assembled extrusions; slip; wood fired, Δ10 reduction. Photo by artist

Bottom right: Lisa and James Tevia-Clark, *Weather Window*, 12" x 12" x 3/4" (30.5 x 30.5 x 2 cm), 1995. Slab, impressed patterns, sprigged medallions; ash glaze, Δ10/11 reduction. Photo by Sean Sprague

SURFACE DECORATION TECHNIQUES

∎

Technical data on surface decoration is so abundant that many novices are tempted to embellish their first few pieces with every technique at their disposal. Experimenting with different techniques is certainly instructive; you're sure to discover, for example, that some will complement your particular personality better than others. But until you've had some practice, the best way to integrate form and surface treatment successfully may be to start with the simplest technique—leaving the natural clay surface unglazed and allowing the inherent qualities of the clay to speak for themselves.

One warning before you start: Whenever you're carving or sanding leather-hard or bone-dry clay or dried slips, engobes, glazes, or underglazes, wear a respirator and either work outdoors or in a glaze booth with an exhaust fan. Inhaling or ingesting any of these substances is dangerous.

TEXTURING THE CLAY SURFACE

Early potters decorated their clay by texturing it. Some used only their hands or found objects to impress or carve textures into the surface. Others allowed their construction methods (pinched coils, overlapped slabs, and clay shapes pressed into the piece's surface, for example) to provide the decoration. English Wedgewood provides the best-known example of texturing by adding clay beads to the surface—a process known as "sprigging."

Left: Michele Ann Rigert, *Green Water*, 17" x 5" x 3" (43 x 12.5 x 7.5 cm), 1994. Slab in drape mold, incised; matt glaze; Δ10. Photo by David Brown

Above: Curtis and Suzan Benzle, *After You're Gone*, 7" x 7" x 4" (18 x 18 x 10 cm), 1993. Inlaid colored porcelain; unglazed; Δ7. Photo by Curtis Benzle

When you use the right tools, carving into stiff but still damp clay to produce crisp, precise designs is a very satisfying process. A pin tool, knife, loop tool, or piece of beveled wood will all work well. As you create a piece, consider its shape and scale and determine what type of carving—delicate or rough—will best complement them. African potters deliberately created thick walls on larger pieces so that subsequent carvings could be deep. On the thin, translucent walls of porcelain ware, however, delicate carved lines or small pierced areas may be more appropriate, as they will allow light to glow through the walls. No matter how large your piece is, if you don't like the results, all you need to do is fill in the carved areas with damp clay and start over.

APPLYING KILN WASH

Oddly enough, kiln wash, which is more often used to prevent glazes from sticking to kiln shelves, can also serve as a surface decoration. The left-hand tile in **Photo 5** was first brushed with kiln wash, and then the ridges of clay were wiped clean, leaving kiln wash in the recesses. For a kiln wash formula, turn to Appendix F on page 148.

APPLYING UNDERGLAZES OVER GLAZES

The right-hand tile in **Photo 5** was first painted with glaze and then with underglazes, a method that helps prevent underglaze designs from smearing when glazes are applied on top of them.

INLAYING COLORED CLAYS OR COLORED SLIPS

The technique known as *inlay* (or *encaustic*) is one in which incised

or carved design lines are filled with colored clay or colored slips. Inlaid surfaces may be covered with a clear glaze or left unglazed. Don't forget that the shrinkage rates and firing temperatures of your slip or colored clay must match those of your base clay, or you'll find that except with very fine lines, you face cracking and separation problems.

To apply colored slip, first carve the clay when it is leather hard. Then paint several coats of slip over its entire surface. When the slip has dried somewhat but is not yet bone-dry (this may take a couple of hours), scrape off the slip-covered surface to reveal the slip-filled incised lines. To use colored clay for inlay work, simply press or roll it into the recessed areas of a soft clay design.

June Kapos, *Bears*, 11" x 13" x 13-1/2" (28 x 33 x 34.5 cm), 1993. Pancake slab, carved; oxides; smoked. Photo by Richard Rodriguez

Linda Owen, *Hanging Slab Platter with Interior*, 1" x 14" x 14" (2.5 x 35.5 x 35.5 cm), 1996. Slab over hump mold; sgraffito; Δ10. Photo by Glen Hashitani

LAYERING AND SANDING COLORED SLIPS OR UNDERGLAZES

As shown in **Photo 6**, colored slips or underglazes may be applied in layers over a textured clay surface, left to dry, and then, after the piece is fired, lightly sanded along the raised clay ridges to reveal the edges of different color layers.

APPLYING DILUTED OXIDES, DILUTED GLAZES, OR UNDERGLAZES

Textured work sometimes looks best with nothing more than a diluted dark oxide, a diluted glaze, or an underglaze. (Underglazes aren't usually diluted, although they certainly can be if you want to apply them in layers.) The oxide, underglaze, or glaze is brushed over the piece and then wiped off so that the coloring remains in the recesses. Copper oxide, manganese dioxide, or red iron oxide mixed with water will all work and may be applied to moist clay, greenware, or bisque-fired ware.

SGRAFFITO

The four tiles in **Photo 7** are examples of a technique known as sgraffito, in which leather-hard or bone-dry ware is first brushed with a layer of underglaze or colored slip. When this coating has dried, lines are scratched through it to the clay beneath before the piece is fired. Be sure to let each coat dry before applying the next and avoid smoothing off any rough areas of the underglaze or clay until the layers have dried thoroughly, or you'll smudge the design. (Several coats may be necessary for underglazes.)

Take a look at the two tiles on the right. The upper one is an unfired tile with an incised layer of underglaze. The lower tile is the fired version of the same tile. Usually, the artist chooses an underglaze or slip that will contrast with the color of the fired clay. A glaze may be applied after the coating has dried but before the piece is fired, or after bisque firing.

The two left-hand tiles in **Photo 7** show

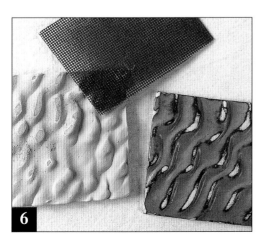

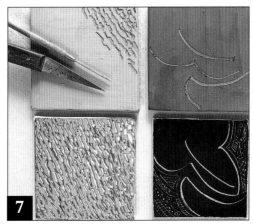

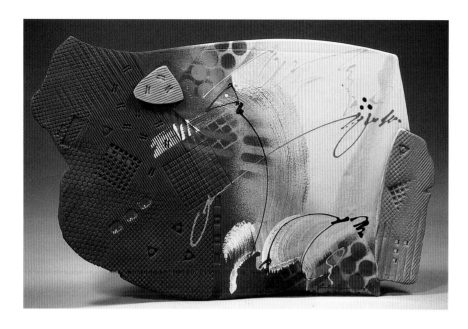

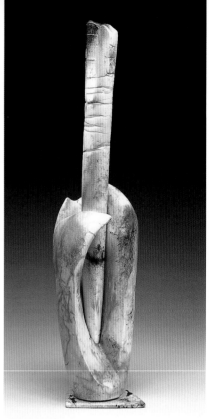

Above: Michael Kifer, *Wall Slab*, 18" x 24" x 2" (45.5 x 61 x 5 cm), 1996. Slab; sprayed, brushed, and slip-trailed underglazes, glaze; Δ05. Photo by artist

Right: Judith E. Motzkin, *Flora*, 32" x 8" x 8" (81.5 x 20.5 x 20.5 cm), 1992. Coiled, carved; terra sigillata, polished; flame painted in saggar. Photo by Meg Landesman

a variation of sgraffito in which the tile is coated with several layers of underglazes in different colors and then incised to reveal the layers of color. Slips may also be used in this fashion.

SLIP AND ENGOBE TRAILING

Slip trailing is the application of thick colored clay slips or engobes through a tube to achieve a relief effect. The technique works best on clay in the early leather-hard stages, but some slip formulas will work on bone-dry or bisqued ware. Run the slip or engobe through a sieve first and then pour it into a syringe or plastic squeeze bottle with a nozzle. (Hairdressers are good sources for the latter.)

You'll need some practice to achieve fluidity and spontaneity and to master the art of making thick and thin lines as you squeeze the slip out onto the clay. Try applying the slip or engobe in dots, as well. When you're through, empty the squeeze bottle if you won't be using it again in the near future and return the slip to a

tightly sealed container so that it won't harden.

A variation of slip-trailed work, one popular in Europe from the fifteenth to the eighteenth centuries, was *combing* or *feathering*. In this technique, slip is first trailed in lines across a flat surface. Then the liquid lines are merged into a pattern by holding a feather or comb at right angles to the lines and brushing it gently across them.

To trail slip-cast pieces, the slip is sometimes applied to the plaster mold before the casting slip is poured in. The still-moist trailed design melds with the surface of the cast form.

BURNISHING

Burnishing clay, a slow tactile process with a long history, appeals greatly to potters who love the warmth and sheen of its results. Before the advent of glazes, this technique helped make pots more impervious (although not completely so) to liquids. By pressing and rubbing the leather-hard or bone-dry clay surface with the

back of a spoon or a smooth pebble, the potter compresses the clay particles, making the object stronger as he does.

Burnishing works best with fine-grained earthenware clay. Because its effects begin to disappear at high firing temperatures, the work should be fired at Δ05. After firing burnished ware, some potters buff the clay surface with a chamois; others apply beeswax or floor polish and buff this coating well.

TERRA SIGILLATA

Terra sigillata refers both to a low-fire surface-decoration technique and to the slip with which the technique is executed. The slip, notable for the fact that it dries and fires to a natural sheen, making glazing unnecessary, contains a very fine-particled clay. Available commercially, either colored or not, the slip may also be hand-mixed (see Appendix I on page 152) and then colored with ceramic stains.

Terra sigillata is usually applied in several thin coats to bone-dry clay.

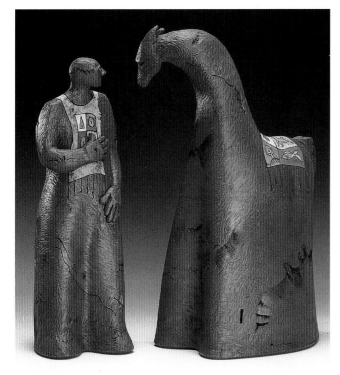

Top left: Dina Wilde-Ramsing, *The Conversation*, 15" x 12" x 4" (38 x 30.5 x 10 cm), 1994. Slab; terra sigillata; Δ03. Photo by Melva Calder

Top right: Mary C. Obodzinski, *Teapot*, 8" x 2" x 8" (20.5 x 5 x 20.5 cm), 1995. Slab, colored clay; unglazed exterior; Δ6. Photo by Ann Nevills

Right: Leah Hardy, *Fruits of Desire: Solace*. With doors closed: 12" x 8" x 2" (30.5 x 20.5 x 5 cm), 1996. Slab; glazes, terra sigillata; Δ04, luster. Photo by Paul Jacques

Because unfired clay tends to be very fragile, some potters first bisque fire their greenware to a very low temperature. (Sang Roberson, whose work appears on pages 53 and 75, recommends Δ018.) Although the slip dries to a natural sheen, burnishing it before firing will make it especially glossy. This type of slip may also be incised or carved for special effects.

The pieces are usually fired to below Δ06 and never above Δ04. A terra-sigillata surface responds well to the carbonization that results from pit-firing, so after bisque firing, the pieces are often loaded into a sawdust-filled pit and smoked. Especially beautiful effects can be created by making masking-tape resists or wrapping the pieces in wet seaweed or other combustible materials prior to firing.

WORKING WITH COLORED CLAY

Perhaps the simplest way to end up with a colored piece is to make it with colored clays. You'll certainly eliminate any potential consternation about how to decorate your finished work! Colored clay may be left unglazed, but a thin coat of clear glaze will brighten it. You may also add a sheen to nonutilitarian pieces by coating them with wax.

The most commonly used method of working with colored clay is to create multicolored tubes of clay from which cross-sections can be cut—a method very similar to *millefiore* (or "a thousand flowers"), a technique used by Venetian glass artists. The multicolored tubes are created by rolling thin slabs around tubes of colored clay so that a single, cross-sectional design runs through the entire length of the tube (**Photo 8**). When disks are sliced off from the completed tube, each one displays a similar color pattern. Working with these slices is one way to achieve intricate designs without having to use a one-hair paintbrush!

8

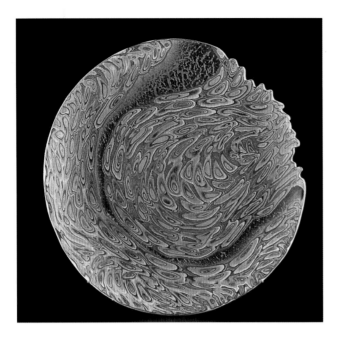

Above: Naomi Lindenfeld, *Platter with Sculpted Edge*. Diameter: 12" (30.5 cm), 1994. Slab, layered colored porcelain, incised, then flattened; unglazed; Δ10 to Δ11 reduction. Photo by Tommy Olaf Elder

Right: Joseph A. Triplo, *Porcelain Jar*, 18" x 7" x 7" (45.5 x 18 x 18 cm), 1996. Cast porcelain slabs; Δ11. Photo by On Location Studios

The slices may be rolled to stretch, flatten, or change the images and then pressed into molds, or combined with coils or other shapes before drying, sanding, and firing. To use the slices in conjunction with a mold, press them into or over the mold and pound them firmly together to eliminate cracks between them (**Photo 9**). The colors may look mushy after you press the disks in place. Don't worry. Allow the clay to dry to just past leather hard and then scrape the surface with a metal rib to define the color pattern more clearly. When the piece is entirely dry, rub the clay surface with steel wool. I made the left-hand bowl in **Photo 10** using this technique and then covered it with a clear glaze and fired it at Δ3. I made the other bowl shown in this photo by rolling scraps of colored clay together on a slab roller, draping the slab into the bisque-fired mold form, and pressing a rim in place around the edge.

For a slightly different effect, coat the mold with a slip before pressing colored clay shapes into it. The slip will act as a grout between the shapes, outlining their edges. Once the pot has dried, scrape the slip off the outside to reveal the pattern beneath.

APPLYING GLAZES

■

When it comes to matching a type of glaze to a type of clay surface, you'll probably find that the minute you try to follow any of the classic rules of thumb, you'll run into an exception. One good example is the commonly accepted belief that highly textured surfaces should be matt glazed. The first time I saw an intricately carved Chinese vase with a shiny celadon glaze pooling in its crevices and highlighting every nuance of detail, down the drain went that guideline. One

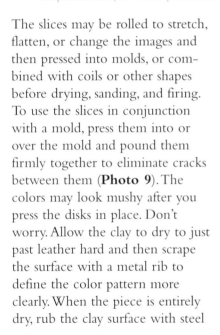

9

10

thing is certain, however. The kiln will always surprise, but no glaze can transform a bad form into a beautiful piece.

PREPARING THE GLAZE AND WARE

Always stir a glaze before you use it. I use a kitchen strainer for this purpose in order to eliminate lumps and debris. I used to stir with my hand—until the day when my hand located a dead mouse in the glaze bucket. Keep those containers covered!

To prevent the ingredients from settling into a rock at the bottom of the container, many glaze formulas contain gums or other glaze suspenders such as bentonite. The gums are usually mixed with warm water and added in small percentages to the glaze formula. Adding these to a glaze that has already settled out will sometimes cure the problem of separated ingredients.

One tool that does a good job of picking up settled ingredients from the bottom of a bucket is a rotary wire paint-stripper attached to a 1'- to 2'-long (30.5 to 61 cm) extension and operated with a drill. For small jars of settled glaze, just use a wire loop tool. Dried-out glaze is sometimes easier to mix if you add a little carbonated soft drink to it.

Although it's possible to apply a glaze to greenware and fire the piece only once, most pieces are bisque fired first in order to make them less fragile. Bisque-fired pieces are still somewhat porous, so they quickly absorb water from the wet glaze to leave a dry coating. For once-fired ware, you may need to use special glaze formulas, which usually contain higher percentages of clay.

Before glazing, make sure that the ware is clean and dust-free. Either

Jeff Irwin, *Love and Junk Mail*, 11" x 15" x 8" (28 x 38 x 20.5 cm), 1994. Slab; engobes, wax resist; ∆04. Photo by artist

brush it off well or use an air-compressor to blow any dust away, doing this outdoors if possible. Avoid handling the work with oily hands; oil on the clay will act as a resist and prevent the glaze from adhering.

APPLICATION METHODS

As you browse through the photos of glazed works in this book, you'll no doubt realize that there are literally hundreds of ways to use glazes, underglazes, and slips. Some artists spray them over stencils. Some use tape, wax, or contact paper to create resists before applying them. Some trail them just like slips. Multiple glazes of the same firing temperature can be applied to a single pot and fired in a single firing. Glazes with different firing temperatures each receive a separate firing. Dry glazes can even be troweled on in chunks. Stains or oxides, metal filings, rust chips, chopped copper scouring pads, or ash can be sprinkled on a fresh glaze. A thin copper wire wrapped around a piece and covered with a glaze will melt if it's fired to ∆04.

Keep experimenting and keep good records so that you can repeat your successes.

Glazes are usually applied by brushing, dipping, pouring, or spraying—or a combination of these methods. The size and type of work will help determine which method or methods to use. Painting, for example, is slow and results in uneven application but may be your only choice if you don't have enough glaze to fill a bucket for dipping.

You'll want to keep several things in mind as you apply a glaze:

■ The longer the glaze is in contact with the clay surface, the thicker the coat will be. Work quickly in order to prevent a thick surface from building up.

■ Glaze dries very quickly. In many instances, you won't have more than a minute or two, so have all your equipment and materials on hand before you start.

■ No matter which glazing method you use, how well you

D. Hayne Bayless, *Tumblers with Tray*, 6" x 16" x 5" (15 x 40.5 x 12.5 cm), 1996. Slab, extruded; matt glazes; ∆10 reduction. Photo by artist

apply a glaze will make more of a difference than whether the formula is great. Certain glazing effects—painting multiple glazes onto a piece is one—leave little tolerance for clumsiness, and sloppy application can end up ruining kiln shelves.

■ In some instances, you'll want to protect one area of a piece while you glaze another. Wax resist, which is available commercially, comes in very handy here. Brushed onto either unglazed or glazed areas, the resist prevents glaze from adhering.

■ Because melted glaze adheres to kiln shelves and can actually "glue" your work to the shelf, the parts of a piece that will touch the shelf are never glazed.

■ Always allow a glaze coating to dry before touching it, or you'll mar its surface; this should take only a few minutes. Remember, too, that the glazed surface will be fragile even after the glaze has dried.

■ The method you choose for glazing a piece will depend a great deal on its shape, size, and the desired effects. For specific techniques, refer to the projects in chapter 6, where you'll find glaze-application tips for particular projects.

DIPPING AND POURING

Pouring is most effective for glazing the interiors of hollow pieces such as cups and pitchers, but will also work when a piece is too large to be dipped in the glaze bucket or is too unwieldy to grip. To glaze the inside of a cup, pour glaze into its interior, swirl the glaze around, tilting the cup as you do so that its interior is covered with glaze right up to the rim. Then pour the glaze back into the glaze bucket, trying not to drip any onto the exterior of the piece. Sponge off any drips on unglazed areas that you plan to leave unglazed or glaze with another color. If you've dripped glaze onto a glazed area, use a razor blade or very sharp craft knife to carefully scrape away the extra thickness. You'll also need to do this when too much glaze collects at the base of a piece, as the excess glaze may run off during firing.

Dipping a piece into a glaze-filled bucket is the best way to get an even glaze coat on the exterior. In order to dip a piece, however, it must be small enough to fit into the dipping container, you must have enough glaze on hand, and you must be able to grip the piece easily, either with your hands or with glaze tongs, without covering any of the areas to be glazed. The longer the dip, the thicker the glaze.

To dip a hollow object such as a cup, after glazing the inside, place the fingers of both hands inside the cup and grip the cup by exerting pressure outward. Then submerge the piece up to its rim in the glaze bucket.

To dip a flat tile with a textured surface, hold it horizontally with two fingers on two opposing edges. Lower the face of the tile into the surface of the glaze and then raise it up just enough to pull up a wave of glaze. Slap the tile back down onto this wave right away in order to force the glaze into the recesses. Then use a brush to paint glaze onto the areas that your fingers covered. Also touch up any pinholes and other bare spots.

To glaze the exterior body of a piece with one glaze and its handle with another, first wrap the handle with plastic and masking tape, sealing it as tightly as possible. Holding the cup by its interior, dip its body down into the glaze. When the glaze has dried, unwrap the handle and apply wax resist to the exterior of the body where the handle joins it. Then either dip the handle into the glaze or hold the piece by its body and pour glaze over the handle. Carefully sponge off any glaze beads on the waxed areas before firing.

When dipping isn't possible, hold or brace the piece over the glaze bucket, dip a smaller container into the glaze, and pour the glaze over the piece so that the excess drips back into the bucket. To pour glaze over a piece without having to hold it, place a coat hanger or a couple of sticks over the bucket rim and rest the piece on top. The main disadvantage to

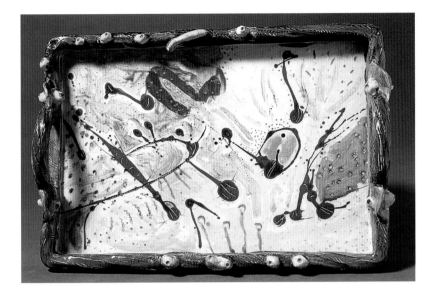

Above: Margo Kren (with Joyce Furney), *Lady Bug Tray*, 1" x 15" x 8" (2.5 x 38 x 20.5 cm), 1993. Porcelain; underglazes, clear glaze; Δ6, Δ018, overglaze. Photo by Joyce Furney

Right: Elyse Saperstein, *Celebration*, 22" x 11" x 8" (56 x 28 x 20.5 cm), 1995. Slab; glazes; Δ05. Photo by John Carlano

pouring is that because you're unlikely to cover an entire piece in a single pouring, the glaze will probably overlap in some areas, obscuring details on the clay surface wherever it does.

Of course, you may want to pour or dip one glaze over another. Thin and thick glaze surfaces render different textures and colors in a finished piece, so the overlapped area may create a completely new look.

SPRAYING

Spraying is often the best alternative for applying glaze to larger pieces, but must be done in a spray booth equipped with an exhaust fan or outdoors with the wind blowing away from you. Regardless of where you work, always wear a respirator and add goggles if you're working outdoors.

Spray equipment ranges from professional-quality airbrushes to hardware-store paint sprayers connected to air compressors. Even small air compressors will work, as

you won't need pressure over 50 p.s.i. Be sure to sieve your glaze thoroughly so that lumps won't clog the sprayer. A thin glaze may work more easily than a thick one.

How can you tell when the sprayed coating is thick enough? You'll learn through experience, of course. In the meantime, very carefully use a pin to gauge the thickness by piercing the glaze and noting the depth to which the pin sinks. An even easier method is to make a few pencil marks on the clay and spray until they're obscured.

A sprayed coating is quite fragile, so load the piece into the kiln very carefully. Adding commercial gums or hardeners to the glaze before spraying will help.

PAINTING

Using paintbrushes to apply glazes, usually in several layers, will also work, but it's difficult to get an even glaze coating this way. Of course, you may be seeking the visual texture that unevenness provides.

ADDING GLAZED SHAPES

An easy way to add colors to a flat piece that will be fired in a horizontal position is demonstrated in **Photo 11**. All the clay parts are allowed to reach the bone-dry stage separately. Then the base is coated with one glaze and the shapes are dipped into another. When the shapes are arranged on the base and the pieces are fired, the glaze will fuse them together. The advantage to this technique is that you don't have to paint glazes onto the shapes and base by hand after the piece is already assembled.

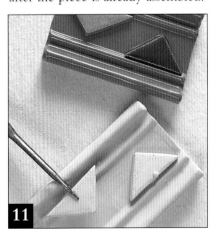

GLAZING PROBLEMS AND SOLUTIONS

Some glazing problems won't become apparent until you've fired your ware. These are treated at the end of the next chapter. Other problems will be obvious right away.

Problem: *A piece has been bisque fired at temperatures so high that the clay is no longer porous enough to absorb water from the glaze. This causes the glaze coating to look uneven or thin.*

Solution: Wipe the unfired glaze off thoroughly and reheat the piece in an oven or kiln set at 200°F (93°C) until it is warm but not so hot that you can't touch it. Apply a thicker coat of the glaze while the piece is still warm.

Problem: *An area of the piece is too thin to absorb water from the glaze. You'll most often notice this after you've glazed the interior of a piece successfully, only to find that the exterior glaze won't go on evenly because thin areas are water-logged from the interior glaze application.*

Solution: Wipe off the exterior glaze and dry the piece thoroughly so that the thin areas will be able to absorb the glaze when you try again.

Problem: *You've glazed your piece and—oops!—just dropped it back into the glaze bucket.*

Solution: Scrape the glaze off and wash the piece thoroughly, submerging it in water if necessary. Either let the water-saturated piece dry naturally or heat it to dry it. Then reapply the glaze.

Problem: *Uh-oh. This time you spilled all the wax resist onto your piece.*

Solution: A propane torch comes in handy here. Burn off the resist, but keep the flame moving so you don't crack the piece. Burning the

Kathy Triplett, *Three Containers*. Smallest: 17" x 10" x 4" (43 x 25.5 x 10 cm), 1992. Slab, wood additions; sprayed underglazes, glazed interior; Δ3. Photo by Evan Bracken

resist off in the kiln or scrubbing it off with a sponge or sandpaper will also work, as will rubbing it off with nail-polish remover.

Some sculptors avoid glazing problems by simply firing their pieces once and then painting them with acrylics or oils rather than applying a glaze. In my first ceramics class, we were so disappointed with our first attempts at glazing that we just polished our next batch of bisqued ware with shoe polish!

GLAZE FORMULATION

■

Glaze formulation is a fascinating area, one unfortunately beyond the scope of this book and probably beyond the scope of most beginners. If you're interested in learning to mix your own glazes or in experimenting with formulas you've found, I'd encourage

you to read as much as you can (many books are available) on glazing and glazes and to get expert help until you're familiar with the chemicals involved.

Understanding the characteristics of individual chemicals will enable you to adjust glazes to suit certain firing temperatures, make matt glazes shinier, and remedy glazing defects when you encounter them. The same understanding will also protect your health. Never forget for a minute that glaze chemicals can be terribly hazardous.

I've had a good bit of experience with glaze formulation and can afford to treat it much as I treat cooking. I bumble along empirically, experimenting with recipes until the results suit my needs, but I do know the properties of the chemicals I choose to handle. Please be sure you do, too!

CHAPTER FIVE

KILNS AND FIRING

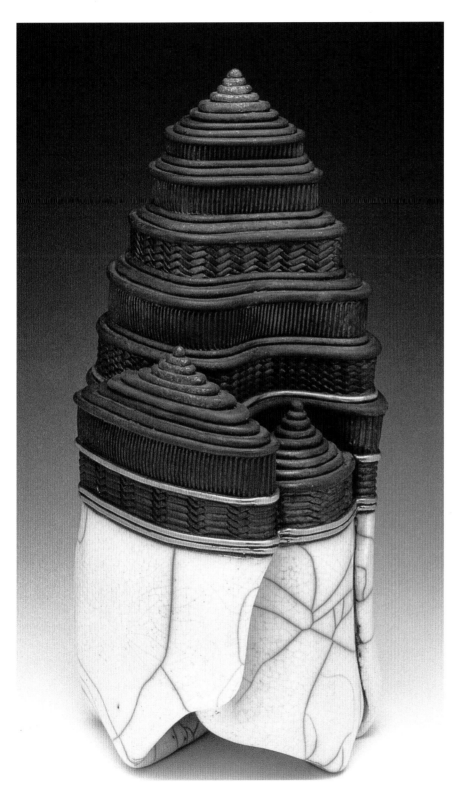

If you're a beginner, it's not likely that you'll be firing your own ware, unless, of course, you've decided to invest in a kiln right away. Until you're sure you want to own one, look for someone who will fire your work for a fee. This fee is likely to be based on the size of your project, measured in cubic inches. Just be sure you know the temperatures to which your clay and glazes will fire. No kiln owner will welcome you back if your glaze melts into a puddle on the kiln shelves! In the meantime, it's well worth knowing a bit about kilns and the firing process.

Candone M. Wharton, *Castillo*, 18" x 8" x 8" (45.5 x 20.5 x 20.5 cm), 1995. Slab, coiled; raku and luster firings. Photo by Jerry L. Anthony

Above: Keith Rice-Jones, *Victorian Tabernacle Box*, 17" x 11" x 8" (43 x 28 x 20.5 cm), 1994. Slab, extruded; oxides, slip, glaze; Δ10 reduction, gold luster. Photo by artist

Right: Pat Taddy, *Salvage Yard Coffee Pot*, 24-1/4" x 11-1/4" x 8-1/4" (61.5 x 28.5 x 21 cm), 1995. Slab, press-molded details; Δ9 reduction. Photo by artist

BISQUE AND GLAZE FIRING

■

Clay pieces usually receive two firings: a bisque firing to harden the bone-dry clay and make it easier to handle during glazing; and a glaze firing to melt the underglazes and/or glazes and fuse them to the bisqued clay. In some instances, however, glazes are applied to greenware and the piece is fired only once. Although this method has its disadvantages (greenware is extremely fragile), it does save time and the expense of a second firing. In other instances, a piece may be fired three or more times. After the piece has been bisque and glaze fired, overglazes are applied, and an additional firing takes place.

In addition to hardening a piece, bisque firing serves other important purposes. First, it releases moisture from the clay. Pieces to be bisqued must be bone dry before they're placed in the kiln, but although these pieces may feel dry and are no longer cool to the touch, they actually contain some chemically bound moisture. Bisque firing must proceed slowly or the clay will harden before that moisture turns to steam and escapes. Too rapid a firing will trap the steam and cause the piece to explode.

Second, bisque firing allows gases within the clay to be released—gases that might otherwise be trapped under a glaze and cause the glaze to bubble or the piece to explode in the kiln. Third, bisque firing also burns out organic materials, carbon, and sulphur from the clay.

The peak temperature of a bisque firing is usually between Δ06 and Δ04. These are relatively low temperatures but are high enough to accomplish the purposes mentioned. A bisque firing will not usually bring clay to the point of vitrification, as it would be very difficult to apply glaze to clay that is no longer porous enough to absorb it. Occasionally, work is high-fired in a bisque so that the setting of the ware will prevent warping during glaze firing. Pieces bisqued in this fashion are then fired with low-temperature glazes on them. They end up having surfaces with the crisp brightness of low-fired work but are very strong. Sometimes, work that hasn't been bisqued at a sufficiently high temperature develops hairline cracks because it isn't strong enough to withstand the stress of cooling in the kiln.

The peak temperature of a glaze firing is generally much higher than that of a bisque firing, as the kiln must be hot enough to melt and fuse the glaze coating with the bisqued clay.

A critical aspect of both bisque and glaze firing is the duration of the firing. No firing takes place quickly. In fact, it's essential that temperatures within the kiln be slowly raised and then slowly lowered.

Above: Josi Bellinger, *Planter*, 4-1/'4" x 4" x 4" (11 x 10 x 10 cm), 1995. Slab; glazed; Δ10 reduction. Photo by Richey Bellinger

Right: Steve Smith, *Dinner Plate*. Diameter: 10" (25.5 cm), 1993. Slab, slump molded, stamped; glazed; Δ10 reduction. Photo by Jerry Anthony

OXIDATION AND REDUCTION FIRING

Two types of glaze firing are possible. An *oxidation firing* is one in which oxygen is permitted to enter the kiln. In a *reduction firing*, however, the kiln atmosphere is deprived of oxygen. As a result, carbon and carbon monoxide develop in the chamber. These draw oxygen from both clay and glazes, changing their colors and creating other special effects. In a reduction firing, for example, brown clays turn warmer in tone, the iron in some clays emerges through the glaze in speckles, and glazes containing copper oxide turn red instead of green.

KILNS

The earliest kilns were simply pits in the ground, fueled with wood or dung. Although the unglazed clay that was fired in them probably remained somewhat porous because it never vitrified, it was still hard enough not to dissolve in water. Today, although some potters still pit fire their work, many types of kilns have been developed, including electric, gas, oil, wood, and raku models. Electric and gas kilns are sold through ceramic suppliers; other types are generally constructed by hand.

ELECTRIC KILNS

Electric kilns (**Photo 1**), which come in many sizes, shapes, and temperature ranges, offer much in the way of simplicity and predictability and will last for years if they're well maintained. With the

1

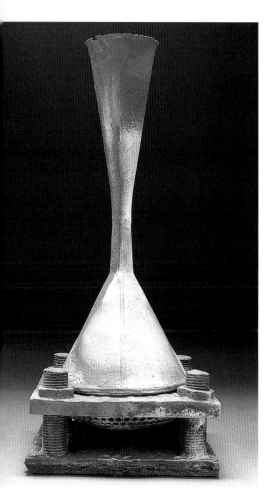

Far left: Matthew T. Wilt, *Sieve I*, 23" x 10" x 10" (58.5 x 25.5 x 25.5 cm), 1996. Slip cast and assembled; slips; reduction cooled stoneware. Photo by artist

Top: Barbara Schwartz, *City from Above*, 10" x 10" x 4" (25.5 x 25.5 x 10 cm), 1989. Hump molded; Δ04, lusters. Photo by Robert Nelson

Bottom: Phyllis Winchester, *House Tea Pot*, 7" x 9" x 3" (18 x 23 x 7.5 cm), 1995. Slab; terra sigillata, wax resist; Δ04 reduction. Photo by Walker Montgomery

new computer controls available on many models, they can almost be programmed to fire themselves, so vigilant tending isn't as necessary.

Electric kilns aren't built for reduction firing, but some potters add combustibles to these kilns in order to reduce available oxygen in the chamber. Unfortunately, this is detrimental to the kiln elements and can shorten their lives.

GAS KILNS

Gas kilns, which run on bottled or natural gas, can achieve very high temperatures. One advantage of gas and other fuel-burning kilns versus their electric counterparts is their capacity for reduction firing. Installing these kilns isn't easy, but the results are well worthwhile.

KILN ACCESSORIES

To keep track of the point at which a kiln reaches the correct firing temperature for your clay, you'll use *pyrometric cones*. These are small, cone-shaped pieces of clay manufactured to melt and bend at specific temperatures and over specific lengths of time; they respond to temperatures in the kiln in much the same way that glazes do. (See Appendix B on page 147 for cone-firing ranges.)

To use these cones in a glaze firing, you'll start by making several *cone packs*—small wads of moist clay, each with a row of three cones protruding at a slight angle. (If you look closely, you'll see a cone pack sitting on the upper rim of the open kiln in **Photo 1**.) The cone in the center, called the *witness cone*, is one that will melt when the correct peak temperature is reached inside the kiln. One cone is the *warning cone*; it will melt just before the correct temperature is reached. The last cone is known

as the *guard cone*. It won't melt unless you've overfired your work. (Usually, only a witness cone is used during bisque firing.) By distributing several cone packs throughout the kiln, you'll be able to keep track of firing temperatures by watching the packs through the kiln peepholes. (Always wear welder's goggles when you look into a hot kiln.) The packs will also let you know whether your kiln has hot or cool spots.

Cone packs should be made up in advance of firing so that the wads of clay are bone-dry when you place them in the kiln. Some potters add vermiculite or grog to the clay, make up the pack, and poke holes through the clay wad so that it won't explode during firing if it's placed in the kiln before it has dried. Cones can't be reused, so discard the packs after the firing.

Right: Lana Wilson, *Ritual Cup*, 8" x 7" x 2-1/2" (20.5 x 18 x 6.5 cm), 1996. Soft slab, stamped; layered glazes; Δ6, Δ06. Photo by artist

Far right: D. Hayne Bayless, *Pitcher*, 12" x 10" x 6" (30.5 x 25.5 x 15 cm), 1996. Slab stenciled with black slip and stretched; extruded additions; glazed; Δ10 reduction. Photo by artist

For monitoring the rising and falling temperatures in a kiln, a *pyrometric gauge* (or *pyrometer*) is also useful. This device, shown with a small electric test kiln in **Photo 2**, has one or more probes, each of which measures the temperature in a different part of the kiln—a very useful characteristic, as temperatures in any kiln are likely to vary from one area to another. The bottom of a kiln, for example, is often cooler than the top. The tips of some pyrometer probes are fragile, so avoid knocking them against ware or kiln shelves when you load the kiln.

What pyrometers won't do is tell you how long the kiln has taken to rise to a given temperature; they register temperature changes immediately. Cones, on the other hand, will melt at different temperatures depending on how long the kiln has taken to rise to those temperatures, just as a glaze may melt at a slightly lower than typical temperature when fired for a longer period of time.

Some experienced potters need neither cone packs nor a pyrometer; they're able to gauge temperatures accurately by the colors in the kiln, which range from dull red at 1000°F (538°C) to bright yellow at 2000°F (1093°C).

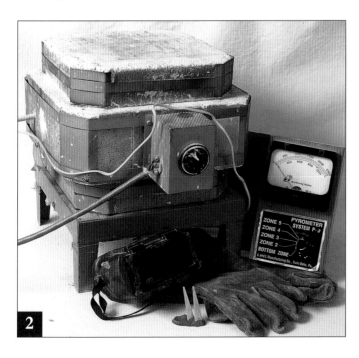

A *kiln sitter* is a mechanism that gives potters with electric kilns a bit of relief from having to constantly monitor the kiln temperatures. The sitter holds a specially manufactured pyrometric cone. (Cones for sitters are different from the cones you'll use in cone packs. Don't interchange them.) When the cone melts, the sitter turns off the kiln automatically. Sitters will prevent you from firing your work at temperatures that are too high, but they aren't always perfectly accurate. You'll still need to keep an eye on the kiln as it approaches its peak temperature.

In addition to kiln sitters, some kilns have back-up timers that can be set to turn the kiln off after a set number of hours. Be sure to set this timer so that it doesn't turn off the kiln prematurely.

Kiln furniture includes heat-resistant shelves, posts, and stilts upon which you'll set your glazed ware in the kiln. By arranging your items on shelves and posts (shown in **Photo 1**), you'll be able to load more pieces into the kiln for a more efficient firing. Shelves are made out of silicon carbide, high alumina, or cordierite. Silicon carbide shelves, which are black, are not used in electric kilns. The other two types are tan in color and can be used in any kiln. Shelf thicknesses range from 1/2" to 1-1/2" (1.3 to 3.8 cm). The heavier your ware and the higher the firing temperature, the thicker the shelf you need. Posts come in lengths ranging from 1/2" to 20" (1.3 to 50.8 cm).

Linda Workman-Morelli, *Memoir of an Earthquake*, 17" x 21" x 5" (43 x 53.5 x 12.5 cm), 1990. Slab; pit fired. Photo by Bill Bachhuber

Kiln stilts, used largely in commercial operations, are made from firebrick or alumina. These special posts keep glazed ware raised above the surface of the shelves so that melted glaze won't cause the fired ware to stick in place. Small, pointed protrusions on the stilts are the only points of contact with the bottom of the glazed piece; they're so small that they don't mar the glaze much. Keep stilts with broken points; you can use them as short posts.

Specialized kiln furniture is available for efficiently firing such items as beads or quantities of flat tiles or plates.

Kiln wash, a mixture of alumina hydrate, kaolin (a white primary clay), *bentonite* (an ingredient that prevents settling), and water, prevents glaze from sticking to kiln furniture. By brushing it onto new shelves and posts and replacing the coating periodically, you'll avoid the problem of accumulated glaze drips or glazed ware sticking to the shelves. (A formula for kiln wash is provided in Appendix F on page 148.) When glaze does adhere to shelves, put on your respirator and grind the shelves smooth with a carborundum grinder wheel attached to a drill.

HANDMADE KILNS

Through the centuries, potters have developed hundreds of kiln designs, from simple pits in the ground to sophisticated fuel-burning mechanisms. Today, sawdust, wood, gas, and raku kilns are still handmade, often with soft firebrick, an insulating material that's easy to cut with a saw. I made my first kiln in Mexico with a hair dryer and a gas burner from an old hot-water heater. It barely made 900°F (482°C)! I have since built gas and wood-burning kilns, using firebrick and sometimes space-age fiber-blanket insulation. It's always a thrilling moment when an arch form is dropped out of a new kiln to leave the curved brick structure standing alone.

PIT FIRING

Ancient pit firing took place in a simple pit dug in the ground. Today, pit kilns are fired with everything from sawdust to cow dung. Some contemporary potters—those who find the glazing process frustrating and glazed ceramics cold and unsympathetic—have turned to this type of firing in order to take advantage of the "gift of the flame," which enhances their ware with smoky flashes of earth-toned colors. The excitement and unpredictability of the results can be fascinating.

Sawdust firing, which takes place in a pit, is a type of reduction firing in which the ware is surrounded by smoldering sawdust. Kilns for this purpose are among the simplest to build and least expensive to fire. A simple trench or pit, covered with kiln shelves or sheet metal, can serve as a kiln. More sophisticated versions consist of brick or metal chambers with holes in the sides to allow some air to enter.

Because sawdust kilns don't usually get hot enough to strengthen the ware, most pit-fired pieces are bisque fired first in an electric or gas kiln. (This preliminary firing must be an oxidation firing.) The pieces are then packed into the kiln and the sawdust is ignited. Sometimes other combustible materials are added as well. Susie Duncan, whose work is shown on the opposite page, gets great color by adding cat food!

A sawdust firing may last from four to forty hours. Burnished and terra-sigillatta surfaces are particularly enhanced by the effects of smoke and carbonization from this reduction firing.

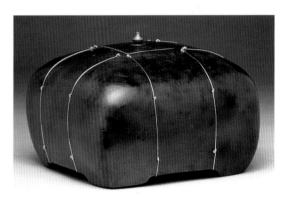

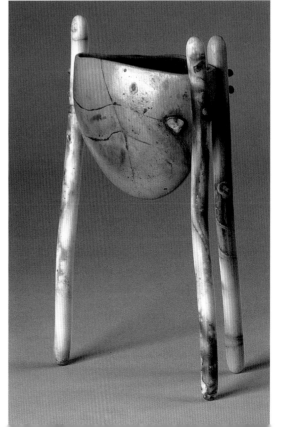

Top left: Susan Bealer Duncan, *Pitcher Form*, 14" x 9" x 6" (35.5 x 23 x 15 cm), 1994. Slab, pinched, press molded, raku parts; terra sigillata; saggar fired, Δ07. Photo by Anderson Flewellen

Top right: Judith E. Motzkin, *Untitled*, 20" x 14" x 8" (51 x 35.5 x 20.5 cm), 1994. Slab; terra sigillata; saggar fired/pit fired, Δ08. Photo by Bob Barrett

Center left: E. Joan Horrocks, *Two Men Walking Four Grey Dogs* (Jigsaw Puzzle Chinese Checkers Set) 14" x 16" x 5/8" (35.5 x 40.5 x 1.5 cm), 1992. Cut slab; raku fired and smoked in sections; marbles handrolled, underglaze, crackle glaze. Photo by artist

Center right: Sang Roberson, *Untitled*, 7-1/2" x 10" x 10" (19 x 25.5 x 25.5 cm), 1992. Cast and altered; burnished with terra sigillata; pit fired; bound wiith copper wire. Photo by Tim Tew

Bottom: Susan Bealer Duncan, *Three Legged Bowl*, 14" x 7" x 4" (35.5 x 18 x 10 cm), 1994. Paddled, pinched, slab legs; terra sigillata. Photo by Anderson Flewellen

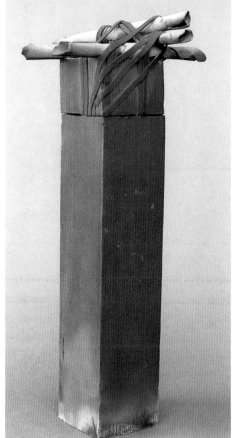

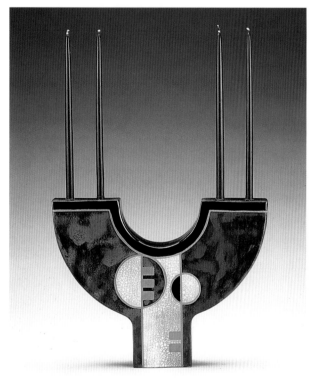

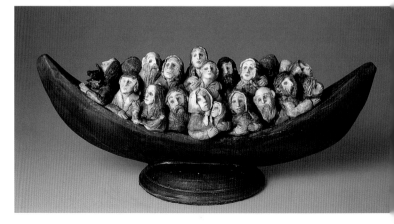

Top left: Peter Rose, *Finding the Arc*, 12" x 10" x 24" (30.5 x 25.5 x 61 cm), 1996. Press molded, extruded; wood fired. Photo by John Cummings

Top right: Janet Leong Malan, *Untitled*, 14" x 4-1/2" x 4-1/2" (35.5 x 11.5 x 11.5 cm), 1984. Extruded, slab; oxides; raku fired. Photo by artist

Center left: Barbara Hertel, *Candelabra*, 8" x 11" x 3-1/2" (20.5 x 28 x 9 cm), 1996. Raku fired after a separate glaze firing. Photo by Bill Bachhuber

Center right: Coll Minogue, *Slab Dish*, 7-3/4" x 6-3/4" x 1-3/4" (20 x 17 x 4.5 cm), 1995. Slab; wood fired, Δ11. Photo by Paul Adair

Bottom: Becky Gray, *Refugee Boat*, 12" x 18" x 6" (30.5 x 45.5 x 15 cm), 1996. Extruded, pinched; underglazes, glaze; raku fired. Photo by John Littleton

Top left: Anne Lloyd, *My Lamp Is Lit*, 14" x 10" x 8" (35.5 x 25.5 x 20.5 cm), 1992. Slab; raku and commercial low-fire glaze. Photo by John Carlano

Top right: Frank Giorgini, *Udu Hadgini Drum*, 14" x 15" x 9" (35.5 x 38 x 23 cm), 1986. Coiled, burnished; raku fired. Photo by Bobby Hansson

Right: Becky Gray, *Rocking Two-Spouted Vessel*, 15" x 18" x 8" (38 x 45.5 x 20.5 cm), 1993. Slumped slab; underglaze and glaze; raku fired. Photo by John Littleton

WOOD FIRING

Potters who wood fire and those who sawdust fire share a similar outlook; they both find joy in the unpredictable mark of the fire and the warm feeling of bare clay and earth colors. Wood-burning kilns play a unique role in the glazing process by depositing ash on the sides and shoulders of pots, where it melts and forms a glaze or creates flashes of color on the clay. Building these kinds of kilns, which often include arches made of bricks, is fun and challenging, but city building codes usually restrict their construction.

RAKU FIRING

Another firing method that involves the unpredictability of the fire is raku, which means "happiness" in Japanese. Raku pots, which are sometimes glazed, are removed from the kiln while red hot and immediately covered with a combustible material. When the material ignites, it carbonizes the clay, turning it black and rendering striking metallic, luster, and crackle-glaze effects. This firing method originated in sixteenth-century Japan as part of the tea-ceremony ritual. Thick, roughly pinched tea bowls were individualized by the shock of their removal from the fire.

Kilns for raku firing (**Photo 3**), which are usually fired by means of a propane tank and burner, are often made by lining a lightweight metal armature with high-temperature fiber insulation. The armature is designed to lift straight off the red-hot ware, making the ware easy to reach for removal.

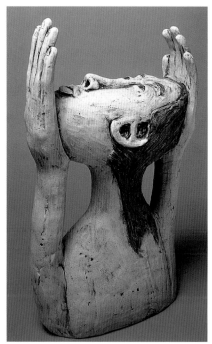

Debra W. Fritts, *Speaking to the Heavens*, 21" x 13" x 6" (53.5 x 33 x 15 cm), 1994. Coiled; layered underglazes and stains, diluted clear glaze; multiple firings, Δ05. Photo by Sue Ann Kuhn-Smith

Andra Ellis, *I'll Eat You Up, I Love You So! ... And So She Did*, 23" x 28" x 2" (58.5 x 71 x 51 cm), 1988. Collection of the Mint Museum of Art, Charlotte, NC. Slab; matt and gloss glazes; multiple firings, Δ04. Photo by Mel Schockner

PURCHASING A KILN

When you're ready to buy a commercial gas or electric kiln, you may want to take a look at the bulletin boards that are often found at ceramic stores and college or university ceramics departments; you may find used equipment listed for sale.

Avoid buying a very large kiln, or you'll have to wait a long time between firings in order to make enough work to fill it up. Frequent firings in a smaller kiln will allow you to experiment more with glaze testing and with firing schedules. I often use a very small electric test kiln to test new glazes. This kiln has one notable disadvantage, however; its rapid cooling can change the appearance of glazes—especially matt glazes. I compensate by *soaking* the ware—using the kiln controls to maintain a steady temperature for a period of time in order to heat-saturate the ware.

Most professional studios have a kiln the interior of which is 23" (58.4 cm) wide and 27" (68.6 cm) deep. A kiln this size will hold more work than you think. If you're just starting out and are making tiles or other shallow pieces, I'd recommend a kiln with an interior 18" (45.7 cm) wide and 18" deep.

Before you buy an electric kiln, consult a licensed electrician about your power options and installation. Some kilns will need special receptacles, while others may be plugged right into your household electrical system. Also note that any indoor kiln will require the installation of an adequate ventilation system.

The automatic shut-off mechanism on an electric kiln may in rare instances malfunction, so it's always a good idea to check the kiln regularly. Heating elements will need occasional replacement as well. You'll know it's time when the kiln heats up more and more slowly after repeated firings. Keep a spare set of elements on hand

and learn how to install them. After installation, watch the next firing carefully as it may proceed too quickly. If the elements occasionally sag out of place, don't try to push them back in. They're brittle and can break. Instead, make sure the kiln is off and use a propane torch to heat them until they're red-hot. Then push them back into their grooves. You can also buy special wires to pin them in place.

Regardless of the make and model of your kiln, follow the manufacturer's installation and operating instructions to the letter! Make sure that your kiln is situated away from both your work place and home, and vent indoor kilns properly in order to draw away the gases released from the clay and glazes. Exhaust fans are essential, as the fumes from clay in the kiln are toxic and can even set off fire alarms. The best solution is to use a downdraft vent that moves air down through the kiln and out, along with toxic fumes and gases. I use both a kiln vent and exhaust fan.

Left: Andrew Van Assche, *Untitled*, 12-1/2" x 7-1/2" x 2" (32 x 19 x 5 cm), 1995. Slab; slips and underglaze pencil; Δ6. Photo by Bob Barrett

Center: Linda Owen, *Footed Covered Jar with Chair*. Height: 12" (30.5 cm), 1996. Slab-built; sgraffito through black porcelain slip; Δ10. Photo by Glen Hashitani

Right: Joan Takayama-Ogawa, *In Memory of Roy Orbison*, 36" x 12" x 6" (91.5 x 30.5 x 15 cm), 1989. Slab; black underglaze, clear glaze; Δ06. Photo by Susan Einstein

OPERATING A KILN

■

In this section, you'll find general instructions for loading and firing a standard electric kiln. These instructions, which will vary somewhat depending upon the kiln you use, will give you some idea of how both bisque and glaze firings take place.

LOADING A KILN FOR BISQUE FIRING

Kilns are usually fired only when they're fully loaded. To make the most effective use of a kiln's interior, the bone-dry pieces are arranged as close to each other as possible and as little kiln furniture as possible is used. Pots are stacked on top of one another, rim to rim or foot to foot, and tiles are positioned on edge. If you do need to use shelves, support each one with three posts, aligning each post with the one beneath it.

You must leave enough space between pieces for air to circulate among them, as your goal is an oxidation firing that will burn out moisture, gases, and organic materials from the clay. If these substances remain in the bisqued clay, they'll try to escape during the glaze firing, causing pinholes, bubbles, and craters in the glaze. Also leave 1/2" (1.3 cm) of space between the ware and the walls of the kiln. Sprinkling grog on the shelves under large flat pieces will help them shrink more evenly.

In most cases, the shorter items are loaded first. One exception to this rule of thumb is large flat pieces. These may crack unless they receive very even heat, which is not often found at the very bottom of a kiln. The top shelf is reserved for taller pieces.

As you load the kiln, handle your greenware with care, cradling it with both hands or within your arms. Don't pick up pieces by their rims. Position cone packs in a few places as you work. (Always use these; pyrometers and sitters can malfunction!) If your kiln has a sitter, don't forget to place a small cone in it before you load the top portion of the kiln. Set the back-up timer now; in my kiln, I bisque fire for 12 to 18 hours.

BISQUE FIRING

Prop open the lid of the kiln, open all the peepholes, and start the kiln with the bottom element on its lowest setting. (Smaller kilns may have only one element and one control; others have two or more to control different levels of the kiln.) I leave the bottom element of my own kiln on low, with the lid cracked, for three to six hours, depending on the thickness of the work I'm firing. During this stage of firing, water remaining in the clay is driven out. If you raise the temperature

Left: Dennis Meiners, *Hard Landing Giraffe Teapot*, 18" x 9" x 6" (45.5 x 23 x 15 cm), 1995. Slab; ash glaze over porcelain slip, barium copper glaze on houses; reduction fired. Photo by Bill Bachhuber

Above: Trudy Evard Chiddix, *Tea for Two*. Teapot: 8-1/2" x 9" x 6" (21.5 x 23 x 15 cm), 1991. Slab, coiled, extruded; colored slips, clear glaze; Δ5. Photo by Allen Bryan

too quickly, trapped steam may cause the clay to explode.

After this gradual warm-up period, close the lid, plug up the peepholes (plugs come with the kiln), and begin to advance the temperature slowly. (Your kiln will have a dial for this purpose.) A slower firing gives oxygen a chance to move into the porous ware and burn the organic materials out. Unless you completely remove the carbon from these organic materials, the bisqued ware may not become dense enough. The resulting pores and open spaces in the clay will weaken your ware and cause it to crack when it's later placed in a dishwasher, oven, or microwave. It's especially important to keep the temperature from rising quickly before temperatures reach red heat (900°F or 482°C), as organic materials and water must leave the ware before the kiln gets this hot.

Continue firing slowly to 1400°F (760°C) and then on to Δ06, Δ05, or Δ04. The total firing time may extend from 12 to 18 hours.

No firing was ever hurt by being too long.

After the peak temperature has been reached, turn the kiln off. (If the kiln has an automatic shut-off mechanism, you obviously won't need to do this.) Allow the kiln to cool slowly. If you're firing large flat objects, which are especially susceptible to the stress of rapid temperature changes, this cooling down period should last at least ten hours or longer. If your ware has a tendency to crack, you may need to slow the cooling down at 437°F (225°C), 1063°F (573°C), and 1598°F (870°C) because these are high-stress stages during the cooling process. To slow down the cooling, just turn one element on at the low setting during these stages.

Unload the kiln when the ware is cool enough to touch. It's easy to detect a cracked piece; tapping it will produce a dull sound rather than a ring. Stack the kiln shelves on edge until the next firing, checking them for cracks as you do. If you find any, you may have fired the kiln too quickly.

LOADING A KILN FOR GLAZE FIRING

I once took a pottery class at a large co-op in Denver, Colorado, where 60 potters shared a large gas kiln. Production was prodigious, so there was no time to waste; everyone participated in running this kiln through a loading, firing, and cooling once every three days. One particular loading of freshly glazed ware was done entirely by students. After the firing, when the kiln was opened (always an exciting day for us), we realized that the glaze firing had been loaded as a bisque. (My class wasn't guilty!) Pots were neatly stacked floor to arch, rim to rim, foot to foot, and all were fused permanently together.

Before you load the kiln, make sure the shelves are coated with kiln wash so that if a glaze does run, you can remove the pot without ruining the shelf. Apply the kiln wash to one surface only, as wash on the bottom of a shelf can flake off onto the pots below it. Potters experienced with particular glazes sometimes eliminate kiln wash so that they can turn the

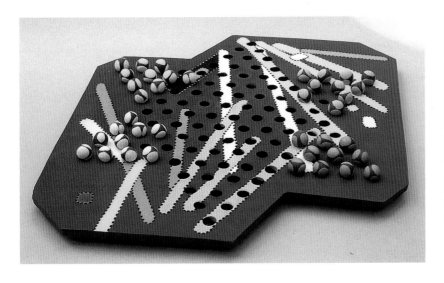

Above: E. Joan Horrocks, *Chinese Checkers Set with Pick Up Sticks and Basketball Marbles*, 11-1/2" x 14" x 1-1/2" (29 x 35.5 x 4 cm), 1995. Footed slab, handrolled marbles; underglazes; Δ06. Photo by artist

Right: Sharon E. Bloom, *Balancing Act*, 17" x 10" x 8-1/2" (43 x 25.5 x 21.5 cm), 1996. Slab, coiled; Δ03; polymer paints. Photo by Steve Twist (Avalon Photography)

shelves back and forth to prevent them from sagging in one direction. Posts should also have kiln wash on their ends. To level kiln shelves that aren't steady, shape a clay shim, adding grog to the moist clay to keep it from exploding. Cover the shim with kiln wash and insert it between the shelf and appropriate post.

Glazed pots must not touch in the kiln, and no glazed area of a piece should touch the kiln walls or shelves. Make a practice of leaving 1/4" (6 mm) of space between the pieces and at least 1/2" (1.3 cm) between any piece and the kiln wall. (Glaze will bubble as it melts, and bubbles can reach nearby surfaces.) To make sure that the underside of a shelf clears the tops of all the pots beneath it, use a small mirror to inspect potential trouble spots. Don't forget to position cone packs as you work.

A sprinkling of grog or silica sand on the shelves will act like ball bearings under large flat pieces and will help them to shrink evenly, but be careful with sand on upper shelves, as it can filter down onto

the ware beneath. One solution is to mix the sand with wax resist and brush it onto the bottoms of the pots. The wax will burn off, leaving the sand just where you want it.

Lids are usually fired in place on their pots, but the areas that contact each other must be free of glaze. When working with clays that are prone to stick, some potters brush these unglazed areas with wax resist that has had a small amount of alumina hydrate added to it. When the wax burns off during firing, a powdery coating of alumina hydrate will remain and will keep the areas from sticking to one another. Just be sure to keep wax resist with sand or alumina hydrate in it separate from wax resist for use on top of a glaze. Alumina hydrate applied on top of a glazed area will make the fired glaze surface rough.

For the most even firing, aim for a uniform load without tight spots. A half-load is neither efficient nor easy to fire. Uniform loading is especially important in a fuel-burning kiln, where the flow of

flame through the chamber both heats it and plays a role in producing the reduction effect on glazes.

Position the pyrometer and set the back-up timer.

GLAZE FIRING

Warm up the kiln for an hour. If you're firing freshly glazed pots, start the glaze firing especially slowly, as moisture turning to steam could pop off some areas of glaze. If you're firing glazed greenware, the firing should proceed as slowly as for a bisque. After an hour, raise the temperature gradually, usually about 392°F (200°C) an hour. Again, a long firing won't hurt. Monitor the temperature rise around 1063°F (573°C) very carefully. This is the temperature at which expansion occurs in the clay and stress cracks are most likely to develop in it.

It's best to soak the kiln at the final stage, slowing it down to maintain an even temperature. This will give bubbles or pinholes some time to heal by smoothing over. The peak temperature is more critical in the glaze firing so pay close attention

CHAPTER FIVE: KILNS AND FIRING **81**

Nerissa G. Regan, *Handle for Sale*, 12" x 8" x 24" (30.5 x 20.5 x 61 cm), 1995. Slab, coiled; underglaze, glaze; Δ9, Δ018, gold and platinum lusters. Photo by Johnathon Roberts

to your cone packs and pyrometer.

How long does the typical glaze firing take? This really depends on the type of kiln and the ware in it. A tightly loaded kiln will require a slower firing than one that is loosely loaded; the latter could be fired to Δ10 in 8 hours. A load of large sculptures, on the other hand, might take 36 hours.

Although both gas and electric kilns can now be equipped with computer-operated controls and often have back-up timers, you must still check at the end of the firing to make sure the kiln has shut off. Leaving a kiln on is much more serious than forgetting to turn off an iron! Keep children away from the kiln, too; its outside does get hot. Likewise be wary of the smoldering debris that may be left after a raku firing. Many tales of studio fires circulate among potters.

Unload the kiln only after it has cooled slowly to below 300°F (149°C), which will take anywhere from 9 to 15 hours or longer. When you do unload it, avoid running your hands across a kiln shelf or you may cut yourself on small, sharp edges of clay fragments that have chipped off a piece.

MULTIPLE FIRINGS

An overglaze or luster applied on top of a previously fired glaze must be fired again. Because overglazes and lusters melt at much lower temperatures than glazes, these third firings are much quicker, perhaps only three or four hours long.

The firing temperature for an overglaze, usually Δ022 to Δ018, is geared to the firing range of the ware to which it is applied, so some testing may be valuable here. Sometimes the ware benefits from a soaking period. You may need to turn the kiln down very slowly after the peak temperature has been reached, at least for the first 100°F (38°C) of cooling, so that any bubbles in the glaze have time to smooth over. Lusters, especially, require that the kiln be well vented; you may even need to fire with the lid cracked open about 1/4" (6 mm). The fumes are highly toxic, so be sure you have adequate ventilation.

GLASS FIRING

Many of my wall-sconce lights include pieces of glass that I slump in the kiln. I do this in two ways: by placing the glass over a kiln-washed bisque mold (with no undercuts) before firing it or by

molding the glass in the fired sconce itself. When I use a mold, I start by cutting ordinary 3/16"- or 1/4"-thick (4.5 or 6 mm) window glass to shape. Then I either place the pieces next to each other on the mold or overlap them slightly (either method will fuse the pieces together). I fire them in a low-temperature firing that proceeds rapidly to 1250°F (676°C) or 1500°F (816°C), depending on the effect desired. I cool the slumped glass rapidly to 950°F (510°C), hold it there for an hour, and then anneal it by cooling it down slowly for about three hours to 750°F (399°C). Finally, I cool the glass rapidly to room temperature.

I also slump glass in cutouts in the glazed and fired wall sconce. Because the required temperature is so low, the Δ6 glaze that I use on my sconces doesn't melt, and its color is only mildly affected. I start by cutting a piece of glass to fit over the opening in the sconce, leaving a glass margin of at least 1" (2.5 cm), so that the piece is bigger than the opening. Then I kiln-wash the areas around the inside of the opening where the glass will touch the bare clay. I position the sconce on kiln stilts, with the opening facing down and place the glass inside, over the opening. (The stilts must be tall enough to prevent the slumped glass from touching the kiln shelf.) I'm careful to place the sconce in front of a peephole, as the glass slumps very quickly and I need to be able to watch it closely.

The glass begins to melt at around 1200°F (649°C) and is finished by 1280°F (693°F.) Keep in mind that because these temperatures are provided by my pyrometer, they could vary from yours! After the glass has annealed and cooled, I remove it from the sconce, sand-blast it, and attach it back in place with a silicone adhesive.

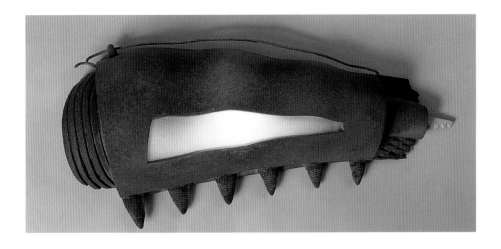

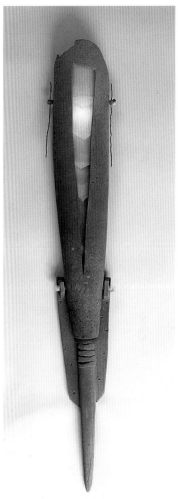

Top left: Kathy Triplett, *Lighted Wall Sconce,* 9" x 19" x 5" (23 x 48.5 x 12.5 cm), 1995. Slab, slumped glass; sprayed glaze; Δ3. Photo by Evan Bracken

Far right: Kathy Triplett, *Lighted Wall Sconce,* 33" x 5" x 5" (84 x 12.5 x 12.5 cm), 1995. Slab, slumped glass; sprayed glaze; Δ3. Photo by Evan Bracken

Right: Trudy Evard Chiddix, *Messages From Fukuoka,* 15" x 20" x 5" (38 x 51 x 12.5 cm), 1993. Slab built; slumped glass encases Japanese paper and coins; black slip, clear glaze; Δ05. Photo by Allen Bryan

FIRING PROBLEMS AND SOLUTIONS

■

Pay attention to your firings and keep notes on every one, so that you can explore the reasons why one succeeds and another doesn't. Try graphing the temperatures for each firing, too, so that you can experiment with making changes in temperatures at given stages. This is how I discovered that my slip-cast tiles and plates had to be cooled with one element kept at the low setting. The ware just couldn't survive the fast cooling of my older kiln without developing small cracks on its edges. The weather can influence the firing results in a fuel-burning kiln. Get to know how by recording the humidity and temperatures when

you fire. When all else fails—or even beforehand—install clay gods and goddesses atop your kiln every time you fire it!

Problem: *You can't remove the lid that was fired in place on its pot.*

Solution: Loosen the lid by giving it a sharp rap with a wooden stick, rubbing a piece of ice around the joint, or placing the fired pieces in a freezer.

Problem: *Your fired piece has small blisters or burrs on it.*

Solution: Use a hand-held grinder to remove them. If a foot rim (the bottom of the pot) is rough, apply a thin layer of silicone sealer, clear lacquer, or polymer emulsion to it.

Problem: *Your fired glaze has fine cracks running through it. This is*

known as crazing *and is sometimes caused by the different expansion and contraction rates of an incompatible glaze and clay body. (Crazing is an effect sometimes created deliberately.)*

Solution: There's not much you can do to save the fired piece. To prevent crazing the next time around, try adding whiting (calcium carbonate) to the glaze formula and regulating kiln temperatures more carefully.

Problem: *The body of your fired piece is cracked. Inspect the cracks carefully. If glaze hasn't flowed over their edges, they may be the result of* dunting—*cooling the piece too quickly or exposing it to a blast of cool air during the cooling period.*

Solution: The piece can't be saved. Avoid rapid kiln cooling the next time around.

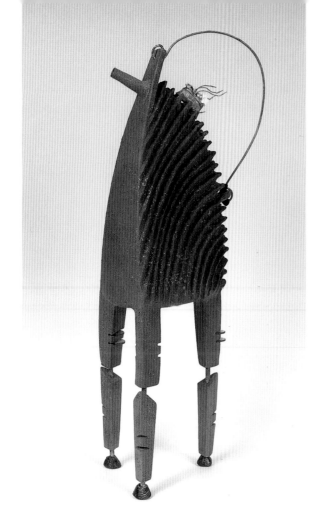

Left: Kathy Triplett, *Teapot*, 26" x 9" x 5" (66 x 23 x 12.5 cm) 1995. Slab, mixed media; sprayed underglazes; Δ3. Photo by Evan Bracken

Above: Linda Bourne, *Untitled*, 14" x 10" x 3" (35.5 x 25.5 x 7.5 cm), 1995. Colored clay; glazed interior; Δ7. Photo by Bill Bachhuber

Problem: *After firing, your glaze has peeled from some areas of the clay. Known as* crawling, *this can result from dusty or oily areas on the bisqued ware or from the glaze shrinking as it dries. Crawling is also caused by glazes with too high a percentage of ingredients with high shrinkage rates and by firing a piece before the glaze has dried. Glazes applied over thick underglazes will sometimes crawl as well.*

Solution: Start over with a new piece or attempt reglazing. You'll need to analyze the possible cause and address it this time around.

Problem: *Your glaze-fired ware has pinholes or blisters in it. These occur in several situations: when a piece has been bisque fired at an insufficiently high temperature; when it has been glaze fired too rapidly to burn out all the glaze impurities; when the glaze coating is too thick; or when the firing isn't soaked at the end. In addition, some common glaze chemicals such as zinc and rutile are prone to blistering.*

Solution: Start over or attempt reglazing. When you fire your next piece, try to avoid the situations that cause this problem.

Problem: *When you fire the piece, the glaze runs down and off its bottom. This will happen when you fire at temperatures that are too high or when the glaze coating is too thick.*

Solution: Try grinding drips away with a carborundum wheel attached to a drill. If this doesn't work, apply a thinner glaze to your next piece, scrape the thick areas of glaze coating from around the base, and monitor kiln temperatures carefully. Slip-cast ware in particular may require a significantly thinner glaze.

Problem: *Your fired ware has dry unglazed areas.*

Solution: Start over or attempt reglazing. On your next piece, use a thicker glaze or fire the pot at a higher temperature.

REGLAZING FIRED WARE

Well, it was a great pot before you fired it, but now it's just olive drab. Can you reglaze it? Yes, but reglazing fired ware is difficult. In most cases, the quickest way to remedy a poor glaze job is to make another piece. If you'd like to experiment with reglazing, however, first heat the fired, glazed piece to help the second coating to adhere. Then apply a thicker layer of either the same or another glaze. Spraying the second glaze coat can also help to even out a glaze application. Sometimes, coating a bad surface with a white engobe and then reglazing it is effective.

It's also possible to refire some glazes that have blistered. Give these pieces a long soaking at the maturation temperature and a very slow initial cool-down. Sandblasting a poor glaze job can yield surprisingly attractive results, too.

CHAPTER SIX

THE PROJECTS

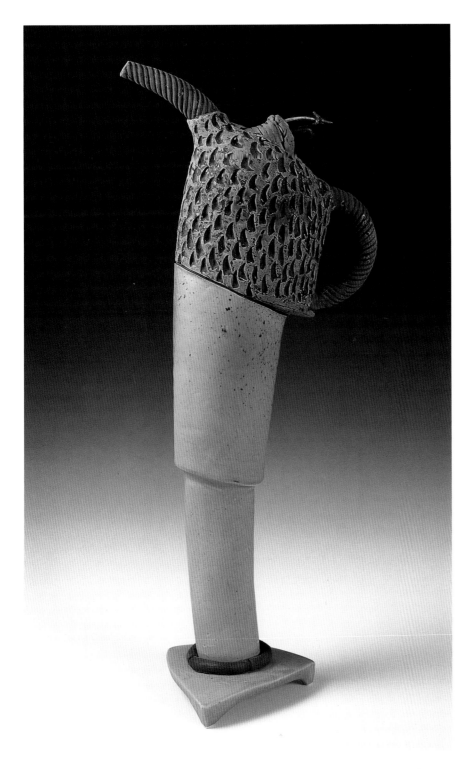

T he projects in this chapter are more than just projects. Think of them as both vehicles and springboards: vehicles for instructions on specific handbuilding techniques and springboards for your own creativity.

Kathy Triplett, *Teapot*, 26" x 10" x 6" (66 x 25.5 x 15 cm), 1996. Slab, carved, extruded, mixed media; layered underglazes, glaze; Δ3. Photo by Evan Bracken

As vehicles, these projects will show you how particular techniques can be used, and by making each one, you'll learn valuable handbuilding methods. Every one of these projects, however, could be made by using a different technique. Take a look at Don Davis's plates, shown on page 94. If you follow Don's instructions, you'll learn how to drape soft slabs over a hump mold, but you could just as well make a similar form by coiling it. Any given technique will impart its own special look to a finished piece. By all means, choose the technique and look that please you most.

Don't be trapped into thinking that the form your project takes has to be—or even should be—the form shown in this book. Use the instructions that come with each project as springboards for your own imagination.

Most important of all, relax. Cut off too much clay? Stick it back on. Clay is a remarkably forgiving material. Obeying the "rules" may prevent you from making mistakes, but if you follow them all—all the time—you won't have any fun.

STARTING TIPS

■ If you're a beginner, you'll probably want to revise measurements and start out with smaller versions of the projects described. I won't tell you not to make a planter that's 2' (61 cm) tall the first time you try coiling, but I will say that you'll probably find it easier to make one 8" (20.3 cm) tall instead.

■ Take the time to make sure a project will fit into the kiln you'll be using!

■ Review previous chapters whenever necessary. There's no shame in brushing up on the basics.

■ Each project comes with a "Have on Hand" list of special tools and supplies. This list doesn't include the hand tools and supplies described in chapter 1, so if your studio isn't fully equipped yet, read through the project instructions to make sure you have what you need. I've offered suggestions as to types of clay, too, but these aren't written in stone. Feel free to experiment.

■ The underglazes, glazes, and engobes on all these projects are ones you can mix up yourself from dry ingredients (formulas are provided for every one), but you may want to start out with commercial glazes and underglazes instead. Just be sure you choose ones formulated for the firing range of the clay you're using.

■ Keep your work surface clear of clay scraps; they'll stick to your project and mar its surface (**Photo 1**). Make special efforts to obey this rule when you're working with more than one type of clay.

■ Many professional potters work in series. If they're making mugs for example, they make several that are similar in style. Instead of waiting for each mug to dry before they start another, they work on more than one at a time. This not only helps them save time, but lets them experiment by making small variations in each one. Try it.

Making mistakes is a great way to learn. The person who makes none usually doesn't make anything! Take the section on warp prevention on page 28. If you want to ignore this tip, go right ahead. Your clay may not warp at all, and if a few cracks develop in it, so what? You'll get the chance to try out crack repairs on a simple project instead of having to test them out on a masterpiece. (For instructions on repairing cracks, turn to Appendix J on page 152.)

Accidents can prompt imaginative solutions and lead you down valuable paths. During the 1980s, I mistakenly glazed a kiln load of pots in a purple and turquoise combination when I'd intended to use only one color. After my shock wore off, I started to like the results, and so did buyers, who labelled these pieces "Miami Vice" pots. I had no idea what this meant at the time; I wasn't a part of mainstream culture, but I did become more aware of the possibilities of startling color combinations and went on to develop even more.

Now, just get your hands on some clay and dive into making your first project. I once read something I'd like to share with you as you do: "Go as far as you can see, and when you get there, you will see farther."

STIFF SLAB WINDOWSILL PLANTER

I've chosen a windowsill planter as the first project because you won't need to concern yourself with the weight of the finished piece, as you might when making a baking dish. As a result, you can create an extravagantly built-up or textured surface on this piece. You'll have an opportunity to be creative with the design elements, too. Glazing, which is sometimes frustrating for the novice potter, is kept simple here but is very effective.

HAVE ON HAND

10 to 12 lbs. (4.5 to 5.4 kg) clay with 10% grog, for Δ3 to Δ6 oxidation firing

Several cups of glaze (Appendix H, Glaze #1, page 151)

1 ounce (29.6 ml) underglaze (Appendix D, page 148)

Alumina hydrate (optional)

Clay ruler (optional)

Design sketch for front and back planter walls (optional)

STARTING TIPS

■ I used a clay with a relatively high grog content (10%) because the grog helps prevents cracking during drying and gives the clay a nice gritty texture after firing. When fired, this clay turns a warm brown color. Any groggy clay will work fine.

■ If you don't think you're ready to prepare your own glazes and underglazes, just buy some from a clay supplier. You'll need a Δ3 to Δ6 underglaze and a Δ3 to Δ6 glaze for oxidation firing on bisqued ware.

■ Many slab-constructed projects are prone to warping during firing. As you make this project,

you'll also learn how to make and use a simple device for warp prevention.

■ Alumina hydrate is available from ceramic suppliers in powdered form. You'll use it to ensure that the warp-prevention braces don't stick to the walls of your planter during firing.

■ A clay ruler isn't necessary for this project unless you want its dimensions to be very precise.

■ You'll notice that I haven't provided a design sketch for the pattern shapes on the front of this planter. Trying to remain rigidly true to a sketch may only inhibit you, and touching the clay will almost always give birth to new ideas or changes in your original design concepts anyway.

I often work without a sketch. I just cut some interesting clay shapes and experiment by laying them out in different ways. Sometimes, I even find useful design elements among the scraps of clay remaining on the table after I cut out the larger project pieces.

To help visualize possible designs, try making a simple viewing frame from wood or cardboard (**Photo 1**). Placing this frame in various positions over a textured slab or a group of arranged elements can help you make design decisions by focusing your attention on a given area.

■ Stiff clay pieces are joined by scoring their surfaces, applying clay slurry to them, and pressing them together. To make the clay slurry, just make up a soupy mixture of water and the clay you're using for this project.

INSTRUCTIONS

1. On a canvas-covered work surface, roll out a slab of clay about 18" (45.7 cm) wide, 24" (61 cm) long, and about 1/4" (6 mm) thick. Cover the slab loosely with a piece of plastic and allow it to dry for a few hours or overnight. Timing is so important! If the slab is too moist and soft when you try to work with it, your project won't hold its shape, but if the slab is too dry, it will crack when you try to bend it.

2. For a finished planter approximately 4" (10.2 cm) wide by 15" (38.1 cm) long, start by measuring out two 4-1/2" x 11" (11.4 x 27.9 cm) slabs for the front and back planter walls. Cut these pieces out with a knife or pin tool (**Photo 2**) and cover them tightly with plastic to keep them from drying out.

3. Before cutting out the short ends of the planter, use a ridged

wooden roller or the tool of your choice to create a texture on part of the remaining slab (**Photo 3**). Then cut out two 4-1/2" x 7" (11.4 x 17.8 cm) end walls from these textured sections. The roller distorts the clay somewhat, which is why I texture the clay before cutting it. (Design decisions are yours, of course. If you'd rather not texture these short walls, leave them smooth.)

4. Bend each of the short ends over a tubular form such as a wooden rolling pin (**Photo 4**). Keep in mind as you do this that clay has a "memory." When it's bent, it will tend to return to its original form. A flat slab that is bent into a curved shape, for example, will attempt to become flat again. To compensate for this tendency, first bend your clay to a slightly tighter curve than you want it to assume. Then open the curved clay to the shape you desire. Cover the shaped pieces tightly with plastic.

5. If this step and the next few take you more than a few minutes, keep the pieces you're not working on wrapped tightly in plastic so they won't dry out. Spraying small pieces with water will also help keep them damp.

If you have a design sketch for the pattern shapes on the front of the planter, transfer the shapes by placing the sketch on top of one of the

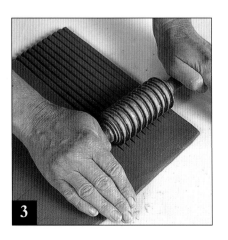

long planter walls and tracing over the design lines with a pencil (**Photo 5**). These lines will serve as placement guides for the clay pattern shapes you're about to cut out. Attractive designs don't have to be complex or made up of many pieces. Consider texturing a single slab to add to the planter wall, as shown in **Photo 6**, or texturing the wall itself. Scribing a line around the textured area will highlight the contrast between it and the non-textured areas and will also give it a neater appearance.

6. Now transfer the same shapes to the remaining, uncut slab in the same manner and cut out the clay shapes with a knife or pin tool. You may want to add a design to the back of the planter, too. If you do, cut out the design shapes now.

7. With a wire scoring tool or fork, score the backs of the design shapes and the areas on the wall slab where they'll go (**Photo 7**).

8. Using a stiff brush, apply clay slurry to the scored areas and firmly press the shapes onto one long planter wall (**Photos 8** and **9**).

9. Paddle the joined leather-hard pieces with any flat wooden tool to make the joints stronger. Then wipe away any excess slurry with a sponge or brush. (Never sponge too vigorously, as doing so will make the surface of the clay gritty.)

10. Clean the edges of the shapes with a 1/2" (1.3 cm) brush dipped in water or with a dampened sponge. A little pressed-in texture here and there can add a delicate touch to the detailing (**Photo 10**).

11. You'll assemble the walls of the planter upside down. Score their short edges (**Photo 11**), apply clay slurry to them, and press them together firmly (**Photos 12** and **13**). Do be careful not to distort the walls, the design shapes on the front, or the details in the texture.

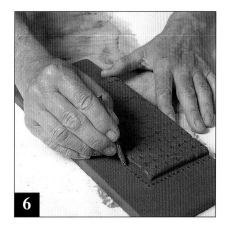

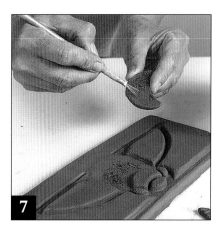

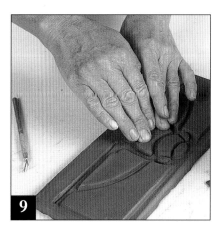

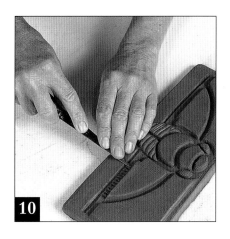

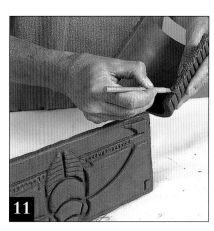

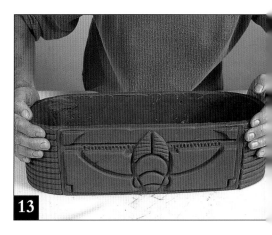

12. Roll out a thin coil of soft clay and press it into the joints on the inside of the assembled walls (**Photo 14**). Smooth the coil well, using your finger, a knife, or—as shown in **Photo 15**—a rubber rib.

13. Before turning the assembled walls over and cutting a slab base for the planter, you may want to adjust the width of the planter to compensate for shrinkage. If the finished width of your planter is to be 5" (12.7 cm), for example,

14

15

compare the 5" mark on a real ruler with the corresponding mark on a clay ruler. For the clay I use, the corresponding mark will be 5-1/2" (14 cm). Adjust the width of the planter to 5-1/2" by bending the short walls in or out, taking care not to disturb the joints.

14. In order to make the assembled walls easier to turn over, stuff the interior of the planter with wadded plastic or newspaper, but don't turn the assembly over yet. First score the upper edges of the assembled walls Then, on the left-over slab, score the areas where the walls will join it (**Photo 16**).

15. Using a stiff brush, apply slurry to the scored edges of the walls. Then, holding the assembly by its short ends, gently, quickly, and in one smooth motion, turn it over and position it on top of the scored outline on the leftover slab.

16. Remove the stuffing from the planter and adjust the walls as necessary. To make sure that the scored areas adhere well and that the upper rim of the planter is even, cover the rim with a scrap of plywood and press down on it firmly (**Photo 17**).

17. To seal the interior joint between the planter walls and bottom, press a thin coil of moist clay into it and smooth the coil out well.

18. Using a knife held at an

angle, cut the excess clay away from the planter base (**Photo 18**). A slightly beveled edge will give your planter some visual "lift" and will add to its appeal.

19. Lightly smooth the rim of the planter with a dampened sponge, but do so sparingly, as excessive rubbing will create a gritty surface (**Photo 19**). Be sure to smooth out any other sharp edges, too, as once the clay is fired, these can be sharp enough to cut (**Photo 20**).

20. To help create an even glaze line on the inside of the planter, scribe a line around the inner walls, about 1/4" (6 mm) down from the upper rim (**Photo 21**). You may use a pencil or any tool with a rounded point to do this, but the handmade implement shown in **Photo 22** will help keep the line even. To make this tool, cut a 3/4" (1.9 cm) length of picture molding, drill a hole though one surface, 1/4" (6 mm) below the inner lip, and insert a small screw until it barely protrudes from the opposite surface. Place the inner lip of the tool on the upper rim of the planter, with the point of the screw facing the inner wall. Then run the tool around the rim; the screw will scribe a line around the interior of the project.

21. Now is the time to make drainage holes if you want them, as drilling these after the planter has

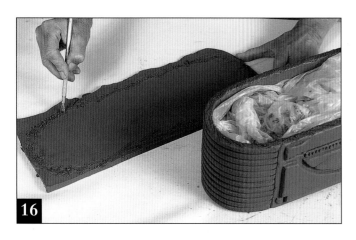
16

17

been fired would be extremely difficult. Even if you're not sure whether you'll fill the planter with potting soil or place smaller containers within it, I'd recommend cutting these holes now. You can always plug them with corks later. To cut the holes, refill the planter with wadded plastic, turn it on its side, and use a hole cutter or knife to remove several pieces of clay from the bottom (**Photo 23**). You may also want to scribe your signature on the bottom of the planter.

22. Long slabs have a tendency to warp inward during drying and firing. The two throwaway braces shown in **Photo 24** are just flat clay bars with two notches cut in their bottom edges. When the notched bars are fit over the upper edges of the long planter walls, they hold the walls apart. Cut out these bars from the leftover slab, making sure that each one is about 1" (2.5 cm) longer than the width of the planter. Then cut a pair of notches in each one, making each

notch slightly less than 1/4" (6 mm) deep and centering the two to match the planter's width. Note that when you glaze the planter, the glaze, which will come up to the scored line 1/4" below the rim of the planter, will stop just short of the bottoms of the braces.

23. Fit the braces over the long walls. Cover the planter lightly with plastic and permit it to dry slowly for a few days. When the planter is bone dry, bisque fire it.

24. Remove the temporary braces from the planter. A gentle tap with a piece of wood should loosen them. Brush all dust from the project and remove any small chunks of clay stuck to the inside. If you've made holes in the bottom of the planter, plug them up with clay, corks, or wads of plastic.

25. Stir the glaze thoroughly. It should be the consistency of cream. Pour it into the planter, right up to the scored line below

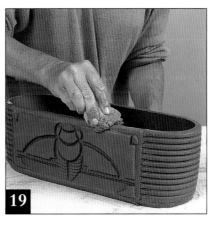

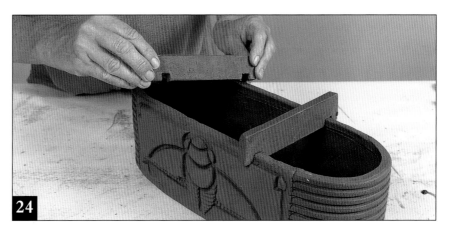

the rim, and then pour it back into the glaze container. If you have only a few cups of glaze, pour them in and coat the inner walls by carefully rotating the planter to swirl the glaze around the interior before you pour the excess glaze back out (**Photo 25**). You may want to hold the piece over the glaze container as you do this in case any glaze spills out.

Experience with particular glazes will teach you how many seconds you have to do this before the glaze dries. In general, you'll have only a few seconds. The longer the glaze is in contact with the piece, the thicker the coating will be. Fortunately, by glazing only the interior of this project, you'll avoid a problem that sometimes occurs when a glaze is applied too thickly to the exterior walls of a piece or

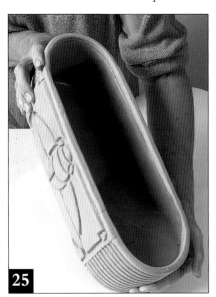

25

when an exterior glaze is fired in a kiln that's too hot: the glaze runs off and causes the piece to adhere to the kiln shelf. Thinning the glaze with some water will give you more time to work.

26. Remove the plugs from the holes in the bottom of the planter. Using a knife, scrape off any dried glaze drips on its outside and around the rim. Then sponge the rim clean down to the scribed line. Touch up any missed or chipped spots by painting the glaze on with a pointed touch-up brush.

27. Using a stiff brush, apply underglaze over the design shapes and texture lines on the short ends. Sponge off the high spots—the underglaze that rises above the recesses—when you're finished (**Photo 26**).

28. If you didn't scribe your signature into the planter earlier, use a fine brush and diluted underglaze to sign the bottom of the piece now. Put the braces back on, making sure they don't touch the glazed area. Sometimes, braces will stick during firing, a problem that's not uncommon with porcelain clay. You can avoid this by rubbing a little alumina hydrate onto the braces and walls where they'll touch each other.

29. Glaze fire the planter to Δ3 or Δ4.

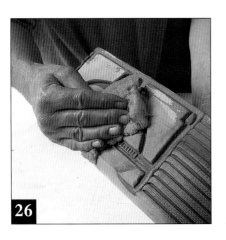

26

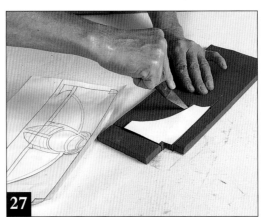

27

TIPS AND VARIATIONS

■ If you're a beginner, start with relatively thick slabs. The thicker the slabs, the stronger the joints will be and the less you'll need to worry about the walls of your planter collapsing.

■ When you plan to duplicate a piece or a series of design shapes, make cardboard, tar-paper, or thin sheet-metal templates of its different parts (**Photo 27**). By using these templates, you won't have to measure and redraw every shape again later. Number each template, marking it on the top so you'll know which side should face up.

■ To support shapes that aren't braced as they dry, fill them with wadded newspaper.

■ When you're making a large sculptural form, building a web of permanent clay buttresses inside it will help prevent warping.

■ When the piece you've made is large, it's wise to let the joined slabs stiffen up for awhile before moving the project to its drying location.

■ Rather than recycling leftover pieces of slab (the odd shapes that remain after pieces are cut), try using them in other ways—as decorative elements or handles, for example, or as temporary spacers in slab boxes to help keep the walls straight while drying.

■ To lift and lighten the visual appearance of slab box shapes, add feet to them.

Top left: Jeri Burdick, *Yellow Pine Polka*, 12" x 9" x 8" (30.5 x 23 x 20.5 cm), 1991. Slab; terra sigillata, underglazes, glazes; Δ04. Photo by Kitty Parrott

Top right: Shari Sikora, *Long Box*, 5-3/4" x 8-1/2" x 4" (14.5 x 21.5 x 10 cm), 1996. Slab; raku fired. Photo by John Carlano

Center left: Chrissie Callejas, *Butter Dish*, 4" x 3" x 7-1/2" (10 x 7.5 x 19 cm), 1995. Slab; copper wash on exterior, glazed interior; Δ5. Photo by Todd Bush

Center right: Joan Rothchild Hardin, *Planter*, 7-1/4" x 7" x 7" (18.5 x 18 x 18 cm), 1995. Slab, press molded; underglazes, glaze; Δ9. Photo by artist

Bottom: Dennis Meiners, *Oval Bowl*, 6" x 22" x 6" (15 x 56 x 15 cm), 1993. Stretched slab; barium copper glaze; reduction fired. Photo by Bill Bachhuber

DRAPED SLAB PLATE

This slab project, shown with and without a transparent glaze coating in the photo above, was designed by Don Davis and brings to mind the simple elegance of many Japanese clay forms. As you make it, you'll probably think of a hundred possible variations you'd like to try. In fact, creating a series is one way in which professionals explore particular design concepts. Studying a piece carefully and experimenting with small variations when making the next one is an excellent way to refine designs.

The one limitation to the method demonstrated here is that in order to remove the clay from the hump mold, the design must be an open one.

HAVE ON HAND

3 lbs. (1.4 kg) brown clay for Δ6 oxidation firing

3-1/2 ounces (103 ml) engobe (Appendix E, page 148)

1 cup (237 ml) transparent glaze (Appendix H, Glaze #5, page 151); optional

Cardboard

Bamboo skewer or any pointed instrument (optional)

Hump mold

If mold is nonporous, a piece of plastic or cloth

Wooden roller (optional)

Several sheets of clean paper

Small, water-filled bowl

STARTING TIPS

■ What can you use as a hump mold? Look around your kitchen, a thrift store, or a junkyard for objects with suitable shapes. A wok, helmet, balloon, or pillow will work as well as a bowl without feet. So will a piece of rigid polystyrene foam that you carve yourself. Just remember that if your mold is nonporous, you must cover it with a piece of lightweight plastic or cloth, or the clay will stick to it. If you know someone who throws clay on a wheel, you might ask them to throw and trim a clay mold like the bisque-fired bowl shape that Don uses for this project.

INSTRUCTIONS

1. Roll out a slab approximately 1/4" (6 mm) thick. For larger pieces or projects that will be carved, the slabs should be closer to 1/2" (1.3 cm) thick.

2. Cut a cardboard template for your plate, in any open shape you desire, and place it on the slab. If you'd rather, you can cut a free-form shape from the slab instead of making a template first.

3. To check for consistent slab thickness, push a bamboo skewer or any pointed instrument through the clay at several locations, noting the depth to which it sinks (**Photo 1**).

4. Mark the shape of the template onto the moist clay (**Photo 2**).

5. Cut the slab to size with a pin tool or knife (**Photo 3**).

6. To make sure that your plate will be centered on the mold, first place the mold upside down on a turntable. Then rotate the turntable while holding a pencil at an even height against the spinning mold (**Photo 4**).

7. Center the slab on top of the mold (**Photo 5**). If your mold is nonabsorbent, don't forget to cover it with a thin sheet of plastic or cloth first.

8. Use your finger or a wooden roller (Don purchased his roller at a paint store) to smooth the edges of the cut slab (**Photo 6**). You may use a sponge for this purpose, but use it sparingly, as excessive rubbing will create a gritty surface.

9. To make the feet, first roll out four balls of clay. Shape these as you like; let your imagination take over here. Don shaped his into cones and textured them by rolling them under a wooden tool (**Photo 7**).

10. Position the feet on the slab to see where they'll look best and offer the best support for the plate. Then score their ends and the sites you've chosen for them on the slab (**Photo 8**).

11. Dip the scored end of each foot into water and press the feet onto the slab (**Photo 9**). For join-

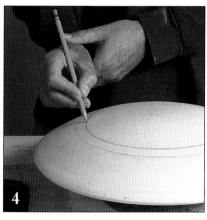

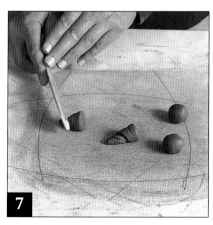

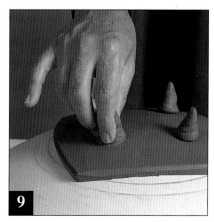

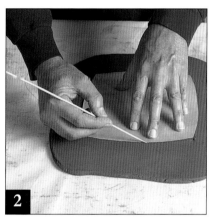

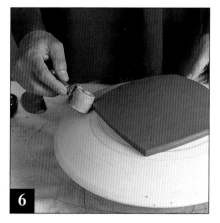

ing clay parts, some potters use clay slurry, others use water, and still others swear by a solution of 1 quart (946 ml) of water and 2 or 3 grams (.07 or .1 ounces) of sodium silicate.

12. To level the feet, place a small board on top of them and adjust them until each one touches it (**Photo 10**).

13. Set the plate and mold aside to dry slowly until the clay can be removed without distorting it. The length of time required will vary, depending on the humidity and the size of the project. Drying may take from one hour to overnight. When the plate is stiff, lift it from the form, set it on its feet, and press gently down on it to even it further (**Photo 11**).

14. Use your fingers to smooth the upper edges of the plate (**Photo 12**).

15. Tear out or cut strips of clean paper, wet them by dipping them into water, and lay them out on the surface of the plate (**Photo 13**).

16. Using a wide paintbrush, apply a layer of engobe over the paper and the exposed clay surface on top of the plate (**Photo 14**).

17. Allow the engobe to dry for about ten minutes. Then carefully peel off the paper strips (**Photo 15**).

18. Allow the plate to dry slowly, under plastic if necessary. For a surface appearance that is flat and dry, simply fire the engobe-coated plate to Δ6 or to the firing range appropriate for your clay. For a shinier plate, bisque fire the engobe-covered plate first, apply a transparent glaze, and then fire the glazed plate at Δ6—or to the temperature that suits the clay and glaze you've selected.

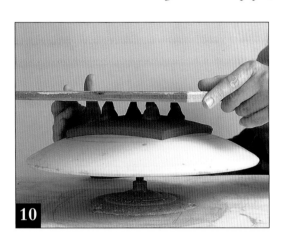

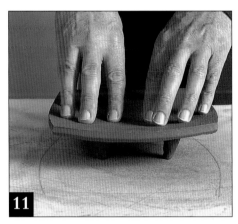

TIPS AND VARIATIONS

■ Alter the shape of the slab by cutting its edge to form a regular or irregular design.

■ Add handles. Both these and feet can be varied by shaping soft thin slabs as if they were material, folding and darting the clay as you do. Just be sure to make holes in any closed, hollow clay piece in order to allow air and steam to vent during firing.

■ Texture the surface of the slab before placing it over the mold or texture the bottom of the plate once the slab is on top of the mold.

■ Add a shaped coil base.

■ To make a closed clay piece, attach two molded pieces together after they're leather hard.

■ Instead of using wet paper strips to create the design, apply the engobe with a brush.

■ Overlap engobes of different colors.

■ After the engobe has dried for ten minutes or so, carve or incise designs into it.

■ Instead of using an engobe, Don often trails a thick glaze onto the bone-dry piece before firing (**Photo 16**). He does this with a few quick strokes of the glaze bottle in the air over the piece (**Photo 17**). Plastic trailing bottles are sold by ceramic suppliers, but an ear syringe will work, too. Fill the bottle with your glaze (try Glaze #6 in Appendix H on page 151, which is mixed a little thicker than ordinary glaze). Make sure there are no lumps in it, as these

can clog up the trailing bottle and squirt out suddenly, along with far more glaze than you wanted to apply. Practice this trailing technique on newspaper, as any hesitation in arm movement will show up in the glaze pattern. This glaze method allows the toasty brown surface of the raw clay to show, providing a pleasant contrast with the shiny, fluid glaze areas.

■ Concave pieces similar to Don's draped plate can also be made with sling molds. I used this type of mold to make the platter shown in **Photo 18**. To create a sling mold, cut a hole out of a piece of plywood or stiff cardboard, shaping it to match the plate or platter you desire. Drape plastic or cloth over the frame and lay the slab on the cloth. The clay—and the cloth supporting it—will sag slightly, forming a natural concave shape. By striking one end of the frame against your work surface, you can accentuate the sag in the cloth and clay (**Photo 19**).

Support the frame over any two objects of equal height and allow the clay to dry (**Photo 20**), trimming the excess clay from the shape in the sling before it's too dry to cut. Add feet, if you like, when the piece is leather hard.

While my piece was still leather hard, I painted a black underglaze on the rim and scratched through it. (Another underglaze was applied to the interior.) When the piece was dry, I sprayed it with a clear glaze and added small, colored clay balls to the indentations on the rim.

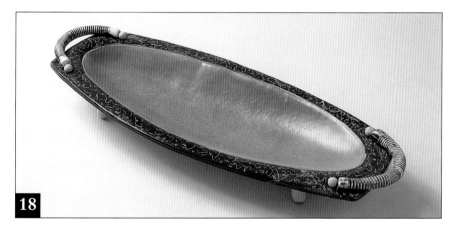

18

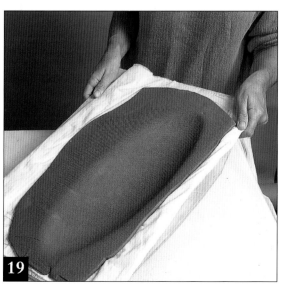

19

Top: Laurie Rolland, *Winged Boat*, 7-3/4"
x 11-3/4" x 6-1/4" (20 x 30 x 16 cm),
1996. Press molded; slip glazes on
interior, underglazes on exterior; Δ6.
Photo by artist

Center left: Ken Sedberry, *Terra-Cotta
Basin*, 21" x 16" x 12" (53.5 x 40.5 x
30.5 cm), 1996. Hump molded; underglazes, clear glaze; Δ04. Photo by artist

Center right: Joanna Borlase, *Vase: Open
Window with Lilacs*, 23" x 15" x 20"
(58.5 x 38 x 51 cm), 1996. Molded
in cardboard cut-out mold, thrown slab,
coiled; slips, stains, underglazes, terra
sigillata, clear glaze; Δ04. Photo by artist

Bottom: D. Hayne Bayless, *Mambo Pot*,
14" x 27" x 4" (35.5 x 68.5 x 10 cm),
1995. Slab pressed into perforated plywood, then stretched; glaze; Δ10 reduction. Photo by artist

COILED AND EXTRUDED PLANTER

This coiled and extruded project is started over a hump mold and then completed by coiling freehand. As you can see in the project photo, the pinch marks on this planter appear on its outer surface, but if you coil a piece on the inside of a form instead of over its outer surface, the pinch marks will be on the interior. As long as the coils are pinched together well, there's no need to smooth them together on both surfaces.

HAVE ON HAND

50 to 60 lbs. (22.7 to 27.2 kg) groggy brown clay for Δ3 oxidation firing

1 quart (946 ml) glaze (see Appendix H, Glaze #2, on page 151)

Extruder (optional)

Small, rounded mold

Large mold, about 20" (50.8 cm) in diameter

Spray-glazing equipment and ventilated spray booth (optional)

STARTING TIPS

■ For this planter (and for any project that will live outdoors), you must select a clay that will be very vitreous when fired and that won't suffer from repeated freezing and thawing.

■ A bowl turned upside down and covered with plastic will work well as the small, rounded mold for the planter base. For the large mold, I use an old, aluminum lighting fixture.

■ Don't worry if you don't have an extruder. Just turn to the "Tips and Variations" section at the end of this project, where you'll find a great alternative explained.

■ Lack of access to a spray booth shouldn't worry you either. Instead of spraying on a glaze, I often brush an engobe or underglaze onto the bone-dry ware, allow it to dry, and then, after carefully moving the planter outdoors and putting on a respirator, use a scrub pad to remove the engobe or underglaze from the high spots. The engobe formula in Appendix E (page 148) will work well, as will any commercial underglaze.

■ As you use the coiling technique, keep a vision of the finished piece in mind so that you can maintain control of the shape. If you don't, your piece will begin to sprawl and bulge in the wrong places. Keep an eye on the real piece, too! Working on a turntable and rotating it periodically will help you keep track of your work's silhouette. Placing the turntable on a stool will keep your work closer to eye level and will let you walk around it. (The huge-oil jars of Crete were made by coiling thick ropes of clay while walking backwards.) Try positioning a mirror so that you can monitor the shape from more than one angle.

■ Coil pots have a tendency to widen as they're constructed, so as the work progresses upward, the coils are deliberately sloped inward by placing each one slightly to the inside of the one underneath.

■ Coiling can become so rhythmic and mesmerizing that you end up

1

adding too many coils too quickly for the pot to support the weight. To prevent the walls of this large coiled project from sagging, stop at regular intervals, cover the last few coils with plastic to keep them from drying out, and allow the coils beneath to stiffen somewhat. (Never allow the pot to dry completely.) To speed up drying, you may use a heat lamp or hair dryer. When the piece has stiffened, if the uppermost coil has dried out too much, score it and apply slurry before adding a new coil.

■ Experience has taught me (and will teach you in time) that the legs of a piece this large can't support the weight of the body before they've been fired. To support the planter in the meantime and to make it easier to move, you'll place a temporary "knock-off" clay pedestal underneath it. To make this pedestal, first roll out a 3" x 12" (7.6 x 30.5 cm) slab, 1/2" (1.3 cm) thick, from the same clay you'll use to make the planter. Then form the slab into a cylinder. Join its edges after scoring them and applying slurry. Cut a few finger-sized holes in the walls; these will allow you to lift the pedestal—and planter—without grasping the

planter itself. Cover the piece loosely with plastic and allow it to stiffen as you construct the body of the planter.

■ As you shape the base, don't forget that when you're using a hump mold, you must remove the shaped clay before it shrinks too much, or the clay will crack.

■ Move this large, unfired piece as little as possible. Spray glazing with a glaze made specifically for greenware and firing the piece only once minimizes the need to move it.

INSTRUCTIONS

1. The rim of this planter consists of three hollow clay tubes that are bent and arranged to form a circle. Start by extruding three tubes, each 16" (40.6 cm) long and about 2" (5.1 cm) in diameter, with walls about 1/4" (6 mm) thick.

2. Bend the tubes while the clay is still moist. When you've completed the body of the planter, you'll adjust their shapes to match its rim exactly.

3. Extrude another tube, 22" (55.9 cm) long, to form the circular planter base, but make its walls thicker, as you'll bend this tube into a tighter shape than the rim tubes.

4. Bend the base tube to make a circle, but don't join its ends yet (**Photo 1**). Cover the four extruded pieces lightly with plastic

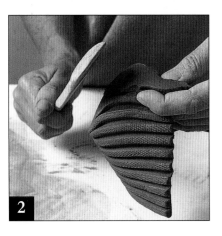

2

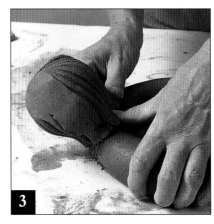

3

4

and allow them to stiffen a little.

5. To make the foot and rim elements, first roll out six small slabs, each roughly 6" x 6" (15.2 x 15.2 cm). I usually make more of these elements than I need so that I can choose the best of the lot. When I'm making more than one pot, I also shape the elements differently for each one.

6. Texture each of the six slabs as desired and then shape them, one at a time, to make the rim and

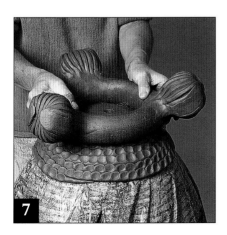

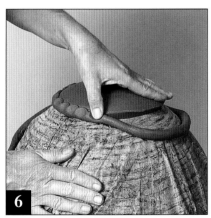

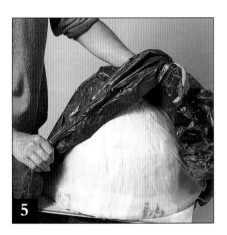

base elements. To create the organic, bulb-like forms shown in the project photo on page 99, pinch and paddle the slabs, using your fingers to push up from the underside of each one (**Photo 2**). Cover these parts lightly with plastic and allow them to stiffen.

7. Score the ends of the base tube, apply slurry to the scored ends, and press them together to form a closed circle.

8. Mark and score the locations for the three feet on the underside of the base. (I angle the feet outward.)

9. Attach the feet to the base by scoring their ends, applying slurry to them and to the scored locations on the base, and pressing the feet into place. Smooth the joints by working on what will be the underside of the legs first (**Photo 3**).

10. Turn the base over, place it on top of a small, rounded mold so that you can reach the upper edges of the feet, and make sure the joints there are pressed firmly together, too (**Photo 4**).

11. Cut a few small holes in the base and feet so that they won't explode during firing. Cover the assembly tightly with plastic to keep it from drying out.

12. Place a piece of plywood on your turntable and position the large mold upside down on top of it. Then cover the mold with two sheets of plastic (**Photo 5**). These

will make it easier to remove the clay later.

13. Roll out a small circular slab of clay, about 6" (15.2 cm) in diameter and 1/2" (1.3 cm) thick. This slab base will make the coiled planter stronger. Place the slab circle on top of the mold, centering it carefully. If you want your finished planter to have a hole in the bottom, cut one out now.

14. Roll out several 1/2"-thick (1.3 cm) coils, tapering their ends so that you can blend the end of one coil with the beginning of the next. To begin making the coiled walls, press one end of a coil onto the slab base and then work around it, joining the coil to the slab by pressing the clay with your thumb (**Photo 6**). Make these indentations at regular intervals, using the same amount of pressure each time. Be sure to keep the coils you're not using wrapped tightly in plastic so they won't dry out.

15. Continue to add coils in this fashion until you've built up several rounds. If you need to take a break, cover the last few coils that you added with plastic to keep them from drying out.

16. Add the extruded base by scoring it and the slab bottom of the planter, applying slurry, and pressing the base in place (**Photo 7**).

17. Press a thin coil into the interior and exterior joints and smooth them in place (**Photo 8**).

18. Place the knock-off pedestal on top of the planter bottom. To make sure that the feet are even, position a sheet of plywood on top of the pedestal. Check to see that the plywood is level (rotating the turntable will help here) and that each of the planter feet

touches its surface (**Photo 9**). You may need to cut the clay pedestal down to size.

19. Remove the plywood, cover the last few planter coils with plastic, and set the project aside, allowing the clay to dry until it's barely leather hard.

20. Set the plywood on top of the planter feet again, carefully turn the project over, and place it—and the plywood—back on the turntable.

21. Remove the mold and the layer of plastic closest to it. You'll find that the other layer of plastic has stuck to the clay; just peel it away.

22. Continue by coiling the planter walls in stages, adding a few more rounds of coils at a time (**Photo 10**). Don't try to build more than 6" (15.2 cm) of height at one time, as the wet clay won't support any more weight than that without collapsing. Instead, allow each batch of added coils to stiffen

before adding another batch. (Don't forget to wrap the uppermost coils in plastic to keep the clay moist.) As you add the coils, position them to lean just slightly inward. It's easier to widen the planter diameter later by pushing them back out than it is to cure wobbling walls by collaring them inward.

As you work, rotate the turntable to check the planter walls for uniformity (**Photo 11**). Correct any bulges or depressions before they get out of hand. To do this, support one surface of the clay wall with a hand, smooth stone, or smooth wad of plastic, and paddle the opposite surface with a wooden paddle or wooden spoon.

23. When the walls have been completed and the last coils have stiffened, level the planter rim by rotating the turntable while cutting through the uppermost coil with a steadily-held needle tool (**Photo 12**).

24. Position the three extruded rim tubes on the planter rim and adjust them until each tube conforms exactly to the shape of the rim. Leave spaces between the ends of the tubes; the three rim elements will fit over these gaps. You'll probably need to bend the tubes slightly and may need to cut clay from their ends as well. Using a template can be very helpful here (**Photo 13**).

25. Score the bottoms of the rim tubes and the planter rim, apply

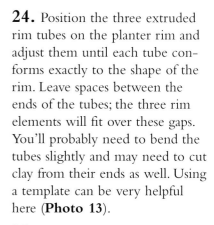

9

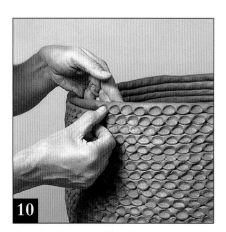

10

11

12

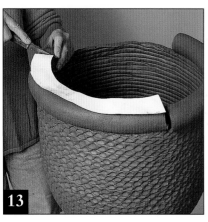

13

14

15

slurry, and press the tubes in place. Then add a coil to the inside and outside of these joints. Next, add the three rim elements in the same fashion (**Photo 14**). Use a pin tool to make holes in both the tubes and the rim elements to prevent these hollow shapes from exploding during firing. Cover the planter loosely with plastic and allow it to dry slowly.

26. When the planter is bone dry, you must move it to a ventilated spray booth for glazing. Lift it carefully by inserting your fingers in the pedestal holes, supporting the planter between your extended arms and against your chest.

27. Put on a respirator and spray the planter with glaze (**Photo 15**). Because the pedestal won't be glazed (it will be protected by the extruded base and feet), it won't adhere to the piece during firing.

28. To move the planter into the kiln after the glaze has dried, lift it up by using the knock-off pedestal again. Spreading a sheet of plastic over your chest will help prevent the fragile glaze coating from rubbing off.

29. Fire the planter to Δ3. (A glazed greenware firing proceeds in the same manner as a bisque firing.)

TIPS AND VARIATIONS

■ If your coils tend to be flat when you roll them out, your clay may be too dry.

■ Potters often speak of the relationship between the rim, shoulder, belly, and foot of a pot. Study this relationship when you're designing the rim of a coiled piece. Should you make the rim with a thick bold coil or finish the pot with a lip that flows in an uneven organic fashion? Resist the tendency to mimic wheel-thrown work and accept the inevitable variations that ensue from hand-forming.

■ If you don't have access to an extruder, substitute a thick slab or coil for the extruded rim and base of this project (**Photo 16**). Keep in mind that in general, a clay piece shouldn't be thicker than 3/4" (1.9 cm) or it will require extremely slow firing. I try to keep all clay pieces no more than 1/2" (1.3 cm) thick.

■ Coiled pots may be textured in a number of ways. Try pinching your coils instead of rolling them out or coil the clay around the interior, concave surface of the form instead of around its convex exterior so that your pinch marks will appear on the inside of the pot (**Photo 17**). Use a tool instead of your fingers to press the coils together, or smooth the coils together, partly or completely, instead of pressing them with your thumb. To create walls without texture, scrape and smooth the coils after adding every few rounds. Pull upwards with each smoothing motion to counter the sagging effect, strengthen the pot, and define its shape.

■ Possible variations on basic coiled shapes are many. They include coiling the clay around a form such as a cardboard roller; applying the coils non-horizontally and incorporating other coiled shapes within them; pressing small clay circles or other shapes into the coils; changing the shape, either as you add coils or by paddling after coiling; enlarging a pinch pot by adding coils to it; and pinching small, short coils to each other to form an openwork, basket-like pattern.

■ To strengthen projects made with small, delicate coils, add thin slabs to one surface.

■ Rather than glazing a coiled piece, you may want to combine coils of colored clay or roll the coils in glaze stains, silicon carbide, iron filings, or glaze opacifiers such as zircon.

16

17

Top left: Candone M. Wharton, *Jarron*, 13" x 15" x 6" (33 x 38 x 15 cm), 1996. Slab, textured coils; raku and luster firings. Photo by Jerry L. Anthony

Top right: Mary Lou Deal, *Animal Fable*, 16" x 10" x 10" (40.5 x 25.5 x 25.5 cm), 1995. Slab, coiled; stains, glaze; raku fired. Photo by Allen Jones

Center left: Phyllis Kudder-Sullivan, *POD 28*, 16-1/2" x 23-1/2" x 11-1/2" (42 x 60 x 30 cm), 1992. Woven extruded coils; glazes; Δ6. Photo by Joseph D. Sullivan

Center right: Sue Abbrescia, *Coil Vessel #2*, 9-1/2" x 7-1/4" x 9-7/8" (24 x 18.5 x 25 cm), 1996. Coiled; underglazes; Δ04. Photo by Tim Rice

Bottom: Paul J. Sherman, *Hydnocerus Series IV (#1)*. Length: 4' (1.2 m), 1993. Coiled double wall; glazes; Δ05. Photo by Tom Eckersley

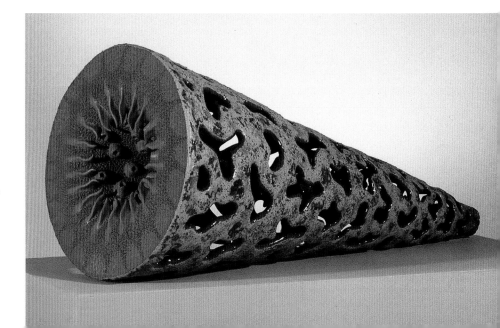

BASIC PINCH POT

Learning to make a pinch pot is a great way to gain some experience with manipulating soft clay. Once you've made this project, you'll be ready to try the extended pinch pitcher on pages 108-110.

HAVE ON HAND

A fistful or more of any type of clay

Terra-sigillata slip, commercial or hand-mixed (Appendix I, page 152)

STARTING TIPS

■ Fingernails will have to be trimmed; they tend to get in the way.

INSTRUCTIONS

1. Take a fistful of clay and indent its center by pressing the clay with both thumbs.

2. Place the indented lump in one hand. Starting at the base of the indentation, press the clay between the thumb and fingers of your other hand while turning the lump slightly in your palm. Continue to shape the clay by repeating this simple slow movement, working around and upward (**Photo 1**) as you do.

3. As you gradually thin the walls, aim for an even thickness. If the heat of your hands starts to dry the clay, it may crack. Just smooth these cracks over. Moisten your

fingers with water once in awhile, but resist the urge to add too much water, as the piece will get so slippery that it will be hard to work. As the walls become thinner, the pot will dry more rapidly, but a few squirts with a mister will help keep the clay moist and workable. Cover the pot with plastic if you have to take a break.

If the form begins to get too wide and floppy, stiffen the clay by letting the pot rest uncovered. (Working on several pots at one time will help you keep a rhythm going.) If you're working with a wide, flared form, you may need to support the clay as it stiffens by setting it on a shape such as a bowl or a stocking-covered balloon or ball. If the pot has a narrow opening, fill it with wadded plastic instead. Don't allow pots placed over forms to stiffen too much or they may crack as they shrink.

4. To collar in the rim of the pot, gather the rim into folds and pinch the folds together.

5. Pinch a strip of clay over the rim to serve as a collar.

6. Dry the finished piece slowly under plastic. As the pot becomes leather hard, you may want to scrape or smooth it with a rib, or—if the clay is thick—use a knife to create facets in its surface. Some potters use hacksaw blades or rasps to shape pieces, although finger marks often form their own expressive finish.

7. To recreate the surface decoration on the pot shown in the photo, when the pot is bone dry, brush on a coat of terra-sigillata formulated with red clay. (I left the rim bare.)

8. When the terra-sigillata has dried, fire the pot to Δ06.

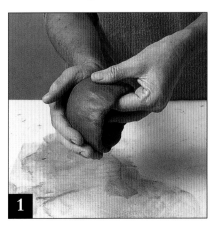

TIPS AND VARIATIONS

■ Pinched forms range from open bowls to completely closed pieces. If you close the rim completely, air trapped inside the form will keep it from collapsing, making it easier to change the shape by paddling it. Just remember to make a hole in the piece before it dries so that air can escape during the firing.

■ One method for shaping a nearly closed form is to wrap the piece with string and then blow—hard—through the small opening until the piece puffs out around the string.

■ If you'd like to make a base for a pinch pot, shape one from a clay coil and press it in place.

■ To square a round pot, use a paddle or hit the curved walls against a table top.

■ Add spouts, necks, feet, and/or handles. If the clay is still plastic, join the pieces by pressing them together well so that the clay at the joints merges together. To join leather-hard clay parts, score and apply slurry first.

■ To make a bowl with a fitted lid, first pinch two separate bowls and then join them together to make a larger sphere. After this form has stiffened somewhat, use a wire to slice off the upper third of the sphere. Turn the smaller piece into a lid by adding a flange to it.

■ You may leave the rim of a bowl irregularly shaped or trim it evenly with a needle tool or knife. (Smooth the edges; sharp edges get sharper with firing.) In either case, the rim should terminate in a purposeful manner.

■ When a pinch pot is just beyond the leather-hard stage, it can also be burnished to create a surface with the feel and sheen of polished wood (see page 62). This ancient technique, which takes the place of glazing, makes the surface more impervious and strengthens the pot as well. Red or white earthenware clay works best here, especially when the piece will be pit-fired after bisque firing. Burnishing has little effect on work fired over Δ06.

■ One variation on the pinching method is the dowel method. Start by pressing a wooden dowel through a lump of clay (**Photo 2**). Then roll the dowel and clay on your work surface. As you do this, the opening in the lump will enlarge. Replacing the first dowel with a thicker one will help keep the walls of this clay cylinder even in thickness. To add height, just squeeze the clay back around the dowel and continue. Texture the clay as desired (**Photo 3**). To form a bottom for the pot, remove the dowel and either pinch and paddle one end closed (**Photo 4**) or add a slab to one end of the cylinder.

■ If you'd like to make feet for a small pinch pot, make several different sets in different sizes so that you can select ones to suit the size of the pot. To add the feet, first make sure they're the same stiffness as the bottom of the pot. Then score them, apply slurry, and press them in place. If the pot is heavy, turn it upside down before adding the feet or use a temporary, "knock-off" pedestal to support the base of the pot (see page 100 for details).

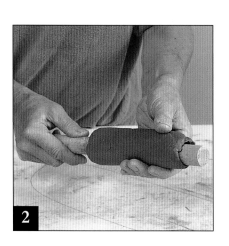

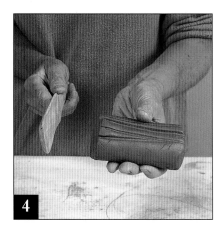

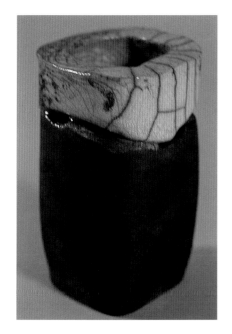

Top left: Mikhail Zakin, *Vase Form*, 10" x 4" x 4" (25.5 x 10 x 10 cm), 1995. Dowel formed; glaze; raku fired. Photo by artist

Top right: Marilyn Andrews, *"One" Teapot with Two Cups*, 9" x 13" x 7" (23 x 33 x 18 cm), 1994. Coiled, pinched, slab; slips, clear matt glaze; Δ6 to Δ7. Photo by Bob Barrett

Center left: Peter Sohngen, *Chess Set*. King: 2-1/2" x 2" (6.5 x 5 cm), 1986. Hand-formed porcelain; stains; Δ10 reduction. Photo by artist

Center right: Elizabeth Smith Jacobs, *Rhinoceros*, 5" x 10-1/2" x 5-1/2" (12.5 x 26.5 x 14 cm), 1992. Two joined pinch pots, draped slab; white crackle glaze; raku fired. Photo by Peter Jacobs

Bottom: Barbara Schwartz, *Lavender Mist*, 8" x 10" x 38" (20.5 x 25.5 x 96.5 cm), 1976. Paddled; glazes; Δ5; low-fire lusters. Photo by Robert Nelson

EXTENDED PINCH PITCHER

Building a project with small wads or handfuls of soft clay allows you just as much freedom of shape and size as coiling but produces more rapid results—at least once you've had some practice. As your skills develop, you'll find there's no limit to the size of the work you can create. I first witnessed this fact at a workshop, where the visiting Japanese "National Treasure," Shiro Otani, built a pot into which he could climb. Because extended pinch work is formed with interlocking clay elements similar to the bones in your skull, it is very strong.

HAVE ON HAND

10 lbs. (4.5 kg) brown clay for Δ3 oxidation firing

1 pint (473 ml) glaze for interior (Appendix H, Glaze #1, page 151)

1 quart (946 ml) glaze for exterior (Appendix H, Glaze #2, page 151)

2 ounces (29.6 ml) commercial underglaze for spout and handle

Rutile and several commercial underglaze colors (optional)

Wax resist

Masking tape

STARTING TIPS

■ One of the drawbacks of working with this technique is that it almost always demands overworking the clay. As a result, the pot will want to become an amorphous blob. To counteract this tendency, it's important to start with a clear image of the final form. I started this pitcher with a cardboard sketch of the profile of the shape I wanted, to guide the form as I made it.

■ As you design the form, consider contrast. A crisp, geometric hard edge against a curving form may

provide the balancing element of contrast that the form needs to define it.

■ Thin spots in any pinched piece may encourage sagging or bulging. Before you start your first extended-pinch project, practice by pinching a few hollow cylinders from individual wads of clay and then slicing across their diameters to see whether the wall thickness is even throughout.

■ I splattered rutile over the exterior glaze, to give it a greenish cast. I also splattered several underglaze colors over it.

INSTRUCTIONS

1. Roll out a clay slab and cut a shape from it for the base of the pitcher.

2. To build the walls, start by pinching a flattened handful of clay onto the base, merging the two pieces together thoroughly. Add more flattened wads, one by one (**Photo 1**) to make overlapping rows.

3. As you continue to add clay, thin the joints where the flattened wads overlap—and the walls themselves—by squeezing the clay with your fingers. Check frequently to see that the walls are uniform in thickness.

4. As the pot grows rapidly upward, sagging and bulging may occur. You can counter this tendency in several ways. Working in stages is one. Allow lower sections to approach the leather-hard stage before adding more clay. Don't forget to keep the uppermost portions moist, however, so that the next pinched row will adhere well. Another way to prevent bulges is to push upward on the clay as you pinch the walls, rather than pushing outward. Paddling the form inward frequently also helps (**Photo 2**), unless, of course, you're making an intentionally flared form.

5. If you like, you can texture the exterior of the shaped pot at this stage. I paddled this piece with the edge of my paddle. When you're finished, cover the pitcher lightly with plastic and set it aside to stiffen a bit.

6. Roll out a slab for the spout and handle and texture the slab as you like.

7. From this moist slab, cut an elongated, rectangular shape for the handle and roll it around a wooden dowel, handling the clay very gently so that you don't mar the texture (**Photo 3**). This shape is more appealing to me when it varies in diameter from one end to the other. I often make more than one handle so that I can select the one that looks best.

8. Form the tubular handle by joining its long edges and pressing them firmly together. Then gently bend the handle to the shape desired (**Photo 4**).

9. To make the spout, first cut a triangular piece from the slab (**Photo 5**). Then bend it to the desired shape. Check it—and the handle—for fit by holding them against the body of the pot and making any necessary adjustments before setting both parts aside to stiffen slightly.

10. Attach the slightly stiff handle and spout by scoring their edges and the body of the pot, applying slurry, and pressing the parts firmly in place (**Photos 6** and **7**). To strengthen the handle, add a small

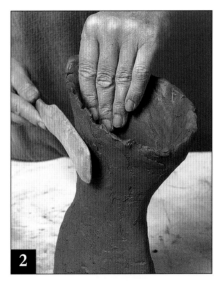

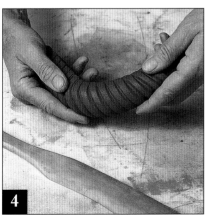

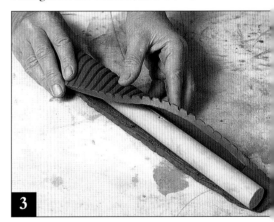

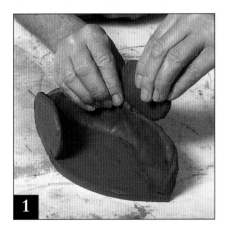

coil of clay around the joint at each end. These will also provide a place later for a small, optional color accent.

11. Use a needle tool to make a small hole in the bottom of the handle so that air can escape during firing. Cover the pitcher loosely with plastic and set it aside to dry slowly.

12. When the pitcher is bone dry, bisque fire it at Δ05.

13. Brush off any dust or bits of clay on the inside and outside surfaces. Pour some glaze into the pitcher and then pour it out while rotating the pitcher to coat the entire interior surface and edge of the rim. If I miss a portion of the interior edge while I'm doing this, I sometimes repeat the glazing procedure but never more than once or the glaze coating will be too thick. If bare clay still remains, use a paintbrush dipped into glaze to touch it up.

14. Sponge off any glaze drips on the outside of the pitcher.

15. To protect the handle, spout, and glazed upper rim from the exterior glaze coating you're about to apply, first paint the glazed rim with a wax resist. Allow the wax resist to dry thoroughly (about 15 minutes should do it) before proceeding. If drops of wax end up where you don't want them, scrub them off immediately with water. If they've dried, use sandpaper instead.

16. Next, mask off the spout and handle by wrapping them tightly in plastic and securing this covering with masking tape. Then hold the piece by the base and position it upside down over your bucket of exterior glaze. (Do as I say and not as I do: Wear gloves! I forgot to bring mine to this photo session.) Dip a cup or ladle into the glaze bucket and pour glaze over

the piece, letting the excess glaze run off into the bucket rather than onto your shoes (**Photo 8**). If your bucket is small, hold the pitcher over a large dishpan instead. Don't turn the piece upright until all the excess glaze has dripped away, or drops of glaze may run down its sides.

17. Very carefully use a wet sponge to clean up any drops of the exterior glaze that sit on waxed areas. Don't rub hard or the glaze underneath will chip or rub off the rim. You may also need to brush glaze over the areas that were covered by your fingers during pouring.

18. Unmask the spout and handle and clean away any glaze that may have leaked onto these areas. Then, with a brush, apply a contrasting color of underglaze. (Note that underglazes remain flat after firing and look better when they're applied with a brush than brushed glazes do.) To give the exterior glaze on the body of the pitcher more interest, I also splattered it with rutile and with a few underglazes. On this piece, I decided to leave the coil around the handle joint unglazed.

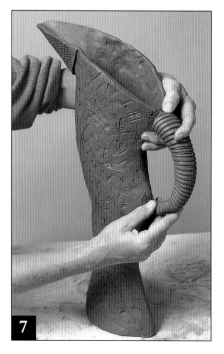

7

19. Double-check the bottom of the pitcher to make sure it's glaze-free. Then sign the bottom with a stain or underglaze and position the pitcher in the kiln for a Δ3 firing.

TIPS AND VARIATIONS

■ To create straight edges in a clay form, use the straight edge of a board.

■ When you're making forms that flare outward, you may need to support the clay as it stiffens in order to keep the walls from collapsing. To do this, prop the walls up (bricks or pieces of wood will help here) or make supporting slings by suspending fabric from wooden frames. Some large sculptural forms may require a permanent inner network of supporting clay ribs.

■ Finger marks and the joints between wads create interesting textures, but you may also smooth the surface completely by scraping it with a flexible rib. Many surface variations are possible. Experiment by using different sizes and shapes of clay wads. Consider leaving open areas in sculpted works.

■ A form too large for the kiln can be sliced apart and flanged when leather hard so that the parts fit together like a jar and lid.

8

Top left: Cynthia Consentino, *Untitled*, 16" x 5" x 5" (40.5 x 12.5 x 12.5 cm), 1993. Oxides, underglazes, glaze; Δ10. Photo by artist

Top right: Wesley Anderegg, *Cups and Saucers*. Each set: 6" x 6" x 4" (15 x 15 x 10 cm), 1995. Pinched; slips, matt glaze; Δ06. Photo by artist

Bottom left: Peter Sohngen, *Box*, 4-1/2" x 6" x 5" (11.5 x 15 x 12.5 cm), 1991. Wads pressed into molds; glaze; Δ10 reduction. Photo by artist

Center right: Marilyn Andrews, *Bird in Trees Teapot with Stand and Cups*, 10-1/2" x 10-1/2" x 10-1/2" (26.5 x 26.5 x 26.5 cm), 1995. Slab, coiled, pinched; slips, clear matt glaze; Δ6 to Δ7. Photo by Bob Barrett

Bottom right: Marvin Sweet, *Guardian of Memory*, 26" x 18" x 11" (66 x 45.5 x 28 cm), 1995. Slab, coiled, pinched; glaze; Δ04. Photo by Dave Bradley

PRESS-MOLDED RELIEF TILE

You're better off handsculpting a simple tile design, but for a relatively complex one, which may take several hours to create, making a mold saves time. The mold will allow you to press or slip-cast as many identical tiles as you like quite quickly. In the project presented here, you'll learn how to make an open-face mold and press clay into it, but the same type of mold is used to make slip-cast tiles as well.

Because timing is especially important at some stages of this project, I've listed all the tools and materials so you can gather them together before you start.

HAVE ON HAND

6 lbs. (2.7 kg) any smooth clay

6 lbs. (2.7 kg) brown clay for ∆3 oxidation firing

12 lbs. 3 oz. (5.8 kg) No. 1 Pottery Plaster

9 lbs. (4.1 kg) water

2 ounces (29.6 ml) each of three underglazes, commercial or handmixed (Appendix D, page 148)

Clay ruler

Flat sheet of nonporous material (glass, clear acrylic, sealed hardboard, or marble), at least 3" to 5" (7.6 to 12.7 cm) larger than the finished tile

Mold form

Release agent such as oil or spray lubricant, for unsealed wooden mold forms

Rubber gloves

Respirator

Level

Scale for measuring plaster

20-mesh screen

Clean-up bucket with some water in it

Empty plastic bucket large enough to hold the plaster and water, with extra space to prevent splashing during mixing

Waste bucket for excess plaster

Variable-speed drill and paint-mixing attachment (optional)

Rasp or knife

Clean, soft brush

Piece of plaster wallboard or plywood that is larger than the tile

STARTING TIPS

■ Before you begin, review the information on making and using molds in chapter 3.

■ When you get to Step 8, if your dry plaster has lumps in it, sift it through a piece of 20-mesh screen as you add it to the water.

■ Appendix C on page 147 provides plaster to water ratios and a tip on bucket sizes. You'll find this information useful when you make molds that are different in size from the one described here.

■ If you're not sure how old your dry plaster is, you may want to mix up a small test batch and pour it into an empty container rather than into your mold form. If this batch sets up too quickly (in less than one minute) or very slowly (over several hours), start over with a fresh bag of plaster.

■ Always wear gloves and a respirator when mixing and pouring plaster.

■ Always mix plaster by adding the plaster to the water. Never add water to plaster.

■ Before making your clay model, you'll need to calculate for clay shrinkage (see pages 26-27). For a finished tile 10" (25.4 cm) square, the model I made here had to be 11" (27.9 cm) square.

■ Keep an extra wad of clay on hand in case plaster begins to leak from the mold form and you need to plug up the holes.

INSTRUCTIONS

1. Using the smooth clay, make a model of your tile. An easy way to do this is to add shapes to a flat slab, as described on page 89. Be very careful to avoid undercuts as you do this. When you look straight down at your tile model, every edge of its design should slope downward and outward at an angle of about 5°.

2. Place the soft or leather-hard clay model on a flat sheet of non-porous material. Make sure that the model adheres to the sheet well so that it won't float up when you pour plaster over it.

3. Secure the walls of the mold form around the model, being careful to position them at equal distances from its edges.

4. Seal the corners and bottom of the mold form by pressing coils of clay into its corners and along its bottom edges, as shown in **Photo 23** on page 43. You may also want to seal the outer corners and edges in the same fashion.

5. If your mold form consists of unsealed wood, be sure to coat its inner walls with a release agent such as oil or spray lubricant so that the plaster won't adhere to them.

6. The mold you're about to cast can be used in two ways: with moist clay or with clay slip. If you plan to make your pieces by pouring clay slip into the finished mold, take the time now to level the flat surface on which the mold form and model rest. This way, as long as the mold sits on a level surface when you pour the slip into it, you won't have to level the mold every time you use it.

7. Put on your dust mask and gloves. You're about to mix your plaster, and after you do, you'll only have a few minutes pouring time before the plaster hardens, so be sure the model and mold forms are prepared before you begin to mix.

8. Plaster can be mixed in different ways. Read this step before starting and choose the method you prefer.

Some people start by weighing out the plaster and water separately. I find it easier to weigh my empty bucket first. I leave the bucket on the scale and add clean, room-temperature (not hot) water until the scale registers the combined weight of the bucket and water. Then I slowly add the plaster by sprinkling it in, stopping when the scale registers the combined weight of the bucket, water, and plaster. Adding the plaster slowly ensures that all the particles are thoroughly wetted and helps prevent lumps.

Other people use the "island" method to add their plaster. They weigh out the water in their bucket and then, rather than weighing the plaster, they slowly sprinkle it into the water until islands of plaster begin to form above the water's surface, waiting from time to time until these islands sink. They stop adding plaster when the islands no longer sink quickly into the water but sit on its surface for at least 10 to 15 seconds.

9. After you've added all the plaster, mix it with your gloved hand or a paint-mixing attachment and a variable-speed drill set at low speed. Be careful not to entrap any air bubbles. After a minute or two, the plaster will turn from a light cream consistency to a heavy cream consistency. This is the point at which it is ready to pour.

Don't add more plaster or water once you've stirred the ingredients. Plaster that is too thin will just take a little longer to set up in the mold form. Plaster that is too thick will thicken while you pour it and may not pick up the impressions from your model very well; you may need to start over if this is the case.

10. Pour the plaster slowly into the mold form, aiming for the space between the model and mold-form walls. Let it flow slowly over the model (**Photo 1**) and avoid splashing. Fill the mold form to about 1-1/2" (3.8 cm) above the uppermost surface of the

model. If you have any excess plaster, pour it into an empty bucket to harden before discarding it.

11. To help the plaster settle into the crevices of the model, jiggle the work surface gently; working on a wobbly table can actually be an advantage here. Do be careful not to jiggle the surface so hard that the mold form shifts position on top of it. Also avoid jarring the table once the plaster has started to set up.

12. Clean your gloves and tools immediately in the waste bucket.

13. As the plaster hardens in the mold, it will start to feel warm, usually after 30 to 45 minutes. Remove the mold form at any time after the plaster has started to cool off again. One tip here: Don't mix the clay that you used to seal the form with any other clay. Either save it for re-use with your mold form or throw it away, as any bits of plaster in it could explode in the kiln.

14. Slide the plaster mold off the nonporous surface and flip it over. Gently, with your fingers or a wooden tool, peel out the clay model as shown in **Photo 2**. (Yes, you're right. The model that I'm peeling out of the mold in this photo is for a different tile, but the process is just the same!) Be careful not to nick the mold surface as you do this.

15. You may notice some very thin fins of unwanted plaster extending from the shaped surfaces of the mold. These will have a tendency to break off when clay is pressed into the mold, so trim them away with a knife. Wait until you've pressed your first tile before making any other adjustments to the mold.

16. Dry the mold by placing it, hollowed side facing down, on flat sticks or a rack in a warm area. The drying process will take several days. A fan can help, but never place a plaster mold in a kiln or oven unless you're sure the temperature will stay under 120°F (49°C). Higher temperatures can make the plaster crumble.

17. Using a knife or rasp, round the outer edges of the mold so that they'll be less likely to chip. If you want to clean the exterior, use a kitchen scrub pad. On the outside of the mold, I also scribe the date and the amounts of plaster and water that I used to make it.

18. To use the dried mold to make a press-molded tile, first dust it out with a clean soft brush and place it, hollowed face up, on a clean flat surface. Then cut or roll out a slab of moist clay and carefully drape it over the mold, as shown in the photo at the beginning of this project.

19. Using your fingers, press the slab firmly into the mold, making sure that the clay fills the edges and crevices (**Photo 3**). Pound the clay in firmly with the heel of your hand. To even out the back, press in additional clay as necessary.

20. To remove the excess clay, slice it off by running a wire across the back of the mold. Scraping the back of the slab with a stick will also smooth out the clay.

21. Set the clay-filled mold aside to dry. Placing a solid block of plaster on top of the clay in the mold will help prevent warping, but this isn't absolutely necessary.

22. When to remove the tile will depend on a number of factors, including the thickness of the clay, the moisture content of the mold (if you've just used it to make another tile, it will still be slightly damp), and the environment in which the mold and clay have been set to dry. The tile must be dry enough to remove without distorting it, but shouldn't be so dry that it cracks as it shrinks in the mold. Drying time can range from 15 minutes to several hours.

To remove the tile, first place a flat board (a piece of plaster wallboard or plywood will work well) on top of the tile and mold. Then flip the mold and board over and lift up the mold (**Photo 4**). The tile may pop right out. If it doesn't, rap the edge of the mold sharply on the work surface. Don't peel the tile out, as this may cause it to warp

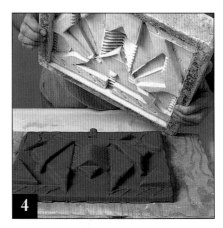

later, even if you flatten it out again now.

23. Examine the tile closely. If you see any pieces of plaster in its crevices, be sure to remove them. Also examine the tile's appearance; now is the time to make any desired adjustments to your mold by carving away unwanted plaster. Some mold makers don't spend much time worrying about small undercuts when they make their models. Instead, they find it easier to carve away mold undercuts at this stage.

You can add plaster to a mold, too, but this isn't as easy. Soak the mold thoroughly with water first, as dry plaster will immediately draw water out of freshly-poured plaster. Then add plaster as you like, pouring, dabbing, or brushing it on.

24. Set the tile on any flat surface, cover it loosely with plastic, and allow it to dry slowly.

25. When the tile is bone dry, bisque fire it to Δ05.

26. To replicate the surface decoration on the tile shown on page 112, first brush a dark underglaze (I used black) into the recesses of some portions of the tile and clean off the high spots after it dries. Then, using the photo as guide, paint red and blue underglazes onto the other portions.

27. Glaze fire the tile to Δ3.

TIPS AND VARIATIONS

■ For instructions on making slip-cast tiles with this mold, turn to page 120.

■ Rather than using your fingers to press a clay slab into a mold, you may also drape the slab over the mold, cover it with a piece of canvas, and use a rubber mallet to pound the clay into the mold. Do be careful not to chip the edges of the mold as you do this.

Top: Red Weldon-Sandlin, *Sir Real No. 1*, 8" x 14" x 6" (20.5 x 35.5 x 15 cm), 1994. Slab, coiled, press molded, hump molded, pinched; underglazes, underglaze pencil, clear glaze; Δ06. Photo by Parish Kohanim

Left: Laurie Rolland, *Vessel*. Height: 10-1/4" (26 cm), 1996. Press molded; stains, glaze; Δ6. Photo by artist

Right: Keiko Fukazawa, *An Ancient Tie*, 9" x 8" x 6" (23 x 20.5 x 15 cm), 1990. Hand formed, molded; underglazes, glazes, lusters; low fired. Photo by Gary Schwartz

SLIP-CAST PITCHER

Any number of mold sections may be necessary to slip-cast certain clay forms, but I've kept life simple here by presenting a small, flat-bottomed pitcher that only requires a two-piece mold. (If you added a foot rim to the base of this pitcher, you'd need a three-piece mold to make it.)

Once again, because timing is critical at some stages of this project, I've listed all the tools and supplies you'll need so that you can gather them together before you start.

HAVE ON HAND

2 lbs. (.9 kg) any smooth clay

9 lbs. 13 oz. (4.5 kg) No. 1 Pottery Plaster

7 lbs. (3.2 kg) water

1 quart (946 ml) Δ6 casting slip (Formula #2, Appendix G, page 149)

1 quart glaze Glaze #4, Appendix H, page 151)

Several underglazes, commercial or handmixed (Appendix D, page 148)

Clay ruler

Flat sheet of nonporous material (glass, clear acrylic, sealed hardboard, or marble), at least 3" to 5" (7.6 to 12.7 cm) larger than the finished tile

Mold form

Mold soap or polyurethane parting compound

Natural bristle brush for applying mold soap

Dry brush for buffing mold soap

Release agent such as oil or spray lubricant, for unsealed wooden mold forms

Rubber gloves

Respirator

Scale for measuring plaster

20-mesh screen

Clean-up bucket with some water in it

Empty plastic bucket large enough to hold the plaster and water, with extra space to prevent splashing during mixing

Waste bucket for excess plaster

Variable-speed drill and paint-mixing attachment (optional)

Dry, stiff brush for buffing mold soap

Rasp or knife

Clean, soft brush

Spoon, knife with curved handle, or a coin and an electric drill

Rubber mallet

Two or three sturdy rubber bands, straps, or rubber strips cut from inner tubes

Bucket for casting slip

Empty container for excess slip and two sticks to place across its top

Glaze bucket and measuring cup

STARTING TIPS

■ Unless you enjoy adrenalin surges, I'd strongly recommend that you start this project by reviewing the information on making molds in chapter 3 and the last project. Next, read all the starting tips and instructions and visualize yourself taking each step. Making molds for slip-cast work isn't all that difficult, but it won't be much fun if you're not well prepared.

■ The amounts of casting slip and glaze specified in the "Have on Hand" list are sufficient for making and glazing three pitchers.

■ Clay slurry (or *water slip*), which is made with nothing more than clay and water, doesn't make a very satisfactory slip-casting material because its high water content causes significant shrinkage. A good casting slip, which has added ingredients, shrinks as little as possible, stays in suspension, accurately produces details in the mold, and is strong when it dries. You can buy ready-mixed slips (but only low-firing ones) from shops where commercial molds are sold and pieces are cast and glazed. For higher-firing slips, try your ceramic supplier or mix your own. I used the Δ6 formula #2 in Appendix G on page 149. You'll find other formulas and tips there as well.

■ Whether you use commercial glazes and underglazes or prepare your own, be sure their firing temperatures match the firing temperature of your casting slip.

■ As clay slip hardens in a plaster mold of the type used here, the mold absorbs water from it, causing the level of the liquid slip in the upright mold to drop. For this reason, the opening in the mold into which you'll pour your clay slip must include a *collar* (or *spare*) that will act as a reservoir for the extra slip you'll add to compensate for water absorption. You'll create this collar when you make the clay model for the mold and will trim it from your slip-cast piece later.

■ When making molds for slip-casting, be sure the opening (or *channel*) is wide enough not to clog up as you try to pour the excess slip out of the mold.

■ Although plastic clay is fine for sculpting models for one-piece molds, this model, because it will be handled more and because it will be positioned in a bed of clay (see Step 5), requires a more durable medium. I bisque fire my clay model before using it and take the clay shrinkage that occurs during bisque firing into consideration when planning its size.

■ When you design a model for a two-piece mold, you must decide where to locate the seam between the two mold sections. Think of this seam as a plane from which the two mold sections can be withdrawn in opposite directions. View your model from every possible angle to make certain that the rigid plaster mold sections won't encounter obstacles (those dreaded undercuts again) as they're removed. Avoiding undercuts is more important with a bisque-fired model than with a leather-hard clay one. You can always peel leather-hard clay out from an undercut in a mold and then modify the mold by carving it, but there's no way to remove a rigid bisqued model that is trapped in hardened plaster.

■ Unlike a leather-hard clay model, a bisque-fired clay or plaster model will stick to the poured plaster unless you coat it with mold soap or polyurethane parting compound, both available from clay suppliers. Oil will also work, but only if detail isn't of much concern to you. Never use mold soap on a bare wooden model; it will make the wood swell. Instead, use polyurethane or shellac.

■ When you're making a hollow cast object such as this pitcher, the longer the slip stands in the mold before you pour out the excess, the thicker the walls of the cast piece will be. Unfortunately, although I can tell you that this 5"-tall (12.7 cm) pitcher generally averages about 15 minutes for me, I can't recommend a specific time, as it will depend on the consistency of the slip you use, the density of your plaster mold, how thick you want the walls of your pitcher to be, and the dampness of your mold. (Casting times get progressively longer if a mold isn't dried between castings.)

■ While some ceramic artists believe that molds are suitable only for industrial production and inhibit the spontaneity of hand-building, others (and I'm one) see the technical possibilities of molds as yet another route to new expressive freedom. Molds can be made from all kinds of found objects and the casts from them combined in all sorts of unusual ways. Molds also help potters produce architectural details with precision and speed. Just one piece of advice: Before duplicating any of your new designs, make sure the design is good enough to justify the time and effort required to make hundreds more.

INSTRUCTIONS

1. Using moist clay, make the model for your pitcher, adding a 1"-high (2.5 cm) collar to its top and taking into account the extra shrinkage that will occur when the model is fired. Check the model very carefully to make sure that it won't create undercuts in either half of your finished mold, and then bisque fire it.

2. Scribe a pencil line around the model to indicate the seam location (**Photo 1**). The simple symmetrical shape of this pitcher is easy to divide in half down its center, but if the shape of your model isn't geometric, the line you draw may not be straight. Thinking of the seam line as a line scribed across the

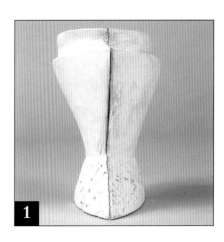

ridge of a mountain range may help you visualize its location.

3. Seal the model with several coats of mold soap or a polyurethane parting compound. Apply either one with a natural bristle brush and use a dry stiff brush to buff each coat to a sheen.

4. Place a small cushion of clay on a flat nonporous work surface that is at least 3" to 4" (7.6 to 10.2 cm) larger than the model. Then rest the model on the clay so that the seam is horizontal. You don't need to level the work surface as you do when making an open-faced mold for a slip-cast tile.

5. Build up a bed of clay around the model, extending it right up to the marked seam line and outward to the future location of your mold-form boards. Note in **Photo 2** that the clay bed doesn't cover the pitcher's mouth.

6. Just to be safe, add one more coat of parting compound or mold soap to the exposed portion of the model and buff it well.

7. Construct a mold form around the model (**Photo 3**), leaving about 1" (2.5 cm) between the outermost edges of the exposed portion of the model and the interior of the mold-form walls. (The mold-form wall at the channel end of the model is an exception; it rests against the collar.) Seal all the joints in the mold form with coils

of clay. If you're using unsealed wooden mold-form boards, coat them with oil or spray lubricant so that the plaster won't stick to them.

8. Mark the mold-form walls about 1" to 2" (2.5 to 5.1 cm) above the uppermost surface of the model so that you'll know how much plaster to pour in.

9. Mix the plaster (see Steps 8 and 9 on page 113). Then pour it carefully into one corner of the mold form until it reaches the marks you made in Step 8. Pour any excess plaster into your waste bucket.

10. Shake the work surface gently to remove any trapped air bubbles in the plaster.

11. Rinse your gloves and tools in the waste bucket.

12. After the plaster has set and has started to cool down (this will probably take about 30 minutes), remove the mold form and turn the mold, model, and moist clay upside down so that the mold rests flat on the work surface. Remove the clay bed to expose the upper half of the model.

13. Using a spoon, a knife with a curved blade or a coin held in a drill, carve three, low, round depressions into any three corners of the plaster mold. These "keyholes," shown in **Photo 5**, will help align the two pieces of your completed

mold when you assemble it and will prevent them from shifting. Just remember not to create undercuts as you make these depressions, or your two mold sections will be permanently locked together!

14. Sand these depressions smooth and thoroughly seal all surfaces of the mold—even the outer surfaces—with mold soap or parting compound. Some potters remove the model and seal the interior portions of their molds as well; others recommend not touching the model at all. I leave it undisturbed.

15. Assemble and mark the mold form walls again, as in Steps 7 and 8, and pour plaster to create the second half of the mold.

16. After the plaster has set up, remove the mold form and separate the two halves of the mold by tapping along the seam with a rubber mallet. If the halves won't come apart, allow them to dry for several hours and try again.

17. Remove the model from the mold section in which it rests and, using a soft brush and water, wash all traces of the sealing agent from the mold sections.

18. With a knife or rasp, bevel the outer edges of the mold. This will help prevent plaster from chipping away from the mold and spoiling your clay.

19. Bind the two halves of the mold together with sturdy rubber

bands, straps, or strips cut from inner tubes, and place them in a dry, warm location (under 120°F or 49°C) to dry. Although solid plaster may strike you as a stable material, it can warp during drying. Keeping the two sections bound during drying will help prevent leaks later.

20. Before pouring the slip into the mold, check to make sure the mold sections are securely banded or strapped together so that the slip won't force them open and leak out. Then pour the slip into the mold channel in a steady stream, without splashing, until it rises into the collar, about 1/2" (1.3 cm) above the rim of the cup. (Jiggling the table will help the slip flow into crevices.)

21. Set a timer for about 15 minutes and allow the slip to rest in the mold for that long. Then check the thickness of the walls by scraping away the slip on the collar or tilting the mold. When the wall thickness appears to be correct, pour the excess slip out of the mold and into an empty container for re-use (**Photo 4**).

22. Place two sticks across the top of a bucket and position the mold upside down, at an angle, on top of the sticks to drain. When slip stops dripping from the mold, turn it upright and allow the clay to dry until it is no longer shiny. This will take from one to two hours. Don't leave a piece in the mold too long, especially when it has a handle, as protrusions can crack off the piece if it shrinks too much in the mold.

23. You may trim off the clay collar now, being very careful not to nick the mold as you do, or you may wait until later (see the next step). Carefully disassemble the mold and gently lift out the cast (**Photo 5**). If the cast feels too soft as you try to do this, leave it in the mold longer.

24. Allow the piece to dry under plastic until it is leather hard. Then use a knife and sponge to trim off the collar if you haven't already removed it (**Photo 6**). Also trim away any slip at the seam and any other rough spots (**Photo 7**). Doing this now will minimize the hazards created by sanding the piece at the bone-dry stage—a process that creates clay dust.

25. When the piece is bone dry, bisque fire it. One tip here: After a lengthy struggle with the problem of small hairline cracks appearing after bisque firing my own slip-cast pieces, I finally realized that slip-cast objects aren't able to withstand the same stresses that other clay objects can. My kiln was creating stress by cooling too fast. Now, when I bisque fire slip-cast pieces, I fire my electric kiln down; that is, I extend the cooling time by leaving one kiln element on the low setting after the peak temperature has been reached, until the kiln temperature has dropped to 600°F (316°C). Then I turn the element off.

26. Mix up your glaze in a bucket. Using a measuring cup, pour some into the pitcher and swirl it gently around, allowing the excess to pour back into the bucket (**Photo 8**). Hold the

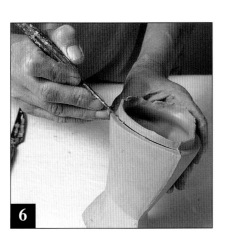

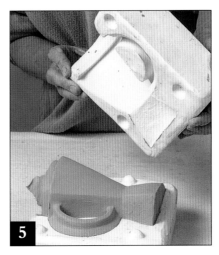

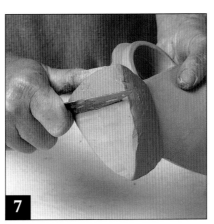

pitcher upside down over the bucket as the last few drops drain out (**Photo 9**). Then dip the pitcher, mouth down, into the glaze bucket until the glaze reaches the indentation at the base.

27. Next, as shown in **Photos 10** and **11**, brush several different underglazes onto the base, one at a time. I spattered the last underglaze color on with a special brush made for this purpose (**Photo 12**).

28. Fire the glazed pitcher to Δ6.

■ Slip-cast tiles are easy to make. Just place an open-face press mold on a level surface and pour casting slip into it (**Photo 13**). Depending on how dry the mold was when you started, the tile should be dry enough to remove in about an hour. When it is, place a board over the mold and flip the board and mold over. Then lift the mold off the tile (**Photo 14**). To replicate the glaze shown in **Photo 15**, just dip the face of the bisque-fired tile into glaze, place the tile face up on the kiln shelf, and glaze fire it. (I used the Δ6 slip-cast formula #2 in Appendix G and Glaze #7 in Appendix H.)

■ When pouring slip back out of a mold with a narrow pouring channel, allow it to run out slowly as air enters the mold. Avoid "glug-glugging," as this can create a vacuum that may suck in a piece of the cast.

■ Slip-casting machines (designed to pump slip into a mold, not to mix casting slip from scratch) make the lifting of heavy buckets of slip unnecessary. A pump in this piece of equipment pushes the slip through a hose and nozzle and into the mold; then the motor is reversed to suck the slip back out.

■ Sometimes, the first few casts in a new mold will stick, but with use, the surface of the mold will become slightly slicker and will release better.

■ If you find that your cast is very hard and brittle, you may need to adjust the slip before making the next cast. See Appendix G for details.

9

10

11

12

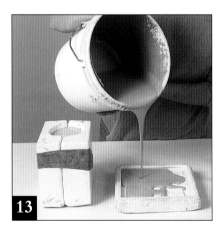
13

14

■ Only a few objects a day can be made with a single slip-cast mold. For production work, you'll need several identical molds, which you can make by casting a urethane mold of the original plaster mold (**Photo 16**) and then using it to make more plaster molds. The urethane, although not available from ceramic suppliers, can be ordered from the manufacturer and comes in several different levels of hardness. Follow the manufacturer's directions carefully, as this material isn't inexpensive. You won't want to make mistakes!

You'll set up your original plaster mold as if it were a model, with a mold-form around it. Then you'll mix the two-part urethane material and pour it in. After the urethane has set up, you'll turn out duplicate plaster molds by pouring plaster into its voids. Undercuts pose no problems, as the flexible urethane just peels off the plaster. These urethane molds can last 20 years.

■ In order to help prevent warping and achieve uniform thickness, some slip-casters use two-piece molds to make flat tiles, plates, and even bowls by filling the mold cavity completely and not pouring the slip out. Large, flat pieces cast in this fashion sometimes tend to stick to the mold. Dusting the mold lightly with talc can help, but wear a respirator when you do this. Shooting compressed air into the area that is sticking and rapping the mold with a rubber mallet will also help loosen the piece.

■ For different effects, try using a slip-trailing bottle to pour thin streams of slip down through the channel of the mold. When these harden, they'll form a weblike, openwork piece.

To decorate the exterior of a slip-cast piece, you may want to trail colored slip into the mold or press leather-hard clay shapes against its walls before pouring in the casting slip. You can build the walls by pouring layers of colored slip into the mold, adding each coat after the last coat applied has lost its shine. Painting designs with under-glazes straight onto the mold surface before pouring in the slip will also work.

■ To create ragged edges on a piece, use wedges to increase the space between the mold sections. These widened seam areas will result in a cast piece with slip-cast fins. Break the fins off to create the ragged effect.

■ The electrolytes in casting slip are corrosive, so a plaster mold will begin to lose some definition after twenty or so casts. In addition, electrolytes absorbed by the mold will cause a fungus-like growth on it. Clean this fuzzy stuff off with vinegar and water. To prevent it from growing inside, store the multiple mold parts banded together, with the channel facing down.

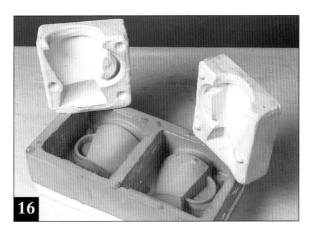

15

16

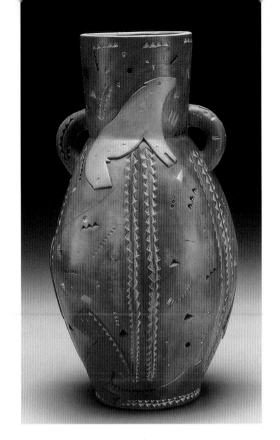

Top left: Matthew Lyon, *Haniwa: Dog with Collar and Bell*, 8" x 3" x 8-1/2" (20.5 x 7.5 x 21.5 cm), 1991. Slip cast; Δ1, then smoked. Photo by Bill Bachhuber

Top right: George Handy, *Mammal, Marsupial, and Giraffe*, 18" x 10" x 10" (45.5 x 25.5 x 25.5 cm), 1996. Slip cast, altered, applied relief; terra sigillata; Δ6; oil pigments. Photo by Tim Barnwell

Center left: Sara Friedlander, *Floating Cubes #2*, 5" x 12-1/2" (12.5 x 32 cm), 1990. Monoprinted colored slips, glaze; Δ06. Photo by Paul Titangos

Center right: Matthew T. Wilt, *Server*, 11" x 13" x 9" (28 x 33 x 23 cm), 1996. Slip cast and assembled; slips; reduction cooled stoneware. Photo by artist

Bottom left: Nick Latka, *Slice*, 24" x 38" x 12" (61 x 96.5 x 30.5 cm), 1990. Slip cast; Δ03. Photo by artist

EXTRUDED AND SLAB TEAPOT

Clay artists create teapots in wildly varying shapes and styles these days. Perhaps some artists are simply responding to the requests of numerous teapot collectors, but many ceramists (and I'm one of them) choose to make teapots because they pose a special challenge.

The teapot is by nature an assemblage. Its various parts (spout, lid, handle, body, and base) must work together to form an integrated whole. Teapots designed for daily use (many are not) must also be properly balanced, comfortable to use, easy to clean, and must pour without gurgling or dripping. The assemblages of nonfunctional

teapots and those intended for only occasional use may be witty, elegant, striking, interesting to touch, or serve only as jumping-off points for forms representing human torsos, animals, or machines. Some contemporary teapots reference historical teapots.

I've made teapots since I first started working with clay. They used to be very geometric and mechanical; now they're taller and more organic. I think of the most recent ones as representing people, possibly dancers striking a pose—sometimes arrogant, sometimes stubborn, sometimes joyful. I deliberately exaggerate certain elements. The bodies, for example, are

too tall and the lids are too small.

Because teapots are one of my specialties, I'm going to present this project in a slightly less formal way, by asking you to join me as I make one. If you don't have access to an extruder, just use another technique to shape this portion of the teapot body.

The many elements of a teapot offer the imagination a vast area within which to play. I start the design process by making a lot of quick sketches, in which I try to integrate the teapot parts and make them more harmonious. I search for ways in which a line in the body might be continued on into the line of the handle, for example.

When I'm through sketching, I choose a few designs that strike me as especially interesting. I don't necessarily stick to these, of course; the clay inevitably contributes its own twists and turns to my original plan. Sometimes these twists take the form of an unexpected crack that appears in a slab as I shape it or a fold that's on the verge of collapse. At other times, the final clay form just doesn't capture any of the life in my sketches, so I start over with new drawings.

Photo 1 shows the parts for this project: two slabs for the upper portion of the teapot body, an extruded tube for its lower portion, a slab for the base, one for the top, a handle, and a spout.

Because I work in series, creating several teapots at once, I extrude tube shapes for six or eight teapots at a time. Attaching the extruder die off-center puts more of a curve

in the extrusions. To keep the tubes from flattening and to help curve them smoothly, I insert a length of foam pipe insulation before cutting them off as they come out of the extruder (**Photo 2**). Holding the ends of the pipe insulation (**Photo 3**), I move the tubes to a smooth surface, cover them lightly with plastic, and allow them to stiffen.

Slabs for six or eight teapots are rolled out next; the ones that will serve as bases are thicker (up to 1/2" or 1.3 cm). I shape some of

the thinner slabs into an assortment of handles and spouts, which I texture and curve while they're still soft. I also texture the slabs that I'll use for the upper body sections and from them cut two shapes for each teapot. All these parts are covered and allowed to stiffen together overnight.

When the slabs and tubes have stiffened sufficiently, I start by shaping the two upper body sections. To make them bulge, I push them out from the inside, curving them as I do (**Photo 4**). Then I join them together and add a coil of moist clay to the inside of each joint to strengthen it.

Next, I place this assembled portion of the body upside down on the table and use one finger to flare out its rim so that I can fit the extruded tube inside (**Photo 5**).

I then add a coil of clay to the inside bottom of the extruded tube (**Photo 6**). The extra surface

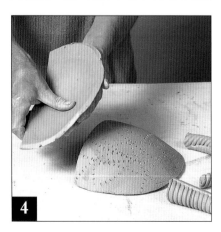

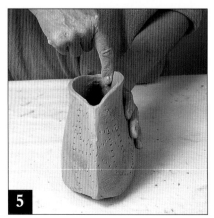

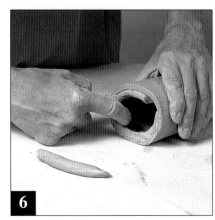

area that this coil provides will strengthen the joint between the tube and the base of the teapot.

To prepare the tube and upper body for joining, I score the outer edge at the top of the tube and the inner edge of the flange of the body. Then I apply slurry and attach the two pieces together (**Photo 7**). In order to reach inside and firm up this joint, I rest the piece gently on its side on a piece of foam or a bed of plastic. If the teapot I'm making is awkward to move because it's especially tall or large, I leave this assembly to stiffen a bit and return to it after an hour or two.

After the body assembly has stiffened, I turn it upside down and join it to the slab that forms the top of the teapot, first scoring and applying slurry (**Photo 8**). Rocking the piece on the table curves the top slightly and also firms up the joint. (I can't do this by adding coils because my hands won't fit down inside the tube!)

Because the handle will eventually be attached to the extended portion of the slab top, I sometimes add a very small coil to the joint between the bulged body section and the top to strengthen it (**Photo 9**).

Most of my teapots have bases; these lift the bodies up and lighten their appearance. To make feet for the triangular base, I pinch three wads of moist clay onto it (**Photo 10**). The feet I design vary in shape and size from teapot to teapot.

A flat base wouldn't complement the curves of this body design. A slight curvature not only does, but also strengthens the base and makes it less likely to sag and warp during firing. I shape the base by placing it on a form and paddling it (**Photo 11**).

To attach the base to the body, I score it, apply slurry, and press the body in place (**Photo 12**). A thick

7

8

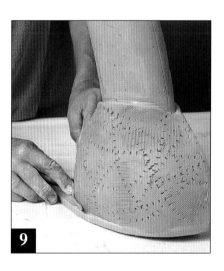

9

10

11

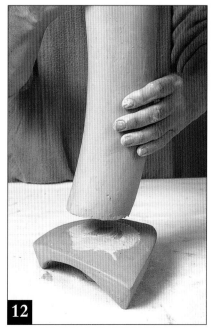

12

coil wrapped around the outside of this joint strengthens it (**Photo 13**). Sometimes the base hasn't stiffened adequately when I'm ready to attach the body to it. When this is the case, I use a clay pedestal to support the base from underneath so that the full weight of the body doesn't flatten out its little feet. If the body is a very tall or heavy one, I'll continue to use this pedestal right through the firings, just as you learned how to do with the base of the coiled planter (see page 100).

Using a round, metal hole cutter, I cut the hole for the lid in the center of the teapot's slab top (**Photo 14**). I use a knife to cut an opening for the spout (**Photo 15**).

I take some time with both the handle and spout, holding those I've made up to the body to gauge whether or not their lengths, sizes, and curvatures are appropriate and making adjustments as necessary (**Photo 16**). Sometimes, when they don't look right, I just make new pieces.

When I've shaped the handle and spout to my satisfaction, I attach them. I add a coil around the base of the handle both to strengthen the joint and to provide a detail where I may want to add a contrasting glaze color.

Then, to prevent the hollow, air-filled handle from exploding during firing, I cut a small hole through the top slab down into it. (Later, to fill this hole, I make a small clay bulb, coat it with underglaze, fire it at Δ05, and glue it in place.)

To make the small lid, I first cut out a circle that's larger than the hole in the teapot top and add a clay cylinder to it. Because this clay cylinder is so thick, I also cut a small hole in it. I love to collect and attach found, nonceramic objects to my lids (**Photo 17**). The elements of contrast they contribute—the tininess of the parts next to the largeness of the teapot and the conjunction of objects as disparate as fossil fragments and electronic circuitry—please me immensely. As soon as I've selected the objects, I decide how I'll attach them later. Drilling into fired clay is too difficult, so if I want to attach the objects with wires, I have to plan ahead and make the required holes now.

I cover the teapot with plastic, wrapping the handle and spout more tightly so that they won't dry out faster than the rest of the assembly. After a few days, I loosen up this tight wrapping. When the teapot is bone dry, it is bisque fired to Δ05, along with the small bulb for the handle. (I was surprised that the fired underglaze on this bulb ended up being so shiny. Low-fire underglazes are usually flat.)

Before glazing the teapot, I brush off any dust and coat the bottoms of the feet with wax resist. On teapots that require a support under the base during firing, I also apply a circle of wax to the bottom of the base where the support will touch it.

The inside of the teapot is glazed first. I pour the glaze in with a cup, swirl it around, and pour it out through the spout. When I'm through, I sponge off any drips on the outside. (For the glaze formula I use, turn to Appendix H, Glaze #1, on page 151.)

On the exterior base and extruded portion, I use Glaze #2 in Appendix H. After making sure that I have a glaze bucket deep enough for the purpose, I dip the teapot into the bucket until the glaze comes up to the textured upper portion of the teapot body. Because the joint between the extruded tube and upper body portion is curved instead of straight and horizontal, I have to wipe off the small amount of glaze that has covered the textured body area. I

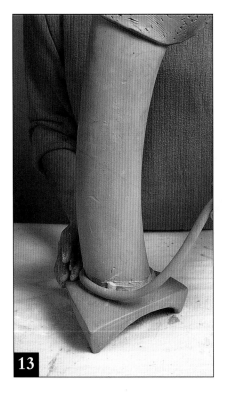

13

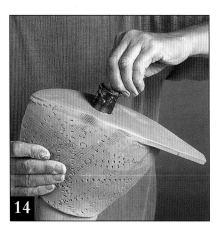

14

15

next dip the top of the lid into the same glaze.

When glazing the upper body portion, I aim for contrast again, this time between the smoothly glazed tubular section and the textured body area above it. To play up this contrast, I apply flat underglazes instead of glazes over the textured area. Before doing this, I place the teapot on its side, on top of a soft bed of plastic so that the

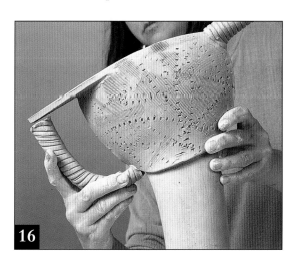

fragile glazed area won't be chipped. Then I brush a black underglaze over all the recesses in the textured area (**Photo 18**).

Next, I brush on a series of three to five different underglaze colors in layers over the black, starting with the darkest and working towards the lightest. On this piece, I made quick, loose, curving strokes with a brush. On others, I sometimes dab on the underglazes with a sponge or paint them on as one solid color. The handle and spout are painted with a one-color coat of underglaze (**Photo 19**). I sometimes splatter additional colors on top of this coat to add more texture. On this piece, I also added a contrasting color underglaze to the little coil around the handle.

The piece is then fired to Δ3 in an electric kiln. I fire the lid separately, next to the teapot. After the firing, I glue the found objects in place.

■ Experiment with using different extruder dies to shape different tubular sections. To widen an extruded section in one area, slice it open and add a slab from the inside.

■ Shape some cups to complement the shape of the teapot.

■ For a functional teapot, a spout with a sharp, angled edge will be more likely to pour without dripping, and a flange on the lid will keep it from falling off when the pot is tipped for pouring.

■ In order to hold the maximum amount of liquid, a teapot should be constructed so that the top of its spout isn't below the level of the lid opening.

■ If you want your teapot to strain out the tea leaves as you pour, instead of cutting a large hole at the joint between the spout and body, pierce small holes instead. Just make sure that these holes don't become clogged when you glaze the interior. Using a thinner interior glaze will help prevent this problem.

■ As you design a functional teapot, you'll need to consider its balance—how it will feel and behave when you lift it by its handle.

■ When I'm working in series and feel I've developed the shapes for various parts just right, I cut cardboard templates of them so that I can duplicate them easily.

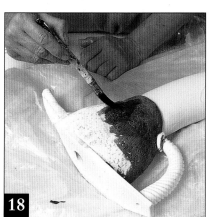

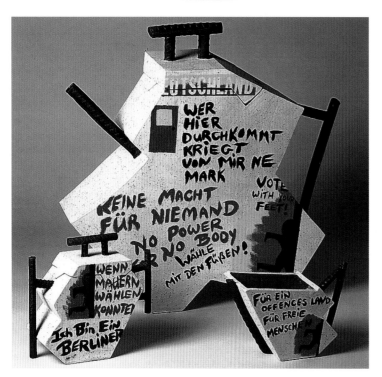

Top left: Bacia Edelman, *Green Teeter I*, 11-3/4" x 16-1/2" x 6-1/2" (30 x 42 x 16.5 cm), 1995. Slab; airbrushed and painted layers of underglazes; multifired, Δ06 to Δ03. Photo by Rick Trummer

Top right: Lisa Mandelkern, *Teapot with Aloes*, 18" x 12" x 7" (45.5 x 30.5 x 18 cm), 1994. Terra sigillata, underglazes; low fired. Photo by artist

Center left: D. Hayne Bayless, *Dzi Teapot with Feet and Hinged Lid*, 8" x 13" x 7" (20.5 x 33 x 18 cm), 1996. Slabs stenciled with black slip applied through perforated metal, then stretched; extruded additions; glaze; Δ10 reduction. Photo by artist

Center right: Bacia Edelman, *Lichen Teapot*, 10-3/4" x 11" x 4" (27.5 x 28 x 10 cm), 1995. Slab, coiled; layered underglazes and lichen glaze; multifired, Δ6, Δ04. Photo by artist

Bottom left: Maery Callaghan, *Berlin Tea Party—Off the Wall!*, 17-1/2" x 19" x 4" (44.5 x 48.5 x 10 cm), 1996. Slab, molded spouts and handles; glazes; Δ04 to Δ05; acrylic paints. Photo by Gregg Eligh

CHAPTER SEVEN

COMMISSIONS

Jane W. Larson, *Out of Chaos, Rings of Life*, 8' x 2' x 2' (2.4 x .6 x .6 m), 1990. Slab, impressed; glazes; Δ6 reduction. Photo by C.E. Larson

A s I worked on this book, I was also working, through a North Carolina Artworks for State Buildings program, on a wall-sculpture commission for Western Carolina University. Fortunately for working artists, many countries, states, and counties have the "percent for art" laws that made this commission possible—laws that require between .5% and 2% of the cost of new or renovated public buildings to be spent on art.

Getting and then executing these and other types of commissions is a fascinating process. Public clients are only one source. Galleries, architects, corporations, interior designers, and private individuals are others. Homeowners are more aware than ever of the ways in which a handmade sink, indoor shrine, lighting fixture, wall piece, or garden column can bring a space alive.

In the United States, some ceramic artists advertise in catalogues distributed to designers and architects, and the American Craft Council maintains a slide registry of artists' work that it makes available to the public. (See "Resources" on page 157.) Galleries and individuals often use the registry to select artists whom they wish to contact.

A PUBLIC COMMISSION

■

The public commissioning process in North Carolina is similar to those in many other areas. Interested artists are first apprised of the budget, the nature of the site, and the type of work being sought. (Often, these projects are open to different media, collaboration among two or more artists, and input regarding specific site location.) In response, competing artists submit slides of their work and a résumé.

The Western Carolina University commission, which was part of a building renovation, proceeded in a typical manner. After reviewing submitted slides, the committee in charge selected three final applicants, each of whom was paid a fee to present a proposal consisting of drawings, models, and budgets.

Successful proposals take into consideration the architectural style of the building, the surroundings, and the function of the space, so that the artwork doesn't end up looking as if it dropped down from outer space.

I chose the interior entryway of the building as my location, because it felt cold, sterile, and institutional as it was. I was sure that the introduction of texture would warm it. In my proposal, I suggested that the design should relate in some way to the function of the building itself—one occupied by six to eight different academic departments. To meet this objective, I planned to interview professors in each department, choose an object representative of that department (a tool, for example), and then focus my design on those objects.

I envisioned two wall arrangements, each consisting of three series of tiles arranged in curves. Each series would focus on one of the department-related objects. It would begin with a simple square tile, amorphous in design, and each successive tile in the series would show the gradual evolution of the object, culminating in a final tile that would reveal the object completely.

There's great satisfaction in creating a piece—public, private, or corporate—that reflects the individuality of a particular situation. A corporation in New York City

asked me to make a piece with flags in it, in order to show their international status. The result was a geometric, quiltlike abstraction of the flags of the United States, Japan, and Kenya. A piece I created for a utilities department depicted the hydrologic cycle and made use of images from their water treatment processes. Sometimes, for private commissions, I incorporate an image of one of the client's personal possessions. I don't think of these requirements as restrictions but as parameters or guidelines. In fact, they make design decisions less overwhelming by keeping my otherwise overactive imagination from circling endlessly around the possibilities.

As an artist considers a possible design for a public or corporate commission and begins to develop a proposed budget, he or she needs to consider a number of important questions. The first is how the space is (or will be) used. If the site is an exterior public space, the commissioned work must be durable enough to withstand harsh weather, the touch of curious hands, and even an occasional climbing body. It may also need to

Above: Beverly Crist, *Lotus Table*, 21" x 26-1/2" x 16-1/2" (53.5 x 78.5 x 42 cm), 1996. Slab; glazes; Δ04. Photo by Richard Anderson

Right: Virginia Scotchie, *Scatter*. Diameters of 157 orbs: 3" to 22" (7.5 to 56 cm), 1995. Pinched, press molded; stain, glaze; Δ04. Photo by Peter Lenzo

be "graffiti-proofed" or at least be easy to clean. Fortunately, clay is such a durable medium that it's often more appropriate than other materials for these types of sites.

If the space is an interior one, how will the proposed work affect or relate to the space it will be in? An office or bedroom site may not be able to tolerate intense color or flamboyance in the way that a shopping mall atrium can.

To what scale should the work be created, and at what angle and distance will the viewer experience it? A number of interim steps can help settle these questions. Design a model or make scale drawings. (A scale ruler is invaluable here.) A large, cardboard cutout of the artwork, positioned in the proposed location, can help determine scale. Keep in mind that what looks large in the studio may be dwarfed when it's surrounded by tall buildings.

The most important issue to consider is the structural integrity of the piece. The utilities department I mentioned earlier requested that a structural engineer approve my installation plan. Fortunately, public commissions are often timed so that the architect and artist can collaborate in order to integrate the artwork with the building design by, for example, incorporating structural changes in the walls to accommodate the extra weight of a ceramic wall piece or sculpture.

Construction drawings and elevations are usually provided to the artist. When they aren't, ask for them, especially for large installations. For the university installation, I had to determine whether the walls were masonry, sheetrock, or plywood before I could propose a budget. My tiles would average six pounds (2.7 kg) apiece and would be installed 15 feet (4.6 m) above floor level, so for safety's sake, I wanted to combine mechanical and adhesive attachment methods.

I was lucky. The walls were sheetrock attached to a plywood base. Installation on a masonry wall would have been much more difficult and time-consuming. As it was, I could use a combination of adhesive and two screws to hang each tile separately so that the overall weight of the tiles would be distributed across the wall. Alternatively, I could have hung each tile by using construction adhesive to attach it to a plywood backing, bolting a beveled 1 x 4 across the back of the plywood, bolting another beveled 1 x 4 to studs in the wall, and hanging one 1 x 4 on the other.

For smaller flat wall pieces, many artists just glue the piece to a plywood backing, attach picture hangers or wire to the plywood, and hang the pieces from nails. Plates and similar clay objects are often made with holes or lugs in the foot rims so that wires can be added for hanging. For more per-

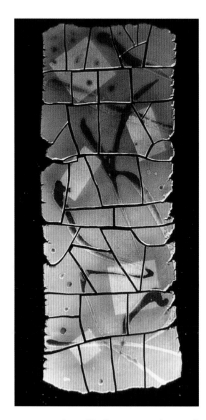

Left: Donald R. Davis, *First Flight*, 24" x 48" x 3" (61 x 122 x 7.5 cm), 1990. Porcelain slab; airbrushed oxides, trailed glaze; Δ9 reduction. Photo by artist

Above: Tom Carbone, *Arc de Triomphe*, 17" x 22" x 17" (43 x 56 x 43 cm), 1995. Extruded, altered, and assembled; slips, glaze; Δ04. Photo by artist

manent installations, mastics and mortar cements are available for attaching clay to interior and exterior masonry surfaces. The joints are filled with grout (different colors are available) to supplement the strength of the mastic or cement. A free-standing piece such as a sculpture may require interior armatures to support it.

In most situations, overengineering by incorporating both mechanical and adhesive solutions is best. These engineering decisions must be made before you can finalize a design.

BUDGETS

∎

Even if you accept a small, private commission, present the client with a drawing and agree on a fee and how it will be paid before you start. Nothing is quite as frustrating as having made a piece that doesn't match the client's preconceived—and unshared—notions of what that piece should be or cost.

Budgets for public, corporate, and large private projects are much more complex. You'll need to ask a number of questions. Will you be responsible for lighting? Must you be insured as you fabricate, transport, and install the piece? (In most cases, the answer will be "yes.") How many meetings will there be with the client? What will it cost to transport the artwork to the site and how will you do this? I once met an artist experienced with corporate commissions who had flown to Singapore with an installation crew to install her tapestry in a hotel, only to find that the tapestry hadn't arrived. It came a week later. Some shipping companies won't insure art, and many have size and weight restrictions, such as no containers over 500 pounds (227 kg). Is there a penalty clause for delays? A time schedule for completion? In any proposal, allow more time than you think you'll need, and then stick to a schedule that leaves you some to spare.

Will one estimate for materials be

sufficient? (Sometimes three are required.) Will a gallery or agent expect a commission from what you are paid? Are you required to provide photographs of the final piece for publicity purposes? What about signage? Will a plaque be placed with the installation and, if so, who will be responsible for its design and cost? Will you need to rent scaffolding for the installation or hire professional installers?

Don't forget to include studio overhead, travel expenses, office supplies, telephone costs, and—of course—the cost of materials and firing. Industry charges for research and development; you should, too! You may have to create new glazes or learn to work with new techniques.

Payment for public commissions is usually divided into four or five installments, the final one made after approval of the installation, submission of maintenance instructions and photographs, and frequently, a formal presentation to the community.

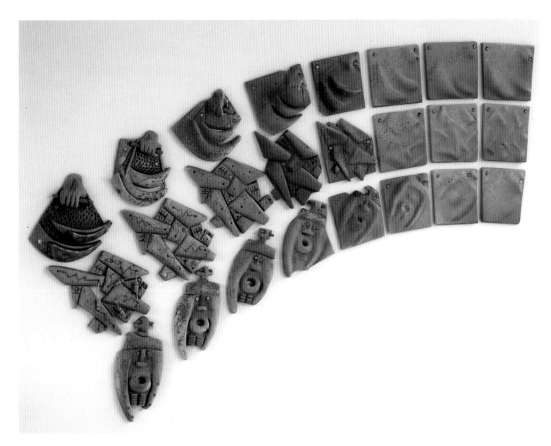

Kathy Triplett, *Tools We Use*, 7-1/2' x 4-1/2' x 3" (22.3 x 1.4 x .08 m), 1996. Slab; sprayed underglazes, glaze; Δ3. Photo by Evan Bracken

MAKING THE PIECE

■

Designing an artwork to include modular repetition of sections will allay a great deal of anxiety during the fabrication and installation process. Having extra sections on hand to use as replacements for ones accidentally broken during an installation far from home will save a lot of time and money. Of course, this isn't always possible.

If you're designing a large piece, consider the ways in which it can be divided into sections so that you can lift it and fit it into the kiln. Wall pieces can be divided into grid patterns or into irregularly shaped sections, the outlines of which follow the design lines. No matter how you divide up the work, be sure to mark each part. Individual pieces may seem easy to identify during modeling, but after firing them, you may find yourself with a puzzling collection of unidentifiable shapes.

After my proposal for the university commission was approved and the contract was signed, I conducted my interviews, took photos of the site, and made drawings of the objects that would inspire my designs, including scissors from the textile design department and a plastics-injection molding machine from the engineering and technology department. I also made a couple of sets of full-size paper cutouts of the two wall areas that the tiles would cover. Because these shapes were curved, the tiles that fit into them couldn't be exactly square. I sketched the tiles directly onto one set of these large templates and cut out the individual designs from them.

I started the tiles, which were constructed of sandwiched slabs, by rolling out slabs of clay, straight from the bag. To make each sandwich, I first scored and applied slurry to one of the slabs. Scoring moist slabs isn't really necessary, but I wanted to take extra precautions.

If I'd been installing these tiles in an airport, where vibrations can loosen up an installation, I would probably have scored the surfaces of both slabs. Then I placed another slab over the scored slab, using my fingers to shape an undulating design into the upper slab by pushing it up from underneath (**Photo 1**). This design reflected the beginning of the shape that would be more fully revealed in later tiles in the series. To help retain the raised, rounded upper surface of the tile, I stuffed newspapers between the pairs of slabs.

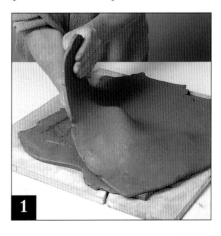

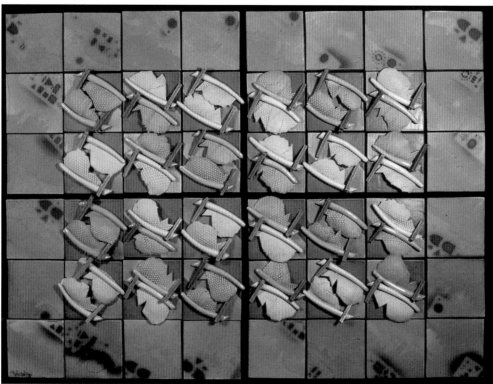

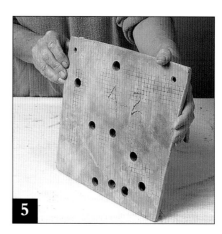

Next, I placed the paper pattern on top of the slab sandwich and cut clay away from the outer edges (**Photo 2**), checking to make sure the slabs were firmly attached to

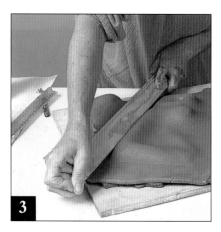

each other where they touched. I continued this process, modeling each tile in a series more distinctly than the last, so that the object I'd chosen to portray would evolve as planned (**Photos 3** and **4**). These tiles wouldn't be touched by the public, so I could afford to include some fragile detailing.

When the tiles were leather hard, I cut holes through the bottom slabs so that air could escape during firing and used tweezers to remove the damp newspaper. (Unfortunately, I've never been able to perform this process without thinking

about how ancient Egyptians prepared bodies for mummification. They pulled the brains out through the nostrils!) I also cut two holes for installation screws in each piece and fired clay plugs for later use as covers for the screw heads. All these holes are visible in **Photo 5**.

After the tiles were bone dry, I applied oxides, ceramic stains, and glazes, leaving much of the clay on each tile bare, but intensifying the colors on each successive tile in a series. Then I fired the tiles to Δ3 in an electric kiln. The color of the bare, fired clay was similar to that of the exterior brick on the building.

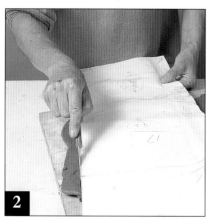

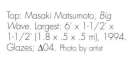

Top: Masaki Matsumoto, *Big Wave*. Largest: 6' x 1-1/2' x 1-1/2' (1.8 x .5 x .5 m), 1994. Glazes; Δ04. Photo by artist

Center: Lorraine S. Capparell, *Three Ages of Women*, 1986. Maiden, Matron (gate), height: 6' (1.8 m); diameter 13" (.3 m); handbuilt. Five Crones (temple), height: 8' (2.4 m); diameter: 26" (.7m); press molded from extruded forms; Δ5; oil paints and sealer. Photo by Lars Speyer

Bottom: Kathy Triplett, *Underwater Waffle*, 2' x 6' x 1" (.6 x 1.8 x .03 m), 1989. Slab; airbrushed underglazes, glazes; Δ6. Photo by artist

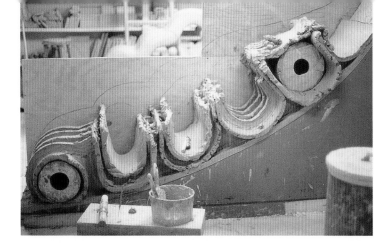

Peter Wayne King, *Annmarie Garden Gateposts*, Solomans, MD, 15' × 13' × 2-1/2' (4.6 × 4 × .8 m), 1995. Slabs; glazes; Δ6. Photos by Stonehaus

Top left: Construction of railings

Top right: Peter "sewing" slabs together

Center left: Completed railing; wet clay

Center right: Detail of finished railing

Bottom left: *Annmarie Garden Gatepost*

Amanda Jaffe, *Scenes and Patterns*. Two rooms: 27' x 12' and 26' x 14' (8.2 x 3.7 m and 7.9 x 4.3 m), 1981. Slip cast; glazes; Δ04; paints. Photo by artist

INSTALLATION

■

Try to arrange for an installation time and date during which you won't be working among swarms of people. If you're installing the job yourself, bring every tool and fastener you can imagine using—

and more. Include cleaning materials to remove marks and prints from walls, as well as touch-up paint and drop cloths. Bring a rope, too; you may be liable unless you rope off the site during installation.

Installing even small wall pieces, including those for homes or galleries, is easier if you make a wall-hanging pattern for the work. As large patterns for this installation, I used one set of the paper templates I'd made, arranging the tiles on top of them and marking their outlines and exact screw-hole locations (**Photo 6**).

This installation was one I was able to do with the help of a great assistant. When an installation must be done by a professional installer, prepare very clear instructions and try to be present, as some installers don't know how fragile clay can be. Although a slab of fired clay has great compressive strength, turning a screw one thread too tight as you install a tile can easily crack it. If you're installing pieces that need electricity or water, such as sinks, fountains, or lit sconces, building codes may require you to retain a licensed electrician or plumber for this portion of the work.

Phyllis Kudder-Sullivan, *Enigma Variation 65*, 16' 8" x 11' x 7" (5.1 x 3.4 x .2 m), 1995. Woven extruded coils, copper pipe; slips, engobes, underglazes; multifired Δ6, Δ06. Photo by Joseph D. Sullivan

With my assistant—and scaffolding borrowed from the university—the installation took a total of six hours, including time spent on photographing the results. We attached the wall-hanging patterns first (**Photo 7**) and transferred the tile shapes and screw-hole locations to the walls. After that, installation of the tiles was relatively easy (**Photo 8**).

Architectural ornamentation has experienced a revival since the 1970s and ceramists have found new opportunities for bringing warmth and texture to contemporary spaces. Here's hoping all your clients are pleased, so we can see more clay enriching our environments!

6

7

CHAPTER EIGHT

INSPIRATION

What keeps people from finding the time and taking the plunge into working with clay? And what keeps professional potters from expanding their scale and trying new techniques? How does anyone decide what to make, and why do ideas get bottle-necked? Let me articulate a few of the problems, first. Then let me offer some solutions that many artists find helpful.

David A. Stabley, *Stacked House with Figure*, 38" x 9" x 8" (96.5 x 23 x 18 cm), 1995. Slab, coiled, pinched, carved; underglazes, glaze; Δ05; colored pencils, wax/oil finish. Photo by Robert Brown

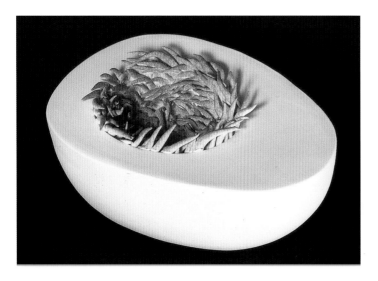

Jinny Hargrave, *Anemone Egg*, 5" x 12" x 8-1/2" (12.5 x 30.5 x 21.5 cm), 1988. Slab; airbrushed stain; Δ04. Photo by artist

Maery Callaghan, *Buffalo Box*, 3" x 3" x 6" (7.5 x 7.5 x 15 cm), 1996. Slab; underglazes, clear matt glaze; Δ04 to Δ05. Photo by Gregg Eligh

Self-doubt often lies at the bottom of our inertia: the fear of failure; the fear of whatever we might discover in ourselves; the fear of being silly. Self-judgment is necessary, of course. In order to refine our work as we create it, we have to make a steady stream of decisions, one at every turning point, but when judgment enters the picture too early, it obstructs the flow of ideas before we have a chance to try them out.

For experienced clayworkers, turning in a new direction is sometimes difficult because unless each new piece is better than the last, we feel we're going backwards. I'm familiar with this fear of being trapped in eddies. I've swirled in them before and have thought I was wasting time, but I've gradually learned that eddies can yield benefits much later. Wrong turns can lead to great discoveries. Penicillin, after all, was the result of contamination in a petri dish.

Perfectionism can be paralyzing. No one can express creative ideas without skill, but getting too wrapped up in struggling for specific outcomes results in rigidity. I often have to remind myself of Degas's belief that only when you

no longer know what you're doing do you do good things. Surrendering to the act of creation and setting aside worries about outcomes can free our imaginations.

Maintaining conviction in what we're doing isn't easy, especially when we've been taught to think that squeezing and poking a lump of clay is just play—something that adults in our culture are often forbidden. Granting ourselves the privilege of play is an important step. We can't allow ourselves to be intimidated by the thought that creativity, often born of play, is something extraordinary—an unusual gift for children and for a few elite adults. It isn't.

Art grows out of facing all these anxieties. Performing unfamiliar acts, taking risks, tapping parts of our unconscious: all this requires courage, discipline, and practice. So how do we cope with self-doubt and anxiety? How do we become inspired?

The craftsperson who exhibits at fairs and in galleries often hears the same two questions over and over: "What's it supposed to be?" and "Where do you get all your ideas?" We'll leave the answer to the first question up to the viewer, but we'll share Bach's answer to

the second. This famous composer replied that the problem was not finding ideas, but getting out of bed in the morning without stepping on them.

Searching for inspiration is less likely to work than clearing a path for its arrival. We tend to think of artists as waiting patiently, tools poised, for the Muse to anoint. In fact, the Muse is more likely to visit not the passive artist, but the one who is not only receptive but active, too. Every artist with whom I've discussed creativity insists that ideas come through the process of doing and making—not beforehand. I once heard the jazz saxophonist Sonny Rollins explain at a concert that he practiced all the time so he could be there when the spirit arrived.

One doesn't "think up" artwork and then execute it. Artists practice until skillful execution is no longer a conscious matter. At that point, their hands often seem to solve problems and provide inspiration on their own. I firmly believe that when we're skilled enough to lose ourselves in what we're doing, we're able to tap our unconscious—a limitless source of inspiration. Not surprisingly, many artists report that when

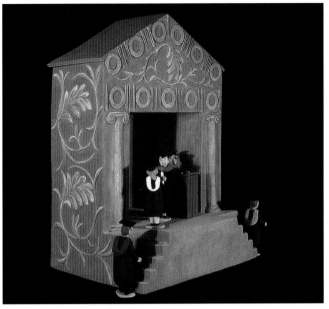

Left and right: Carrie Anne Parks, *Alma Mater* (front and back views), 20 x 18 x 10" (50.5 x 40.5 x 25.5 cm), 1996. Slab, pinched; slips, underglazes; Δ04. Photo by artist

insights do emerge, they're often directly related to areas in which the artists have practiced diligently.

Of course, even experienced artists hit roadblocks occasionally. When they do, they often find that turning away from the work at hand to do something relaxing or physical is more useful than puzzling over the problem at hand. Einstein claimed that he experienced his finest insights while shaving. Rest and diversion don't produce insights, but they do help remove the inhibitions that keep inspiration at bay. A daily walk, periods of solitude, breaks for dart-throwing—breaks during which we're quieting our minds rather than trying to solve problems—are often productive. We can't force inspiration, but we can prepare the right conditions to coax it along.

One useful preparation is setting limits. As potters, many are set for us: the size and type of kiln we have, how much weight we can lift, and the natural properties of clay itself. Others we can choose voluntarily. We can decide, for example, to explore a new method intensely or to focus on one micro-aspect of a technique in order to master it. At one time, Monet focused his attention by limiting himself to painting haystacks, exploring the ways in which light played on them as he did. Recently, a gallery asked me to make a series of teapots, all under 10" (25.4 cm) tall, for an exhibition of small works. I found that changing scale (I'd never made such small pieces) opened up a whole new way of working, one which enabled me to reapproach my large teapots with a new perspective. When a particular territory is mapped out and we don't have to worry about it, inspiration is free to flow in other directions.

One way to begin granting yourself permission to "play" is to make a quick series of thumbnail sketches—very quick. The point isn't to think about or judge what you're drawing, but to tap your unconscious. Don't expect the drawings to be beautiful and don't evaluate or criticize them. Only after you've done a series should you go back and check to see if any of them offer ideas that you'd like to explore (**Photo 1**).

Sometimes your idea library may just need restocking. Traveling to a new environment or culture is rejuvenating for many people. I find that driving somewhere, alone, and allowing myself to daydream often leads to new discoveries. I'll occasionally visit the local junkyard, where the shapes and forms of objects, once concealed by their specialized functions, are now accessible and can be seen anew.

Top left: Kelly Lohr, *Innocence*. Height: 58" (1.5 m), 1994. Coiled; unglazed; Δ10 reduction. Photo by artist

Top right: Laurie Spencer, *Toad Hall Habitat*, 10' x 10' 6" (3 x 3.2 m), 1990. Coiled; wood fired on site for three days. Photo by artist

Bottom left: Heinz Kossler (Design: Boraev/Kossler), *Slosman Fireplace*, 66" x 72" x 40" (1.7 x 1.8 x 1 m), 1996. Slab on hump mold; unglazed. Photo by Neil Pickett

Bottom right: Larry Brow, *Hays Chair*, 30" x 28" x 20" (76 x 71 x 51 cm), 1995. Modified paddle and anvil; glazes; Δ6. Photo by artist

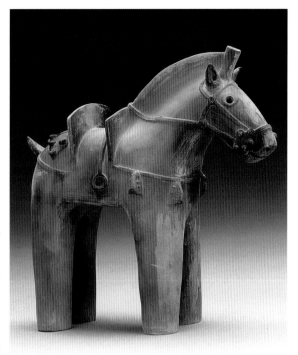
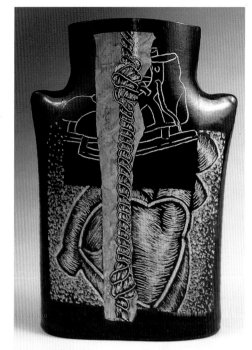

Right: Matthew Lyon, *Haniwa, Horse with Parade Tack,* 9-1/2" x 3-3/4" x 10-1/2" (24 x 9.5 x 26.5 cm), 1991. Slip cast; unglazed; Δ1, then smoked. Photo by Bill Bachhuber

Far right: James Klueg, *Chinese Whispers,* 15" x 10" x 4" (38 x 25.5 x 10 cm), 1995. Slab; sgraffito, majolica; Δ03. Photo by artist

Your own personal repertoire of interests and your own environment may be the first library to consult for ideas. Studying clay work from the past is inspiring to me, whether I'm looking at museum pieces or shards discovered in my neighbor's backyard. Clay artist Matthew Lyon, whose work is shown above and on pages 58 and 122, directs his interest in historical claywork towards a study of ancient methods and forms. Other artists find that political or social change is an impetus for commentary in clay. Still others find inspiration closer to home. I once had a student who was a retired electrical engineer. Stymied by what sort of decoration to use on the outside of his bowls, he finally landed on the brilliant solution of forming a design with the electrical symbols with which he was so familiar. Even a new tool can return enthusiasm to the studio. When my new extruder pumped out its first long, square tube, I lost track of time completely. I played with the extrusion for hours, thinking of all the new things I could do with it.

Taking a short workshop is a good way to try out new methods and techniques. Exploring new materials is worthwhile, too. *Paperclay,* for example, which is a mixture of paper pulp and clay, has made it possible to construct very thin slabs, and *metal clay* allows potters to use clayworking techniques to create objects made of silver and gold.

Developing new tools can be inspirational as well. In my own neighborhood, Michael Sherrill (whose work is shown on pages 17 and 145,) has designed and fabricated a turning electric extruder that permits him to shape the extrusions as they come out. Heinz Kossler (see the opposite page) makes very large slabs, without a slab roller, by packing his clay into a 4' x 4' x 4' (1.2 x 1.2 x 1.2 m) cube and then slicing off slabs with a handmade cutter large enough for the job.

Even though I know that the claywork will be fun once I start, anxiety over the start of a big new project will send me straight out into the garden. The first mark of the day is definitely the hardest to make. Hemingway coped with this problem by deliberately stopping each day's work before he'd finished the section he was writing because he liked to know that he could start work the next morning without hesitation or struggle. I make a deal with myself: I tell myself that I won't start the project today—not really. I'll set today aside for making a few preliminary sketches. Before I know it, I'm elbow-deep in clay.

Conquering inertia and self-doubt takes courage, but courage can be fragile. If you invite people to see your work, especially work in progress, make sure they're people who can appreciate and discuss it. If you notice your friends' or relatives' eyes glaze over as you explain your newest piece, or if one of them says, "But, honey, do people really buy this stuff?" change the topic—or audience. Conversations with people whose opinions of claywork you respect can be valuable. One caution, however: Listen well and speak less, or you won't benefit from what those people have to offer.

If overcoming inertia demands that we confront such hard edges, why pick up a ball of clay at all? For

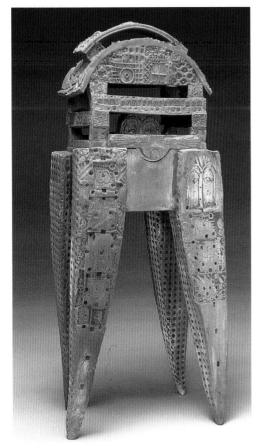

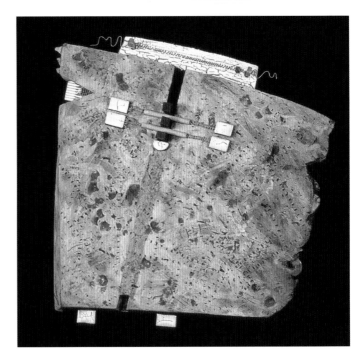

me the answers are simple. Working with clay is fun, difficult, and good, all at the same time. We're changed—and so is the world—by the objects we make. Through them, we communicate ideas on a gut level, in the same way that myths communicate. I also believe that if we seek authenticity and grace in this life, we should surround ourselves with objects that share these qualities.

Through the repetitive processes of our work, we enter a state of heightened concentration—a contemplative state. When work goes well, time stops, and hunger is forgotten. We surrender to the spell that clay has cast upon us and are lost in it. I once heard a famous major-league baseball player make a comment about his sport that is just as relevant to working with clay: "All along, I thought I was learning to play the game, but in the end, it was really just playing with me."

Top left: Carol Gentithes, *My Mother's a Fish*, 9-1/2" x 7" x 14" (24 x 18 x 35.5 cm), 1995. Coiled; underglazes, glazes; multiple low firings. Photo by Pennsylvania State University Photo Dept.

Top right: Tom Latka, *Extruded Vase*, 18" x 4" x 4" (45.5 x 10 x 10 cm), 1995. Δ01. Photo by artist

Bottom left: Lana Wilson, *Ritual Box*, 18" x 10" x 6" (45.5 x 25.5 x 15 cm), 1995. Soft slab, stamped; engobe, iron sulfate; Δ6. Photo by artist

Bottom right: Kathy Triplett, *Tools for the Future*, 15" x 14" x 3" (38 x 35.5 x 7.5 cm), 1993. Layered underglazes; Δ3. Photo by artist

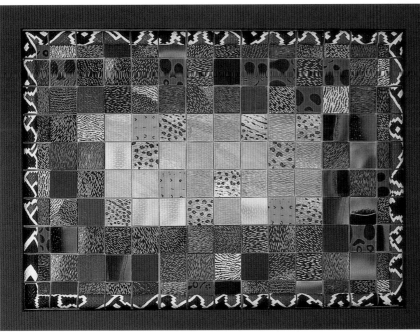

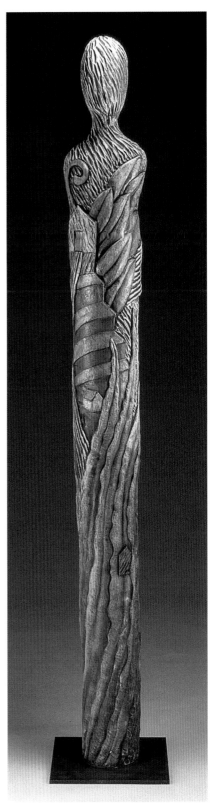

Top left: Michael Sherrill, *The Garden* (set of seven). Shortest: 8" x 8" x 3" (20.5 x 20.5 x 7.5 cm), 1995. Extruded and pulled forms, carved; glaze; low fired. Photo by Tim Barnwell

Center left: Amanda Jaffe, *Model for the Rainforest Wing of the Staten Island Zoo*, 26" x 18-1/2" x 1-1/2" (66 x 47 x 4 cm), 1989. Cast and carved tile; terra sigillata, under-glaze, stain; Δ4. Photo by artist

Bottom left: Jennie Bireline, *Chamas River Origami Pot*, 30" x 17-1/2" x 7" (76 x 44.5 x 18 cm), 1994. Slab; terra sigillata painted freehand; Δ04, gold and silver leaf. Photo by George Bireline

Right: Christine Federighi, *Long River Way*, 71" x 8" x 7" (180.5 x 20.5 x 18 cm), 1994. Coiled, carved; Δ05; oil patina. Photo by Bridget Parlato

SAFETY PRECAUTIONS

Working with clay and glazes doesn't have to be hazardous, but scrupulous attention to safety precautions is a must. Read the following advice carefully and—please—take it!

■ Working with clay produces a fine dust that should never be inhaled or ingested. Respirators can help and should certainly be worn by most people, but they're not as effective as professionally installed ventilation systems designed to filter out clay dust. (These are available from ceramic suppliers.) Respirators are downright ineffective if you wear glasses or have a beard and

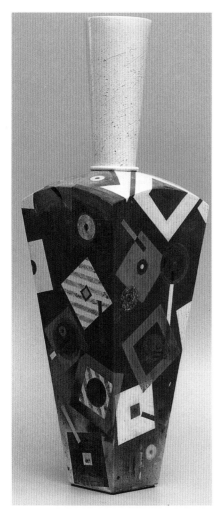

Right: Jeffrey R. Patterson, *Raku Columnar—Black and Rust*. Height: 6' (1.8 m), 1992. Raku fired. Photo by artist

shouldn't be worn by people with heart or lung problems.

Inhaling or ingesting powdered glazes is also dangerous and the fumes produced when a kiln is fired can be lethal. Among the dangerous fumes emitted are sulphur dioxide, carbon monoxide, hydrogen chloride, ozone, nitrogen oxides, chlorine, and fluorine. Many of the metal oxides and compounds in glazes are poisonous, and luster glazes, which produce toxic fumes as well, are the worst of the bunch. Any kiln you use should have its own local exhaust system, one that sucks in contaminated air right at the source and deposits it elsewhere. Keep ventilation systems well maintained.

■ Even if your ventilation system is in top working order, wear a respirator whenever you work with dry clay, plaster, or glazes.

■ Never disturb the dust in a studio by sweeping or vacuuming, unless you're using a vacuum made specifically for clay dust. Clean the work area frequently, but use mops and sponges and plenty of water. Always clean "wet" rather than "dry."

■ Wear protective clothing and shoes in your studio and remove them before you eat or drink anything. In fact, remove them before you reenter your household space. Never smoke, eat, or drink in your studio. Wash your hands thoroughly before you leave and take a shower as soon as you get back home.

■ Looking into a kiln peephole without wearing welder's goggles is an invitation to severe eye burns.

■ Unless you're an expert, don't build your own kiln. If you are an

expert, don't forget that raku, wood-firing, oil, and salt kilns should never be installed in an enclosed area.

■ Fire, although less of a danger with electric kilns than with fuel-burning kilns, is a major studio hazard. Keep the appropriate fire extinguishers on hand and if you use an oil-fired kiln, keep a bucket of sand available too. Never use water to put out an electric, gas, or oil fire.

■ Sawdust remaining after a sawdust firing can reignite on its own. Be sure to dampen it after you've removed it from the kiln.

■ Pregnant women shouldn't work with clay, and children should only work with it under the strictest of supervision.

■ When you buy commercial glazes and underglazes for use on dinnerware, check the labels to make sure they're safe for this purpose.

■ Find out which of the substances you have on hand contain toxic materials. Your ceramic supplier can direct you to sources for this information. Carefully label every substance in your studio.

■ Two excellent sources of information related to studio safety, both written by Monona Rossol, are *The Artist's Complete Health and Safety Guide*, 2d. ed. (New York: Allworth Press, 1994) and *Keeping Clay Work Safe and Legal* (Bandon, Oregon: National Council on Education for the Ceramic Arts, 1996). Ms. Rossol provides accurate and easy-to-read information on the potential health hazards faced by all ceramists and explains how to avoid them.

CONE-FIRING RANGES

The ranges provided here are for large Orton and Seger cones, fired at a temperature rise of 270°F (132°C) per hour. Note that the temperature at which a cone will melt will vary depending on the rate of temperature rise in your firing.

ORTON	SEGER	DEGREES F	DEGREES C
022		1112	605
021		1137	615
020		1175	635
019		1261	683
	019	1265	685
	018	1301	705
018		1323	717
	017	1346	730
017		1377	747
	016	1391	755
	015a	1436	780
016		1458	792
015		1479	804
014		1540	838
013		1566	852
012		1623	884
011		1641	894
010		1661	905
09		1693	923
	09a	1715	935
08	08a	1751	955
	07a	1778	970
07		1784	984
	06a	1803	990
06		1830	999
	05a	1832	1000
	04a	1847	1025
05		1915	1046
	03a	1931	1055
04		1940	1060
	02a	1955	1085
03		2014	1101
	01a	2021	1105
02		2048	1120
	1a	2057	1125
01		2079	1137
	2a	2102	1150
1		2109	1154
2		2124	1162
3		2134	1168
	3a	2138	1170
4		2167	1186
	4a	2183	1195
5		2185	1196
	5a	2219	1215
6		2232	1222
7	6a	2264	1240
	7	2300	1260
8		2305	1263
9	8	2336	1280
	9	2372	1300
10		2381	1305
11		2399	1315
	10	2408	1320
12		2419	1326
	11	2444	1340
13		2455	1346

PLASTER AND WATER RATIOS

WATER		PLASTER		WATER	PLASTER
Lbs.	Oz.	Lbs.	Oz.	Grams (Kg)	Grams (Kg)
0	8	0	11	227 g	311 g
1	0	1	6	454 g	624 g
2	0	2	13	908 g	1.3 kg
3	0	4	3	1.4 kg	1.9 kg
4	0	5	10	1.8 kg	2.6 kg
5	0	7	0	2.3 kg	3.2 kg
6	0	8	6	2.7 kg	3.8 kg
7	0	9	13	3.2 kg	4.5 kg
8	0	11	8	3.6 kg	5.2 kg
9	0	12	3	4.1 kg	5.5 kg
10	0	14	0	4.5 kg	6.4 kg
12	0	16	13	5.4 kg	7.6 kg
14	0	19	10	6.4 kg	8.9 kg
16	0	23	6	7.3 kg	10.6 kg
18	0	25	8	8.2 kg	11.6 kg
20	0	28	0	9.1 kg	12.7 kg

For future reference when mixing plaster, a 2-1/2 gallon (9.5 l) bucket will hold 12 pounds (5.4 kg) of water, with room to spare for mixing. A 5-gallon (18.9 l) bucket will hold 22 pounds (10 kg). One gallon of water weighs 8.3 pounds (3.8 kg).

UNDERGLAZE FORMULA

By mixing commercial ceramic stains with other ingredients, it's possible to make up, test, and adjust your own underglazes.

KATHY'S UNDERGLAZE

Δ3 to Δ6

For application to bisqued ware

Mix together two parts ceramic stain (any color) with one part Frit 3134. Then add water until the mixture is the consistency of thin cream. For every 100 grams of this mixture (about 1/2 cup), add a few drops of gum solution to prevent settling.

Test the underglaze on a small bisqued tile. If the fired underglaze is too shiny, add less frit to the next batch. If it rubs off the clay after firing, add more frit.

To make an underglaze that is more opaque and lighter in color, first mix the dry ingredients below:

Feldspar	30%
Kaolin	60%
Flint	10%
	100%

Then add these dry ingredients to the stain and frit (a ratio of 50:50 works well for me) before adding the water and gum solution.

ENGOBE FORMULA

DON DAVIS'S ENGOBE

Δ5 to Δ7

For wet to leather-hard clay. May be used under a clear glaze or left unglazed for a matt dry look. For a variety of effects, try colorants and stains others than those mentioned.

EPK (Florida kaolin)	30 g
Ball clay	10 g
Tile #6 clay (Georgia kaolin)	15 g
Nepheline syenite	15 g
Talc	10 g
Silica	20 g
	100 g

For white, add no other ingredients.

For red-brown, add 7% red iron oxide.

For black, add 10% Mason 6600 stain.

For an alternate black, to 1000 g of basic formula, add:

Cobalt oxide	20 g
Red iron oxide	50 g
Manganese dioxide	50 g
Copper carbonate	30 g
	150 g

KILN WASH FORMULA

This mixture may be used on kiln shelves or as a dry white, flat underglaze to accentuate texture on dark clay.

Alumina hydrate	65 g
Kaolin	35 g
Bentonite	2 g
	102 g

CASTING SLIP

An ordinary clay slurry made with nothing but clay and water contains about 60% water and shrinks a great deal when it's dried and fired and also tends to saturate plaster molds. A good casting slip, on the other hand, usually contains between 25% and 45% water. Because it shrinks less and doesn't dampen molds as much, it's more appropriate for use in slip-cast work.

For two good reasons, beginners will do better to purchase ready-mixed commercial casting slip for their first few slip-cast projects. First, using a commercial slip will give you some sense of the correct consistency of a good slip. Second, although many formulas are available for slips, the quality of the water you use and variations in the clay ingredients will affect the quality of the slip produced. Mixing your own slip, however, does save a good bit of money. If you'd like to give it a try, read the following explanations and instructions carefully before starting. Also make sure you have a gram scale.

THE THEORY

The electrical charge in clay particles causes them to stick together (or "flock"). By adding electrolytic substances to the clay, the particles are made to disperse and the clay becomes fluid and pourable—a process known as deflocculation. Sodium silicate and soda ash, electrolytes that work well in combination, are best for this purpose. Both are available from ceramic suppliers. Store the soda ash, which is an absorbent powder, in an airtight container. Sodium silicate is sold in liquid form under various trade names.

MIXING SLIP FROM FORMULAS

Many formulas are available for slips for different firing temperatures. You'll find three in this section. Note that ball clay (a very plastic secondary clay) is called for in all of them. If you don't have access to ball clay, try substituting a different kind. Not all clays can be deflocculated; white clays are usually much easier than darker ones.

The first two formulas will each yield about 5 gallons (18.9 l) of slip; the third will yield about twice that amount. For smaller batches, just reduce the amounts proportionately.

To mix any of these recipes, first place the required amount of water in a large bucket. Then add the sodium silicate and/or soda ash and mix well. In a separate container, mix the dry clay ingredients thoroughly, adding grog if desired. Then gradually add the dry ingredients to the water and electrolytic substances, and mix well.

FORMULA #1: KATHY'S LOW-FIRE CASTING SLIP

Δ05

Warm water	38 to 42 lbs. (17.3 to 19.1 kg)
Soda ash	20 g
Sodium silicate	130 g to 168 g

(Note: Add only 130 g of the sodium silicate to start, keeping about 38 g in reserve. Add the reserve, drop by drop, until the slip is the right consistency.)

Talc	50 lbs. (22.7 kg)
Ball clay	50 lbs.
	100 lbs. (45.4 kg)

Add 3% to 5% grog if desired.

FORMULA #2: KATHY'S HIGH-FIRE CASTING SLIP

Δ6

Warm water	38 to 42 lbs. (17.3 to 19.1 kg)
Soda ash	20 g
Sodium silicate	130 g to 168 g

(Note: Add only 130 g of the sodium silicate to start, keeping about 38 g in reserve. Add the reserve, drop by drop, until the slip is the right consistency.)

Ball clay	37 lbs. (16.8 kg)
EPK or other kaolin	15 lbs. (6.8 kg)
Feldspar	33 lbs. (15.0 kg)
Silica (200-mesh)	15 lbs. (6.8 kg)
	100 lbs. (45.4 kg)

Add 3% to 5% grog if desired

FORMULA #3: RICK HENSLEY'S CASTING-SLIP

Δ5 to Δ7

Water	10.5 gallons (39.7 l)
Sodium silicate	360 g
Nepheline syenite	70 lbs. (31.8 kg)
Ball clay (Tennessee recommended)	50 lbs. (22.7 kg)
EPK clay	36 lbs. (16.3 kg)
K-200 feldspar	18 lbs. (8.2 kg)
6-tile clay (Georgia kaolin)	10 lbs. (4.5 kg)
Silica (200-mesh)	14 lbs. (6.4 kg)
	198 lbs. (89.9 kg)

TIPS

■

■ Recently, rather than mix up dry ingredients, I've found it simpler to buy a dry clay mix recommended for deflocculation by a supplier. This mix is slowly sifted into the weighed-and-mixed water and deflocculant and is then stirred with a drill and paint-mixing attachment. (The longer the slip is mixed, the better.)

■ Mechanical slip-mixing machines for production studios are available through commercial suppliers, but some potters construct their own models, attaching small outboard motors from motorboats to 55-gallon (208 l) drums with spigots added to their bottoms.

■ To color casting slips, add oxides or ceramic stains to the dry ingredients before adding them to the water. To make blue, add 4% cobalt carbonate; for green, add 4% chrome oxide; and for brown, add 5% red iron oxide.

■ Casting slip that you mix yourself should be aged for a few days in a closed container before you use it.

■ Store your slip, including any liquid slip that you recycle, in a closed container. If the slip thickens over time, try a thorough but slow mixing, being careful not to incorporate any air bubbles. A few additional drops of sodium silicate may also help. If the stored slip is lumpy, pass it through a 40-mesh sieve or kitchen strainer. Most slips will last for a long time if they're protected from freezing, but a few may ferment over time and cause pinholes in the casts.

■ Molds absorb some of the electrolytes in a slip. As a result, recycled slip may not be fluid enough to re-use. You can solve this problem by adding more sodium silicate from time to time.

■ You may recycle scraps of dried slip (but only in small quantities) by returning them to the liquid slip. Some potters prefer to throw scraps away rather than risk upsetting the delicate balance of the slip. I make a plastic clay with mine, which I use to make additions to cast pieces.

When I tried using my normal plastic clay to do this, the difference in firing shrinkage between the slip and plastic clay additions was too great and caused cracking.

TEST BATCHES

■

Before you mix up a full batch of slip, you may want to make a smaller test batch. Use the dry ingredients listed in one of the formulas in this appendix, a dry clay commercial slip mix, or your own dry clay scraps. Make sure that you have a large bucket for mixing dry clay and water, a graduate, and a gram scale.

Mix together 1000 g of the dry clay mixture and 400 g of water. In a graduate, dissolve 3 g each of sodium silicate and soda ash in 25 cc of warm water. Then add another 35 cc of warm water to the graduate to make 60 cc of solution. Each .1 cc of this solution will now contain 1 g of deflocculant.

Add this solution, drop by drop, to the mixed clay and water, stirring as you do. As soon as you've added the correct amount, the sticky mass of clay should turn, quite miraculously, into a liquid. To help prepare you for making future batches, record the amount of solution you added. By translating this amount into a percentage of the weight of the dry ingredients, you'll be able to calculate how much to add to larger batches made with the same dry clay ingredients.

The electrolytic substances are usually measured as percentages of the weight of clay to be deflocculated. From 1/10th to 3/10ths of 1% of that weight will do the job. Too much electrolyte will cause the clay to jell rather than liquify.

The type of water you use may affect the properties of the slip ingredients, so in order to achieve the correct fluidity, some minor adjustments may be necessary after mixing. If your clay liquefies after you've added the electrolytic solution, but still isn't thin enough to pour, add not more than 100 g of water, a little at a time. (The water content must remain under 50%

of the total weight of the slip.) Adding a commercial water softener can also help to thin the slip. If neither method works, start over with a different dry clay mixture.

Testing the specific gravity of a slip can help you decide whether to add more water or more deflocculant. To perform this test, weigh 1 pint (473 ml) of deflocculated slip; it should weigh between 28.9 ounces (820 g) and 29.2 ounces (828 g). If it weighs more, you can safely add more water. If it weighs less, add more deflocculant diluted with water, again a drop at a time.

PROBLEMS AND SOLUTIONS

■

Some slip problems can only be identified by casting with the slip and studying the results. Following are a few examples:

■ A hard brittle cast may be the result of excessively high amounts of sodium silicate. Add less to the next batch.

■ If your slip shrinks too much, you've probably used too much ball clay. Unfortunately, the less ball clay you use, the less plastic and strong the slip will be, so when you make your next batch of slip, try including a coarser ball clay instead of increasing the amount of clay you use.

■ Uneven thicknesses of slip within the mold can cause uneven drying. If your slip is failing to fill small areas of the mold, carve small hairlines in the mold to draw air away from crevices you want to fill with slip.

GLAZE FORMULAS

In the glaze formulas that follow, if you measure 1 gram for each percentage point in the basic formula, you'll end up with about 1/2 cup of glaze. When additional ingredients are listed, the amount to add is given as a percentage of the total weight of the main ingredients. Note that all these glazes are formulated for oxidation firing.

GLAZE #1: KATHY'S SATIN CLEAR

Δ3 to Δ6

For application to bisqued ware, this glaze may be used by itself, or under or over underglazes. It may also be colored with certain stains such as the teal in this recipe and chrome-tin stains (stains in the red zone).

Custer feldspar	26%
Silica	23%
Whiting	15%
Kaolin	10%
Frit 3134	22%
Bentonite	2%
Tin oxide	2%
	100%

For teal, add 6% teal ceramic stain.

For dark crimson, add 10% crimson ceramic stain.

For other colors, add 5% to 10% ceramic stains.

GLAZE #2: KATHY'S TEXTURED SEMI-MATT

Δ3

For application on greenware or bisque

Lithium carbonate	8.9%
Strontium carbonate	18.4%
Nepheline syenite	55.2%
Ball clay	9.2%
Flint	8.3%
	100.0%

For copper/turquoise green, add 5% titanium dioxide and 4% copper carbonate. The fired colors will vary from turquoise to green to brown, depending on how thickly the glaze is applied.

For bright purple-blue, add 1% cobalt carbonate instead of titanium dioxide and copper carbonate.

GLAZE #3: GREEN/BLACK MATT

Δ6

Although it's not used on the projects in this book, this glaze for bisqued ware is one of my favorites. It will be green where it's applied thinly and black wherever it's thick.

Whiting	18.6%
Feldspar	25.0%
Nepheline syenite	22.5%
Kaolin	18.5%
Flint	6.0%
Zinc oxide	2.9%
Copper carbonate	3.5%
Bentonite	.5%
Frit 3134	2.5%
	100.0%

GLAZE #4: KATHY'S STONY MATT

Δ6 (or Δ3; see formula)

For application on bisqued ware. Try spraying, splattering, or sponging different colors of underglazes or ceramic stains on top of this glaze or adding stains to the formula as you mix it.

Dolomite	13%
Wollastonite	22%
Nepheline syenite	43%
Kaolin	22%
	100%

To change this formula to a Δ3 glaze, add 15% frit 3134.

For blue, add 1% cobalt carbonate.

For other colors, add 5% to 10% ceramic stains.

GLAZE #5: DON DAVIS'S CLEAR

Δ5 to Δ7

A transparent glaze for use on bisque

EPK clay	7.5%
F-4 feldspar	25.0%
Silica (325-mesh)	27.5%
Dolomite	5.0%
Whiting (calcium carbonate)	5.0%
Gerstley borate	10.0%
Frit 3124	20.0%
	100.0%

GLAZE #6: DON DAVIS'S FLOATING BLUE

Δ5 to Δ6

Provides a nice texture for trailing on bone-dry clay or on bisque

Nepheline syenite	47.3%
Gerstley borate	27.0%
Silica	20.3%
EPK clay	5.4%
	100.0%

For blue, add 2% cobalt oxide and 4% rutile.

GLAZE #7: BLUE SPRUCE

Δ6

For application on bisque

Whiting	16.8%
Frit 3124	20.9%
Nepheline syenite	20.9%
EPK kaolin	12.6%
Flint	12.6%
Zircopax	8.4%
Copper carbonate	1.8%
Cobalt carbonate	1.8%
Rutile	4.2%
	100.0%

TERRA-SIGILLATA FORMULA

For use on bone-dry ware

FORMULA #1

■

Place 28 lbs. (12.7 kg) of water in a 5-gallon (18.9 l) bucket.

Add 14 lbs. (6.4 kg) of clay of your choice, red or white, and a few tablespoons of sodium silicate. Allow to settle for one or two days.

Siphon off the water that will rise to the top and separate the slip from the coarser particles at the bottom.

FORMULA #2

■

Mix either 70% or 80% water with 30% or 20% dry clay, red or white.

Add .1% to .3% sodium silicate.

Siphon off the water that will rise to the top and separate the slip from the coarser particles at the bottom.

For a colored terra sigillata, add 1% to 10% oxides or stains to either formula.

APPLICATION

Brush several layers onto bone-dry clay, buffing each one with paper towels, chamois, or the palm of your hand.

REPAIRING CRACKS

The formulas in this section will work on both clay and slip-cast pieces.

FORMULA #1: CRACKS IN GREENWARE

■

Mix up a clay slurry with the same clay you've used to make your project (or use the same slip). Then add any one of the following ingredients:

1/2 tsp. of vinegar

A few drops of sodium silicate

Paper pulp (one part pulp to one part slurry)

A commercial additive, following the directions that come with it.

FORMULA #2: CRACKS IN GREENWARE OR BISQUE

■

Mix one part kiln repair cement with one part matching clay.

APPLICATION

Press the mixture into the crack, adding more as it dries and making sure to press each layer in as deep as possible. Carve or sand away the excess after it has dried.

GLOSSARY

Alumina. One of the main ingredients in clay and a refractory ingredient in glazes. Imparts strength to the clay and mattness and viscosity to glazes during firing.

Ball clay. A very fine-grained plastic secondary clay that fires to white or near white.

Bentonite. A very plastic clay added in small amounts to clay bodies to increase their plasticity and to glazes to aid in glaze suspension.

Bisque firing. The first firing of unglazed ware at a low temperature, usually Δ010 to Δ05. Bisque firing removes all moisture from the clay and makes it easier to handle.

Blistering. A bubbled, crater-like surface in a glaze (usually considered a defect) that is caused by too fast a firing or by eruption through the glaze of residual gases in the clay body.

Bloating. The warping, bursting, or bubbling of clay when it undergoes too rapid a firing.

Bone dry. The condition of unfired clay when it is as dry as possible prior to firing.

China paint (or **enamel**). A low-temperature overglaze fired onto previously fired glazed ware.

Clay body. A mixture of clay and other materials selected to produce particular characteristics to meet the ceramist's needs.

Cones. *See* Pyrometric cones.

Crawling. Separation of the glaze from the clay during firing. Leaves bare areas. Most often caused by dust or oil on the bisqued ware, too thick a glaze coating, or too rapid a warm-up in the glaze firing.

Deflocculant. An ingredient of casting slip that reduces the amount of water necessary to make the clay fluid, therefore reducing shrinkage of the slip during drying and firing.

Dunting. The cracking of fired ware during cooling that results from too-rapid lowering of the kiln temperature.

Earthenware. Pottery fired to below Δ2; usually red and porous.

Enamel. See China paint.

Engobe. A type of slip applied to damp or bisqued ware to color its surface.

Flint. Main source of silica in glazes; increases their viscosity and hardness.

Flux. A substance that reduces the melting point of silica in a clay or glaze.

Frit. A glaze that is melted and reground in order to render certain ingredients less toxic. Frits are used as fluxes in glazes and in some clays.

Glaze. A compound of minerals that is applied to the surface of greenware or bisqued ware and that forms a glassy coating when fired.

Glaze firing. A kiln firing that reaches temperatures at which glazes will melt. A glaze firing is usually higher than a bisque firing and will usually bring the clay body to its maturation point.

Greenware. Pottery that has not been fired.

Grog. Ground fired clay that is added to a clay body to reduce shrinkage and warpage. Available in different mesh sizes.

Kiln. A furnace, built of a refractory material, for firing ceramic ware.

Kiln furniture. Heat-resistant posts, shelves, and other devices upon which ware is supported in a kiln during firing.

Kiln sitter. A kiln mechanism that automatically turns off the kiln when a small pyrometric cone in it slumps.

Kiln wash. A refractory coating applied to kiln shelves to prevent excess glaze from fusing ware to the shelves.

Leather hard. The condition of a clay body that has dried somewhat but can still be carved or joined.

Luster. A type of metallic coating that is applied to a glazed surface or clay body and fired to a low temperature to give an iridescent sheen.

Majolica (or **Maiolica**). A term used today to describe earthenware with a tin-lead glaze. Originally, a Spanish surface decoration technique in which a tin opacified glaze was often colorfully painted.

Maturing point (or **maturity**). The firing temperature and time in firing at which a given clay body reaches maximum hardness or at which a given glaze melts to the desired point.

Model. The original clay form from which a mold is made.

Mold. A form, usually plaster, that contains a hollow negative shape of an object such as a model.

Overfire. To fire a glaze or clay body beyond its maturation temperature.

Overglaze. A low-temperature glaze that is applied on top of previously glazed and fired work and then fired again. Also called *enamels* or *China paints*.

Oxidation firing. A firing with an ample oxygen supply. Electric kilns provide oxidation firings.

Peephole. A hole in a kiln chamber, covered with a removable plug, through which one can observe the pyrometric cones, color, or atmosphere inside the kiln. Welder's goggles should be worn during viewing.

Plaster. A calcium sulphate material that hardens when mixed with water. Used in ceramics for mold-making because it is absorbent and able to reproduce fine details.

Porcelain. Ceramic ware or the clay from which it is made. The fired ware (porcelains are traditionally fired above 2300°F or 1260°C) is very hard, and white and translucent where thin. Lower-fire porcelains have been developed in recent years.

Press mold. A one-piece mold into which clay is pressed or casting slip is poured.

Primary clays. Clays that are found in the ground at their source of origin.

Pyrometer. An instrument for measuring the temperature in a kiln during firing and cooling.

Pyrometric cones. Small, pyramid-shaped forms, made with ceramic materials and formulated to bend and melt at specific temperatures. Used to gauge temperatures in kilns.

Raku. A method of low-temperature firing, Japanese in origin, in which the pot is withdrawn from a red-hot kiln and then carbonized by placing it in a closed container of combustible material.

Reduction firing. A firing in which the deliberate reduction of oxygen in the kiln results in incomplete combustion of the fuel. This in turn causes carbon monoxide to rob the oxides in clay and glazes of oxygen, thereby causing them to change color.

Refractory. Resistant to heat and melting.

Resist. A material or method in which a coating such as wax or oil is applied to bisqued or glazed ware to prevent a glaze applied on top of the resist from adhering to the clay or glaze underneath it. The resist burns off during firing.

Salt glazing. A glazing method in which salt is introduced into a hot stoneware kiln, where it forms a glaze on the exterior of the ware. Salt glazing produces toxic fumes.

Sandblasting. A method of etching the surface of a material by spraying it with compressed air and sand. A respirator and protective eyeware should always be worn when sandblasting.

Secondary clays. Primary clays that have been moved from their source of origin by natural forces such as wind and water.

Sgraffito. A surface decoration technique in which the ceramist scratches through a layer of slip to reveal the clay body underneath.

Silica. *See* Flint.

Slip (or **slurry**). A mixture of clay and water. Called an *engobe* when additional materials are added, and called *casting slip* when a deflocculant is added for fluidity.

Slip casting. The process of pouring casting slip into a plaster mold to create a clay shape.

Slip trailing. A surface decoration technique in which the ceramist uses a nozzle to apply slip to the ware.

Soaking. Holding the temperature in a kiln at a certain level in order to allow clay and glazes to mature.

Sprigging. A surface decoration technique in which pieces of clay are attached to the surface of damp clay in order to form a relief.

Stains. Commercially processed coloring oxides that are used as additives in clay and glazes.

Stilts. Heat-resistant supports used to raise glazed ware above the kiln shelf so that melting glaze won't fuse the ware to the shelf.

Stoneware. A type of clay (or ware made from that clay) that is fired to a temperature above 2100°F (1149°C), causing the body to become dense and vitrified. Buff to brown in color.

Temper. The coarse material added to a clay body to make it more porous, more resistant to thermal shock, and less likely to warp. (Also refers to the process of adding the material itself.)

Template. A pattern or cutting guide used to shape or cut clay.

Terra-sigillata. A fine, precipitated slip used to coat the surface of ware in order to make it smoother and more impervious.

Undercut. A negative space that creates an overhang in a solid form. When matched with its corresponding positive space, a locking form results. To be avoided when making models for molds.

Underglaze. A material colored with stains or oxides that is usually applied under—but sometimes over—a glaze.

Vitreous. Glasslike; hard, dense, and nonabsorbent.

Wedging. Kneading clay by cutting and reforming it in order to expel air and make the clay homogenous.

CONTRIBUTING ARTISTS

The artists whose works appear in this book may be contacted directly or through Lark Books.

Kathy Triplett (Front cover, pages 3, 5, 6, 13, 43, 45, 68, 83, 84, 85, 87, 97, 99, 103, 105, 108, 112, 116, 121, 123, 130, 133, 134, 135, 144), Weaverville, NC

Sue Abbrescia (page 104), Kalispell, MT

Cristina Acosta (page 27), Cristina Acosta Design, Bend, OR

Kathryn Allen (page 30), Kathryn Allen Clay Studio, Seattle, WA

Wesley Anderegg (pages 32 and 111), Denver, CO

Marilyn Andrews (pages 107 and 111), Andrassche Handbuilt Stoneware, Plainfield, MA

Gordon R. Andrus (pages 14 and 35 and back cover), Gordon Andrus Pottery, Hardin, KY

Theresa M. Archuleta (page 39), Colorado Springs, CO

D. Hayne Bayless (pages 8, 66, 73, 98, and 128), Sideways Studio, Ivoryton, CT

Josi Bellinger (page 71 and back cover), Portland, OR

Curtis Benzle (pages 25 and 60), Hilliard, OH

Suzan Benzle (pages 25 and 60), Columbus, OH

Craig A. Bird (page 40), University Heights, OH

Jennie Bireline (page 145), Bireline Studios, Raleigh, NC

Sharon E. Bloom (page 81), Blooming Creations, Chico, CA

Joanna Borlase (pages 21, 41, and 98), Vancouver, BC, Canada

Mary Kay Botkins (pages 34 and 38), Highwater Clays, Asheville, NC

Linda Bourne (pages 26 and 84), Linda Bourne Pottery, Sherwood, OR

Janet Braley (pages 33 and 35), Real Desert Pottery, 29 Palms, CA

Judy Brater-Rose (page 44), Knoxville, TN

Larry Brow (page 142), Please Touch Pottery, Lawrence, KS

Jeri Burdick (page 93), Radcliffe Street, Inc., Eutawville, SC

Jon Burke (page 16 and back cover), Jon Burke Pottery, Seaside, OR

Maery Callaghan (pages 128 and 140), Victoria, BC, Canada

Chrissie Callejas (pages 50, 59, and 93), Vilas, NC

Geri Camarda (page 20), West Palm Beach, FL

Lorraine S. Capparell (page 135), Capparell Design, Palo Alto, CA

Tom Carbone (page 132), Grosse Pointe, MI

Joan F. Carcia (pages 6-7 and 51), Reading, MA

Elaine Carhartt (page 47), Pasadena, CA

Mark Cavatorta (page 33), Interwoven Clay, Hebo, OR

Trudy Evard Chiddix (pages 33, 51, 80, and 83), Wilton, CT and Evergreen, CO

Michael Cohen (page 45), Amherst, MA

Cynthia Consentino (page 111), Northampton, MA

Diana Crain (page 57), Diana Crain Porcelains, Petaluma, CA

Tim Crane (pages 30 and 39), Brownsville, MN

Beverly Crist (page 131), Hollowed Ground Ceramic Studio, Ft. Lauderdale, FL

Donald R. Davis (pages 54, 94, and 132), Davis Studio Pottery, Asheville, NC

Mary Lou Deal (page 104), Ashland, VA

Barbara Elaine Doll (page 42), Atlanta, GA

Patrick L. Dougherty (page 40), Patrick Dougherty Studio, Penland, NC

Susan Bealer Duncan (page 75), Atlanta, GA

Ken Eastman (pages 15 and 48), Herefordshire, England

Bacia Edelman (page 128), Madison, WI

Andra Ellis (pages 5, 28, and 78), Philadelphia, PA

Christine Federighi (pages 14, 56, and 145), Miami, FL

Antonio Fink (page 11), The Clay Studio, Philadelphia, PA

Steven Forbes-deSoule (page 22), Forbes-deSoule Studio, Weaverville, NC

Mark W. Forman (pages 5 and 13), Boca Raton, FL

Patz Fowle (pages 44 and 49), Hartsville, SC

Rebecca Fraser (page 12), Tate Studios, Santa Barbara, CA

Sarah Frederick (page 50), Sarah Frederick, Potter, Louisville, KY

Sara Friedlander (page 122), Santa Cruz, CA

Debra Waddell Fritts (page 78), Roswell, GA

Keiko Fukazawa (pages 55 and 115), Pasadena, CA

Richard Garriot-Stejskal (page 50), Albuquerque, NM

Carolyn Genders (page 44), Sussex, England

Carol Gentithes (page 144), Johnston and Gentithes Art Pottery, Seagrove, NC

Terry Gess (page 50), Penland School, Penland, NC

Frank Giorgini (page 77), UDU, Inc., Freehold, NY

Becky Gray (pages 76 and 77), Burnsville, NC

Glenda E. Guion (pages 22 and 39), Easley, SC

Larry Halvorsen (page 30), Seattle, WA

George Handy (page 122), George Handy Pottery, Asheville, NC

Joan Rothchild Hardin (page 93), New York, NY

Leah Hardy (page 63), Laramie, WY

Jinny Hargrave (page 140), Carolina Clay Connection, Charlotte, NC

Barbara Hertel (page 76), Hillsboro, OR

MaryLou Higgins (page 52), Pittsboro, NC

Georgina Holt (page 24), Hand Built Porcelain (Albertson-Peterson Gallery), Winter Park, FL

Hanna Lore Hombordy (page 49), Ventura, CA

E. Joan Horrocks (pages 75 and 81), State College, PA

Jeff Irwin (page 65), San Diego, CA

Elizabeth Smith Jacobs (page 107), Montclair, NJ

Amanda Jaffe (pages 40, 137, and 145), New Mexico State University, Las Cruces, NM

Marcia Jestaedt (page 9), Marcia Jestaedt Designs, Bowie, MD

Leroy Johnson (page 43), The Clay Studio, Philadelphia, PA

Randy James Johnston (pages 51 and 56), McKeachie-Johnston Studios, River Falls, WI

Jeffery Kaller (page 26), Philadelphia, PA

June Kapos (page 61), Kapos Pots, McLean, VA

Michael Kifer (pages 13 and 62), Richland, MI

Peter Wayne King (page 136), Stonehaus, Pensacola, FL

James Klueg (page 143), University of Minnesota, Duluth, MN

Karen Estelle Koblitz (pages 16 and 57), Los Angeles, CA

Rebecca Koop (page 54), Back Door Pottery, Kansas City, MO

Heinz Kossler (page 142), Heinz Kossler Architectural Ceramics, Asheville, NC

Margo Kren (page 67), Kansas State University, Manhattan, KS

Phyllis Kudder-Sullivan (pages 13, 104, and 138), Shoreham, NY

Meg Largey (page 44 and back cover), Northampton, MA

Jane W. Larson (page 129), Bethesda, MD

Nick Latka (pages 14 and 122), Latka Studios, Pueblo, CO

Tom Latka (pages 13 and 144), Latka Studios, Pueblo, CO

Marc Leuthold (pages 5 and 58), Leuthold Ceramics, New York, NY

Naomi Lindenfeld (page 64), Brattleboro Clayworks, Brattleboro, VT

Anne Lloyd (page 77), Bryn Mawr, PA

C. Kelly Lohr (page 142), Studio of C. Kelly Lohr, Churdan, IA

Mark Lueders (pages 30 and 55), Philadelphia, PA

Matthew Lyon (pages 58, 122, and 143), Matthew Lyon Studio, Portland, OR

Janet Leong Malan (page 76), Cupertino, CA

Lisa Mandelkern (page 128), Las Cruces, NM

Linda Marbach (page 42), East Quogue, NY

Ginny Marsh (pages 23 and 25), Borden, IN

Masaki Matsumoto (page 135), Koga Shiga, Japan

Marsha McCarthy (page 31), Holliston, MA

Anita McIntyre (page 14), Fadden, A.C.T., Australia

Dennis Meiners (pages 21, 80, and 93), Jacksonville, OR

Coll Minogue (page 76), Perthshire, Scotland

Richard Montgomery (pages 18 and 59), Boone, NC

Judith Motzkin (pages 62 and 75), Cambridge, MA

Eric Nelsen (pages 39 and 53), Vashon, WA

Laura Jane Nuchols (page 23), Laura Jane Nuchols Pottery, Spokane, WA

Mary Carolyn Obodzinski (page 63), Crystal Lake, IL

Karen Orsillo (page 23), Karen Orsillo Porcelain, Kittery Point, ME

Alena Ort (page 48), New York, NY

Linda Owen (pages 61 and 79), Martell-Owen Pottery, Salem, OR

Carrie Anne Parks (pages 23 and 141), Alma College, Alma, MI

Jeffrey R. Patterson (page 146), Patterson Ceramics, Vernonia, OR

Margaret F. Patterson (page 38), Callanwolde Pottery, Atlanta, GA

Jane Peiser (page 55), Jane Peiser Pottery, Penland, NC

Jane Perryman (page 53), Cambridge, England

Lynn Peters (page 49), Plainfield, NJ

Sandi Pierantozzi (pages 24 and 59), Philadelphia, PA

Roddy Brownlee Reed (page 32 and back cover), Tampa, FL

Nerissa G. Regan (page 82), New Albany, IN

Marjolaine Renfro (page 15), Ketchum, ID

Keith Rice-Jones (page 70), Wildrice, Burnaby, BC, Canada

Jan Richardson (page 20), Windy Meadows Pottery, Knoxville, MD

Michele Ann Rigert (page 60), Portland, OR

Sang Roberson (pages 53 and 75), Ormond Beach, FL

Laurie Rolland (pages 54, 98, and 115), Sechelt, BC, Canada

Peter Rose (pages 40 and 76), Knoxville, TN

Hazel Mae Rotimi (page 34), Minor Miracles African Pottery, Gloucester, MA

Amedeo Salamoni (page 51), Lula, GA

Elyse Saperstein (pages 11 and 67), Elkins Park, PA

Barbara Schwartz (pages 72 and 107), West Palm Beach, FL

Virginia Scotchie (page 131), Columbia, SC

Ken Sedberry (page 98), Sedberry Clay Studio, Bakersville, NC

Phillip Sellers (pages 9 and 46), River Hill Pottery, Madison, OH

Carol Sevick (page 24), Seaforms in Porcelain, Putney, VT

Kaete Brittin Shaw (page 49), High Falls, NY

Paul J. Sherman (page 104), Le Roy, NY

Michael Sherrill (pages 17 and 145), Mud House, Hendersonville, NC

Shari Sikora (page 93), Havertown, PA

J. Paul Sires (pages 10 and 28), Center of the Earth Gallery, Charlotte, NC

Richard Zane Smith (pages 29, 46, and 50), Glorieta, NM

Steve Smith (pages 6, 39, and 71), Smithwork Studio, Ney, OH

Peter Sohngen (pages 107 and 111), Memphis, TN

Laurie Spencer (page 142), Tulsa, OK

David A. Stabley (pages 10 and 139), Danville, PA

Bernadette Stillo (pages 23, 24, 41, and 44), Philadelphia, PA

Carol Stirton-Broad (page 33), Elkins Park, PA

Suzanne Storer (page 19), Ogden, UT

Hiroshi Sueyoshi (page 49 amd back cover), Wilmington, NC

Natalie Surving (page 18), Surving Studios, Middletown, NY

Marvin Sweet (page 111), Merrimac, MA

Pat Taddy (page 70), Vancouver, BC, Canada

Joan Takayama-Ogawa (page 79), Pasadena, CA

Lisa and James Tevia-Clark (page 59), Brasstown, NC

Joseph Anthony Triplo (page 64), Triplo Studios, Stone Ridge, NY

Penny Truitt (pages 19, 37, and 55), Santa Fe, NM (winter); Rosedale, VA (summer)

Andrew Van Assche (pages 52 and 79), Andrassche Handbuilt Stoneware, Plainfield, MA

Red Weldon-Sandlin (page 115), Decatur, GA

Candone M. Wharton (pages 69 and 104), Sanford, FL

Dina Wilde-Ramsing (pages 21 and 63), Wilmington, NC

Lana Wilson (pages 5, 30, 73, and 144), Del Mar, CA

Matthew T. Wilt (pages 72 and 122), Philadelphia, PA

Phyllis Winchester (page 72), Atlanta, GA

Linda Workman-Morelli (pages 37 and 74), Two Bears Pottery Studio, Newberg, OR

Mikhail Zakin (page 107), Closter, NJ

Mary Lou Zeek (page 52), Salem, OR

METRIC CONVERSION CHARTS

Inches	CM
1/8	0.3
1/4	0.6
3/8	1.0
1/2	1.3
5/8	1.6
3/4	1.9
7/8	2.2
1	2.5
1-1/4	3.2
1-1/2	3.8
1-3/4	4.4
2	5.1
2-1/2	6.4
3	7.6
3-1/2	8.9
4	10.2
4-1/2	11.4
5	12.7
6	15.2
7	17.8
8	20.3
9	22.9
10	25.4
11	27.9
12	30.5
13	33.0
14	35.6
15	38.1
16	40.6
17	43.2
18	45.7
19	48.3
20	50.8
21	53.3
22	55.9
23	58.4
24	61.0
25	63.5
26	66.0
27	68.6
28	71.1

Inches	CM
29	73.7
30	76.2
31	78.7
32	81.3
33	83.8
34	86.4
35	88.9
36	91.4
37	94.0
38	96.5
39	99.1
40	101.6
41	104.1
42	106.7
43	109.2
44	111.8
45	114.3
46	116.8
47	119.4
48	121.9
49	124.5
50	127.0

Volumes

1 fluid ounce	29.6 ml
1 pint	473 ml
1 quart	946 ml
1 gallon (128 fl. oz.)	3.785 l

Weights

0.035 ounces	1 gram
1 ounce	28.35 grams
1 pound	453.6 grams

Temperatures

To convert Fahrenheit to Centigrade (Celsius), subtract 32, multiply by 5, and divide by 9.

To convert Centigrade (Celsius) to Fahrenheit, multiply by 9, divide by 5, and add 32.

RESOURCES

AGENCIES, ORGANIZATIONS, AND ASSOCIATIONS

American Ceramic Society
735 Ceramic Place
P.O. Box 6136
Westerville, OH 43086
(See *Ceramics Monthly* below)

American Craft Council
72 Spring Street
New York, New York 10003
(Exhibitions; 8000-volume library; slide registry; bi-monthly magazine; seminars and audio-visual materials)

Craft Emergency Relief Fund
P.O. Box 838
Montpelier, VT 05601
(Emergency loans)

National Assembly of State Art Agencies
1010 Vermont Avenue N.W., Suite 920
Washington, D.C. 20005
(Directory of arts agencies throughout the U.S.)

National Council on Education for the Ceramic Arts
P.O. Box 158
Bandon, OR 97411
(Annual conference; student fellowships)

National Endowment for the Arts
1100 Pennsylvania Avenue, NW
Washington, DC 20506
(Grants)

Orton Firing Institute
P.O. Box 460
Westerville, OH 43081
(Bi-monthly publication; quarterly; newsletter; technical tips for studio artists)

Tile Heritage Foundation
P.O. Box 1850
Healdsburg, CA 95448
(Bi-annual magazine; quarterly newsletter)

continued on following page

Tiles & Architectural Ceramics Books
3 Browns Rise, Buckland Common,
TRING
Herts, HP23 6NJ
England
(Free book list on request)

PERIODICALS

American Ceramics
9 East 45th Street
New York, NY 10017
(Quarterly)

Ceramic Review
21 Carnaby Street
London WIV IPH
United Kingdom
(Monthly)

Ceramics Monthly
American Ceramic Society
1609 Northwest Blvd.
Columbus, OH 43212
(Monthly)

Clay Times
P.O. Box 365
Waterford, Virginia 20197-0365
(Bi-monthly)

The Crafts Report
300 Water Street
Wilmington, DE 19801
(Monthly)

Studio Potter
Box 70
Goffstown, NH 03045
(Semi-annual)

BUSINESS RESOURCES

Ceramic artists may advertise in the following sourcebooks (see Bibliography)— *The Designer's Sourcebook II: Art for the Wall, Furniture, and Accessories*; *Burridge Index: The Design Center in a Book*

BIBLIOGRAPHY

Ball, F. Carlton and Janice Lovoos. *Making Pottery Without a Wheel.* New York: Van Nostrand Reinhold Co., 1965.

Blandino, Betty. *Coiled Pottery: Traditional and Contemporary Ways.* London: A & C Black, Ltd., 1984.

Brady, Harvey. *The Book of Low-Fire Ceramics.* New York: Holt, Rhinehart, and Winston, 1979.

Burridge Index: The Design Center in a Book. Carpinteria, CA: Burridge Index Corporation, 1995.

Casson, Michael. *The Craft of the Potter.* Hauppauge: Barron's Educational Series, 1979.

Ceramics Art and Perception. no. 22 (1995).

Ceramics Technical. no. 2 (1996).

Chaney, Charles and Stanley Skee. *Plaster Mold and Model Making.* New York: Prentice Hall Press, 1986.

Clark, Kenneth. *The Potter's Manual: Complete, Practical-Essential Reference for All Potters.* Secaucus, NJ: Chartwell Books, 1983.

Cowley, David. *Moulded & Slip Cast Pottery & Ceramics.* London: B.T. Batsford, Ltd., 1984.

The Designer's Sourcebook II: Art for the Wall, Furniture, and Accessories. Madison, WI: The Guild, 1996.

Giorgini, Frank. *Handmade Tiles: Designing, Making, Decorating.* Asheville, NC: Lark Books, 1994.

Hamilton, David. *The Thames and Hudson Manual of Architectural Ceramics.* London: Thames and Hudson, 1978.

Hessenberg, Karin. *The Complete Potter: Sawdust Firing.* Philadelphia: University of Pennsylvania Press, 1994.

Hopper, Robin. *The Ceramic Spectrum: A Simplified Approach to Glaze & Color Development.* Radnor, PA: Chilton Book Company, 1984.

Khalili, Nader. *Ceramic Houses: How to Build Your Own.* San Francisco: Harper & Row, 1986.

Laguna Clay Company: Product Catalog and Reference Guide. City of Industry, CA: Laguna Clay Company, n.d.

Laidman, Roberta. *Slab Building Illustrated: A Technical Guide for the Ceramic Sculptor.* San Francisco: Laidman Dog Press, 1995.

Leach, Bernard. *A Potter's Book.* Albuquerque: Transatlantic Arts, 1946.

Lundstrom, Boyce. *Kiln Firing Glass: Glass Fusing Book One.* Colton, OR: Vitreous Group, 1994.

Lyle, David. *The Book of Masonry Stoves: Rediscovering an Old Way of Warming.* Amherst: Brick House Publishing Company, 1994.

May, Rollo. *The Courage to Create.* New York: W.W. Norton & Company, 1994.

McCarthy, Bridget Detie. *Architectural Crafts: A Handbook and a Catalog.* Seattle: Madrona Publishers, 1982.

Nachmanovitch, Stephen. *Free Play: The Power of Improvisation in Life and the Arts.* New York: G.P. Putnam's Sons, 1990.

Nelson, Glenn C. *Ceramics: A Potter's Handbook.* 3rd ed. New York: Holt, Rhinehart and Winston, 1978.

Nigrosh, Leon I. *Low Fire: Other Ways to Work in Clay.* Worcester, MA: Davis Publications, 1980.

Perry, Rosemary E. *Potters Beware: Control of Hazards Encountered in Making, Glazing, and Firing Ceramics.* Tauranga, New Zealand: The New Zealand Society of Potters, 1996.

Rhodes, Daniel. *Clay and Glazes for the Potter.* New York: Greenberg, 1957.

——. *Kilns: Design, Construction, and Operation.* Philadelphia: Chilton Book Company, 1968.

——. *Stoneware & Porcelain: The Art of High-Fired Pottery.* Philadelphia: Chilton Book Company, 1973.

Rogers, Mary. *On Pottery and Porcelain.* Radnor, PA: Chilton Book Company, 1986.

Rossol, Monona. *The Artist's Complete Health and Safety Guide.* 2nd ed. New York: Allworth Press, 1994.

——. *Keeping Clay Work Safe and Legal.* Bandon, OR: National Council on Education for the Ceramic Arts, 1996.

Sapiro, Maurice. *Clay: Hand Building.* Worcester, MA: Davis Publications, 1979.

Speight, Charlotte F. and John Toki. *Hands in Clay: An Introduction to Ceramics.* 3rd ed. Mountain Vie, CA: Mayfield Publishing Company, 1995.

Waller, Jane. *Hand-Built Ceramics.* London: B.T. Batsford, Ltd., 1996.

Williams, Gerry, Peter Sabin, and Sarah Bodine, eds. *Studio Potter Book.* Warner, NH: Daniel Clark Books, 1978.

Wilson, Lana. *Ceramics: Shape and Surface.* n.p., 1996.

Woody, Elsbeth S. *Handbuilding Ceramic Forms.* New York: Farrar Straus Giroux, 1978.

Zakin, Richard. *Electric Kiln Ceramics: A Potter's Guide to Clays and Glazes.* Radnor, PA: Chilton Book Company and VNR Publishers, 1981.

——. *Hand-Formed Ceramics: Creating Form and Surface.* Radnor, PA: Chilton Book Company, 1995.

ACKNOWLEDGMENTS

Thanks

To all the artists around the world who so generously contributed more than 3,000 photographs of fine work and who answered my many questions about their innovative processes. Because these photos were of such high quality, my publisher agreed to expand the scope of this book. Even so, some excellent work had to be excluded, but that work, too, helped to inspire the whole process.

To **Brian McCarthy** of Highwater Clays, for his participation as a jury member during the selection of photos for this book, and for always finding the answers to my endless and obscure technical questions.

To **Don Davis**, who so kindly demonstrated his draped slab plate project for this book. Don, who holds an M.F.A. from the Rhode Island School of Design, has been an artist for more than 20 years and has served as the founding director of the Odyssey Center for the Ceramic Arts in Asheville, NC. His work, which appears in both residential and commercial settings, is also represented in galleries around the United States and in the collections of the Mint Museum, in Charlotte, NC, the Rhode Island School of Design, and Shirakawa Public Hall in Japan.

To **John Cram** and **Andrew Glasgow** at the Blue Spiral I gallery in Asheville, NC, for permitting me to photograph several of my pieces on display.

To my editor **Chris Rich**, who helped organize my reams of scribbled data. Her good humor, patience, and encouragement kept me on track when the lure of clay started to overpower that of pen and paper.

To art director **Kathy Holmes**, whose own experience with clay surely helped her inspired organization of so many images.

To photographer **Evan Bracken** (Light Reflections, Hendersonville, NC), for his outstanding work and for his ability to make photo sessions so much fun.

To publisher **Rob Pulleyn**, whose commitment made this book possible. I first realized that Rob had a great eye for ceramics when he proved to be an exceptionally talented student in one of my handbuilding classes a few years ago.

The editor thanks assistant editor **Laura Dover**, whose remarkable skills and unfailing good humor make my job possible; and Lark employees **Rosemary Kast** and **Evans Carter**, for having handled the hundreds of photo submissions so capably.

INDEX

INDEX

clay rulers. *See* clay, shrinkage

clay slabs
    drying, 37, 38, 88
    making, 12, 15, 34-36, 143
    moistening, 38
    moving, 9
    thickness of, 92, 103
    working with soft, 36-38, 94-97
    working with stiff, 37, 38, 87-92, 124-26
    See also clay, joining pieces of; clay, texturing;
        slab rollers

combing (or feathering). *See* slip trailing

commission work
    acquiring, 130
    creating, 133-34
    designing, 131
    estimating costs of, 132
    See also installation

cone-firing ranges. *See* clay, firing ranges of

cone packs, 72, 79

cut-off wires, 10, 34-35

Einstein, Albert, 141

enamels. *See* overglazes

engobes, 51, 96, 97, 99, 148. *See also* slip trailing

extruders and dies, 11, 15, 99, 127. *See also* clay extruding

firing
    bisque, 32, 63, 65, 70, 74, 79-80
    drying projects before, 46
    explosions during, 19, 80, 103, 110, 126
    glass, 82
    glaze, 32, 53, 70, 72, 80-82
    glazed greenware, 103
    multiple, 82
    oxidation, 57, 71, 74, 79
    pit, 63, 71, 74
    problems related to, 83-84
    raku, 77
    reduction, 57, 71, 74
    slip-cast work, 32, 119
    soaking during, 78, 81
    vitrification during, 22, 70
    wood, 77
    See also clay, shrinkage; clay, firing ranges of; kilns

frits, 48

glaze application methods
    brushing, 61, 65, 66, 67, 91-92, 103, 110
    dipping, 65, 66, 110, 120, 126-27
    pouring, 66, 91-92, 110, 119-20, 126
    spraying, 59, 65, 67, 103

glazes
    ash, 54, 76
    colors of fired and unfired, 25, 56, 71
    commercially prepared, 53, 87
    crystalline, 55
    diluted, 61
    firing ranges of, 53-54, 57, 69, 70
    formulas for, 65-66, 68, 151
    for greenware, 53, 70, 100
    ingredients in, 53, 57
    majolica, 54
    matt, 54, 78
    melting of, onto kiln shelves, 66, 69, 74, 80-81
    preparing, from powdered ingredients, 56, 57-58, 65
    problems related to, 22, 53, 68, 78, 81, 82-84
    raku, 54
    reapplying, 84
    resists used with, 65, 66, 81, 110, 126
    salt, 54
    slip, 54
    storing, 58, 65
    test firing, 56, 78

trailing, 65
types of, 54-55
as waterproofing, 25, 53
on white clay, 25
See also firing, glaze; frits; hydrometers

glaze sieves, 57, 58, 62

greenware, 31. *See also* glazes, for greenware

grog, 26, 42, 72, 79, 81, 87

gum suspenders, 48, 65

handbuilding methods. *See* clay; clay slabs

health and safety
    clay dust, 10, 16, 20, 31, 59, 119, 146
    cleanliness, 10, 146
    disposal of waste, 16, 114
    engobes, 59, 99
    fire prevention, 82, 146
    glazes and underglazes, 10, 16, 57, 59, 66, 146
    kilns, 72, 78, 146
    lusters, 82, 146
    physical fitness, 15-16, 19
    plaster, dry, 10, 113, 146
    pregnancy, 146
    respirators, 146
    slips, 59
    talc, 121
    underglazes, 59, 99

Hemingway, Ernest, 143

hydrometers, 58

inlay (or encaustic), 60

installation, 131-32, 137-38

lusters. *See* overglazes

kaolin, 74

kikumomi. *See* wedging

kilns
    early, 71
    furniture for, 73-74, 79, 80
    installing, 78
    loading and firing electric, 79-82, 119
    purchasing, 9, 78
    sitters for, 73, 79
    test-firing in, 56
    types of, 71-72, 74, 77
    See also cone packs; firing; pyrometric cones;
        pyrometric gauges; kiln wash

kiln wash, 60, 74, 80, 148

loop trimming tools, 11, 38, 60, 65

maturation point. *See* clay, maturation point of

metal clay, 143

mold forms, 43, 46, 113, 117, 118

molds
    collars on, 117, 118, 119
    corrosion of, 121
    hump, 36, 41, 94-97, 99-102
    materials for, 43
    models for, 42-43, 46, 113-14, 117-18
    modifying plaster, 114, 115
    open-face press, 36, 41, 42-45, 112-15, 120
    sling, 36, 41, 97
    for slip casting, 31, 41-42, 113, 117-19, 120
    slump, 41, 64
    two- or more-piece, 41-42, 46, 116-121
    undercuts in, 42, 113, 117
    urethane, 121
    See also mold forms; plaster; releasing agents

Monet, Claude, 141

overglazes, 55, 82

oxides, 48, 51, 61

paperclay, 143

"percent-for-art" laws, 128

pin tools, 11, 60

plaster
    in clay, 19, 114, 115
    dry, 10, 43-45
    lumps in, 112
    mixing, 10, 12, 45-46, 113, 147
    pouring, 43, 113-14, 118
    slabs for wedging, 19
    storing, 45, 112-13
    See also molds

pyrometric cones, 72

pyrometric gauges (or pyrometers), 73, 78

releasing agents, 43, 113, 117, 118

ribs, wooden, rubber, and metal, 11, 34

Rollins, Sonny, 140

Rossol, Monona, 146

rutile, 108, 110

scoring tools, 10, 11, 31

sgraffito, 61-62

Shiro Otani, 108

slab rollers, 12, 20, 36

slip casting, 31, 42. *See also* casting slip; molds, for slip
    casting

slip-casting machines, 121

slips, colored, 51, 61, 121. *See also* inlay; sgraffito; slip
    trailing

slip trailing, 62, 97, 121

sodium silicate, 96

spray booth. *See* glaze application methods, spraying

stains, 10, 48, 51, 65

teapots, 123-27

templates, 11, 92, 94, 127

terra sigillata, 53, 62-63, 75, 105, 152

turntables, 11, 95, 100

undercuts. *See* molds, undercuts in

underglazes
    brushing, 61, 92, 99, 110, 115, 120, 127
    effects of firing on, 52
    formulas for, 148
    with or without glazes, 52, 60
    ingredients of, 48, 52
    layering, 61
    spattering, 110, 120
    sponging, 92, 120, 127
    testing, 56
    See also sgraffito

vitrification. *See* clay, vitrification of fired; firing, vitri-
    fication during warp prevention, 22, 28, 70, 91,
    92, 121

Western Carolina University, 129, 130

work spaces, 8, 10, 16, 146

work surfaces, 9, 12, 19, 86